WISCONSIN 5-0

From High-Risk Police Calls to Comic Cop Stories

Hilary Dickinson

Trails Books
BOULDER

Published by Trails Books
a Big Earth Publishing company
3005 Center Green Drive, Suite 225
Boulder, Colorado 80301
1-800-258-5830
E-mail: books@bigearthpublishing.com
www.bigearthpublishing.com

Cover and text design by D.K. Luraas

ISBN: 978-1-934553-50-3
Library of Congress Control Number: 2014943600

9   8   7   6   5   4   3   2   1

Printed in the United States of America

Contents

INTRODUCTION

M aybe you saw a squad car zoom past you on your way home from work, its lights flashing and sirens blaring. Perhaps you scanned the headline in your morning newspaper or watched it on the nightly news. Most of us are aware when a major crime happens in our community, but we don't know much beyond what was reported in the newspaper or on the news.

We didn't feel the adrenaline rush racing to the scene. We didn't discover the victim or confront the weapon-wielding suspect. We didn't know what it was like when the incident was over and you went home, sometimes struggling to come to terms with what happened. We also don't understand how these incidents can stay with you for days, months, and even years. What I didn't realize when I set out to write this book was how much the officers wanted—and needed—to tell their stories. It made me proud to be able to share them.

Wisconsin 5-0: From High-Risk Police Calls to Comic Cop Stories gives you an inside look at what it's like being a law enforcement officer in the state of Wisconsin. These true stories of officers' most memorable calls detail their involvement in the case every step of the way from the time they responded to the call to the time the investigation was complete. For some officers, however, they emotionally were not finished with the incident even after the case was closed. They experienced long-lingering effects, and *Wisconsin 5-0* explores those emotions.

While conducting interviews with the thirty-plus law enforcement officers featured in this book, ranging from rookies to retired officers and from beat cops to sheriffs, it quickly became apparent that their most memorable calls often centered on the same type of subject matters. *Wisconsin 5-0* is subsequently divided into the following categories: Mass Shootings, High-Risk Calls, Homicides, One of Their Own, Rescues, Calls Involving Children, 10-50 Fatal Accident, Stranger Than Fiction, and Comic Cop Stories.

The first section on mass shootings examines two of Wisconsin's most recent prominent incidents that made national news: the 2012 Oak Creek Sikh Temple shooting and the Brookfield Azana Salon and Spa shooting that occurred later that same year. While many of the stories were ripped from the headlines so to speak, some are lesser-known (or even unknown), yet arguably just as compelling in their own ways.

Throughout the stories, readers will no doubt come across new terms like suicide by cop, post-traumatic stress disorder, and use of force. These subjects and more are briefly explored in fact sheets that accompany each story. Other fact sheets provide statistics on issues that play a role in the stories, while some offer interesting information on topics, including female law enforcement officers in Wisconsin and the Badger State's first sheriff. Lastly, a few fact sheets give safety tips related to matters in the book, such as how to prevent a child from drowning.

Although the stories appearing in *Wisconsin 5-0* can be grim, they also highlight the good in people. For instance, you'll read about the victims of the spa shooting, who stuck together assuring each other that they'd be okay. You'll meet the lieutenant who washed off a child's bloody shoe so her parents wouldn't have to relive what happened, and you'll learn about how a police chief formed a lifelong relationship with a girl who always needed a family.

Through the tragedy and heartbreak, the officers interviewed in this book often found the silver lining. For many, it reaffirmed their calling to do police work or taught them not to take their families for granted. For others, it encouraged them to do what they've always wanted or made them appreciate life more.

As one said, "You have to enjoy what you got because you just don't know when it's going to be done."

Located on the Capitol Square in Madison, Wisconsin,
the Wisconsin Law Enforcement Memorial (seen close
up and from afar) remembers and honors Wisconsin law
enforcement officers killed in the line of duty (photos by
Hilary Dickinson).

MASS SHOOTINGS

*"It just deepened my faith that there's more
to this world than random chance."*

—Oak Creek Officer Sam Lenda

1

"The Battle for Murphy's Ridge"

Milwaukee Journal Sentinel

The mass shooting at the Sikh Temple of Wisconsin in Oak Creek happened on August 5, 2012, but to Oak Creek Officer Sam Lenda it started a month earlier.

His car mechanic called him up one day in July, telling him, "My dad's here, and he's got something for you. Can you stop over?"

The mechanic's father is a former marine whom Lenda befriended due to his love for the Marine Corps. Lenda's own father and brother were marines, but an injury prevented him from becoming one himself.

Lenda always gives his mechanic's father a hard time and jokingly calls him one of Uncle Sam's Misguided Children.

When Lenda arrived, the man handed him two books: *Flags of Our Fathers* and *Lone Survivor.*

The officer wondered what was wrong with him. *Is he sick and dying and giving away his possessions?*

"You got to promise me you'll read these," the former marine said.

"Okay," Lenda answered, unconvincingly.

"No, you promise me you're going to read these books."

Lenda stashed the books on a shelf where they sat for the next month or so until guilt set in. He also knew that if his car broke down and he needed his mechanic's services, his father would ask him about the books.

He figured that he'd read the first and last chapters of each book so he'd sound somewhat knowledgeable discussing them if they came up. He opened *Lone Survivor* first and found himself unexpectedly engrossed.

Written by retired Navy SEAL Marcus Luttrell, the book tells the story of Operation Red Wings, a 2005 mission to capture or kill a Taliban leader. Luttrell and three other SEALS got ambushed in the Hindu Kush Mountains, and all sixteen special-forces troops died trying to rescue them when a rocket-propelled grenade brought their helicopter down. Luttrell was ultimately the only one to make it out alive.

Lenda stayed up until the early hours of the morning finishing the book, and when he was done all he could think was, *Wow.*

As a thirty-two-year veteran of the police force, he thought he was pretty cool. He's a member of the SWAT team, a high-speed operator, and a sniper. Plus, he'd been through two shootings. Yet, that night he realized that he "wouldn't make a pimple on their ass."

Luttrell's story was truly one of courage, honor, and duty.

That was the night of August 4, 2012.

———

The next day, with the book still on his mind, he went to work.

It was early Sunday morning and already very hot. Lieutenant Brian Murphy was in charge. It wasn't his scheduled day to work, but he switched with another command officer so the latter could attend his son's graduation.

During roll call, Murphy learned that some of the officers hadn't watched a training video that they'd been assigned, so he ordered them all across the hall into the break room to watch it.

"Lieutenant, I have to be at Kohl's at seven-thirty to pick up a tape from security," Lenda told him.

"I don't care. Go watch the video," Murphy said.

Lenda reluctantly did as he was told, keeping an anxious eye on the clock. At seven twenty-five, he left in a hurry, leaving behind his SWAT gear at the station.

Once he took care of the call at Kohl's, dispatch sent him to a hotel for a fight between two transvestites and he never made it back to the department to get his gear.

He sat in his squad car in the parking lot of the hotel at South 13th Street and West College Avenue typing his report on his laptop computer when a call came over the radio just before ten-thirty.

It was for a disturbance at the Sikh Temple at 7512 South Howell Avenue, less than three miles away. Within ten seconds, dispatch reported shots had been fired and people were injured.

Lenda glanced at the computer in his squad, displaying the location of all the Oak Creek police cars. He knew he wouldn't be the first to arrive, but he'd likely be second or third.

Murphy arrived at the scene when Lenda reached the intersection of Rawson and Howell Avenues, still half a mile from the temple.

"I have victims. Send an ambulance," Murphy said over the radio. "I don't see the shooter."

Assuming the parking lot would be safe, Lenda shifted from active shooter mode to rescue mode. He later learned what a mistake that was.

Gunman Wade Michael Page killed six people and himself at the Sikh Temple of Wisconsin. He also wounded four others during the shooting rampage, including Oak Creek Lieutenant Brian Murphy (photo by Hilary Dickinson).

He veered over a median and up the hill leading to the parking lot of the temple, arriving about a minute after Murphy. Sixty to seventy-five yards ahead of Lenda was a bald man wearing black pants and a white shirt. He was marching straight toward Lenda.

Lenda briefly looked around for Murphy. He was nowhere to be seen. *What is going on?* Lenda wondered. He reversed his squad down the hill and stopped to retrieve his rifle from the rack in his squad. He had left his personal weapon along with the rest of his gear at the station, but this one would have to do.

"I've got someone walking out the driveway toward me," Lenda said over the radio. He pulled forward a couple of yards before stopping again. The faint sounds of sirens echoed in the distance.

Suddenly, Lenda realized that the man was shooting at him. He had arrived on scene expecting to help the injured people—not to respond tactically. He could clearly see the man raise the gun against his white shirt and reload.

"I got a man with a gun in the parking lot!" he said over the radio.

Lenda pulled his squad forward to engage him.

"Drop the gun!"

The sounds of the sirens grew louder and louder.

The shooter, a man on a mission, ignored the command and ran toward Lenda firing in his direction.

Dodging the bullets whizzing over his head, the officer grabbed his rifle and took cover in what is called the "tactical v" position between the open door and the door frame.

The scream of approaching sirens became deafening.

"Drop the gun! Drop the gun!"

One of the assailant's bullets struck Lenda's windshield, peppering him with glass. The round hit directly above the steering wheel and lodged into the headrest.

BANG! BANG! BANG! BANG! BANG! BANG! Lenda shot back six consecutive times until the shooter was down. He didn't realize until he watched the squad dash-cam video later that the second shot was the one that took the assailant down, striking him in the hip area.

"Shots fired! Shots fired at officer!"

The man fell behind a berm, but Lenda couldn't see exactly where.

"Don't move! Don't move!" Lenda shouted.

"Can you see him?" he asked Officer John Finco. Finco, who now stood on the other side of Lenda's squad, had arrived just as Lenda fired.

"Yeah I've got him."

"Can you see him?"

"Yes. I see him. He's moving ... He's moving!"

"Is he crawling?"

"He's behind the berm."

Then they heard another BANG!

Lenda thought the assailant was still shooting at them. He hopped back in his squad. *This was ending now.* If he couldn't shoot him, he would run him over. He wouldn't let the man leave the parking lot or get back inside the temple. They needed to find their lieutenant, and they needed to get these people help.

Once Lenda got to him, he saw that the shooter—who wore black combat boots with red shoelaces and whose arms were covered in tattoos—was down. He had been shot in the head, whether it was self-inflicted or from one of Lenda's shots. He didn't know if he was dead, but he did know he was no longer a threat.

He just didn't know if he was the only shooter—maybe there were more.

Lenda kicked the gun away and, as other officers tended to the shooter, set off in search of Murphy, who wasn't answering his radio. The whole time, Lenda found himself thinking about a chapter in *Lone Survivor* called "The Battle for Murphy's Ridge," which tells the story of how Luttrell would have likely died if not for his lieutenant named Michael Murphy, who had sacrificed himself for his team.

They found Murphy on the ground of the parking lot in between cars two aisles over from where the shooter went down. His face and hands were bloody. He was pushed up on his elbows, waving the officers inside the temple to help the other victims.

Lenda wanted to pick him up and carry him away, but he knew he couldn't. As the most senior officer on scene now that Murphy was incapacitated, Lenda was in charge.

He shifted into officer down rescue mode and, as the lead officer, stepped over Murphy to provide cover from any oncoming danger, while the two officers behind him—Officer Kelly Romel and Officer Michael Schultz—lifted Murphy up and put him in a squad car to begin rendering aid.

Lenda jumped back in his squad and drove down the hill to Howell Avenue where the ambulances were staged. Two followed him up to the lot, and the paramedics immediately loaded up Murphy and rushed him to the hospital.

Then Lenda discovered two more victims, later determined to be brothers, in the parking lot. One of the men's eyes appeared glassy and wet; the other man's were hazy and dry. He'd seen enough deceased people throughout his career—over three hundred to be exact—to know that the latter was dead or near death.

Lenda ran over to the other ambulance to get the paramedics, but unbeknownst to him all four paramedics left in the one ambulance because of the severity of Murphy's injuries. Frantic, Lenda and the other officers started dragging the two men into the unattended ambulance.

Around the time that Lenda ran back down to Howell Avenue to bring up another ambulance, he learned that another person had been shot. This victim was a street over from the temple, which meant there could indeed be more than one shooter.

What they didn't know at the time was that the wounded man had run from the temple to a nearby house to pound on the door for help. It just so happened that a retired Oak Creek firefighter lived there and was able to provide him with lifesaving medical attention.

People inside the temple meanwhile began rushing out the front doors screaming and yelling, including one woman who latched onto Lenda's arm and refused to let go. The language barrier and her rapid, excited speech prevented him from understanding anything she said. He peeled her fingers off of him and sat her down next to another officer.

Lenda next started to instruct everyone to gather up their rifles, helmets, and extra ammunition because they were going into the temple. Before they did though, a sergeant grabbed him by the shoulder and asked if he was the officer who shot the assailant.

"Yes."

"You're coming with me."

"No. I want to get up there."

"No. You're out of it. You're done."

Since Lenda fired his weapon, he had to be removed from the rest of the incident. (In fact, he was subsequently placed on administrative leave until an investigation determined that his actions were justified, as is customary police procedure.) The sergeant yanked him from the scene and put him in a van where he waited helplessly. He was frustrated. It's not in him or any officer not to help. "We run toward everything when most people run away," he said.

For the next three hours while police secured the scene, Lenda—who was active on the scene for thirty to forty-five minutes before he got pulled—watched everything.

He saw approximately two hundred police officers arrive from thirty agencies, including twenty-seven local, one state, and two federal agencies. He observed the command post set up, the media arrive, and the helicopters search the surrounding areas for additional victims. "I watched our SWAT team make the entry, and I didn't get to play," he said.

Still, he knew other people were handling it. He did his part to end it, and now everyone else was picking up the pieces.

Six people died that day in what became one of Wisconsin's deadliest shootings. Those killed were Satwant Singh Kaleka, sixty-five, the president of the temple; Prakash Singh, thirty-nine, a priest; brothers Sita Singh, forty-one, and Ranjit Singh, forty-nine, both priests; Suveg Singh Khattra, eighty-four, a former farmer from India; and Paramjit Kaur, forty-one, a mother of two.

A memorial honoring the six victims from the August 5, 2012, mass shooting sits outside the Sikh Temple of Wisconsin in Oak Creek (photo by Hilary Dickinson).

Gunman Wade Michael Page, forty, died from a self-inflicted gunshot to the head. According to the FBI, Page—an army veteran and white supremacist—acted alone and had no help. No evidence suggested that he was directed or facilitated by any white supremacist group, and there was no evidence indicating the attack was part of any ongoing threat to the Sikh community.

Page also wounded four others during the shooting rampage, including Murphy who was struck twelve times at close range (three more hit his bulletproof vest).

Murphy retired due to his injuries in mid-2013 after twenty-two years at the department. According to the *Milwaukee Journal Sentinel*, Murphy, who was one of First Lady Michelle Obama's guests at the State of the Union Address, still suffers from physical issues with his left thumb, has no feeling in his right forearm and leg, and his voice remains raspy due to a throat wound.

———

After the incident, Lenda thought he had better read the other book his mechanic's father gave him. Telling the story of the flag raisers from Iwo Jima, *Flags of Our Fathers* talks about how they hated to be called heroes—something Lenda would relate to after the temple shooting.

"To this day I still hate being called a hero," Lenda said. "We do what we do because of who we are. I don't want to be thought of as a hero. I want to be thought of as a warrior, and there's a difference."

When Lenda was a child his father had a cigar box. He never knew what was in it until one day he saw it open when his dad was cleaning the room. Inside he found ribbons that his dad had earned from serving in World War II.

"Dad, are you a hero?" Lenda asked.

"Remember this, heroes have their names on the wall," his father said. "We're just the unlucky ones that made it home."

That stuck with Lenda for his whole life, although he never understood what it meant until he attended his first police funeral. Then he realized that the survivors are the unlucky ones because they have to carry the memory of all those who died.

Since the books the former marine gave Lenda proved to hold such significance, he wanted to know what possessed him to give them to him at that moment in time and to make him promise to read them.

He went back to him and asked.

"Because you just needed to read the damn things," the man barked.

So why does Lenda believe he gave him the books?

"It just deepened my faith that there's more to this world than random chance," he said. "All the bullets that Brian took and all the bullets that missed me ... was that for a reason? Brian survived, I believe, because his mission here isn't done. Neither is mine. That has just instilled my faith that life is more than just a blob of amino acids. There's something higher."

Lenda also finds it interesting that on the day of the shooting he left roll call without putting his SWAT gear into his car. If he would have done that, he would have been fifteen seconds later to the call.

"And what would the ramifications have been if I had gotten there fifteen seconds later?" Lenda asked rhetorically. "He [Page] would've been out of that parking lot, and Brian would have been dead because he [Page] would have been standing over Brian finishing executing him. He would have gotten in his car and drove away before I even got there or he would have gotten back inside the temple."

People often ask Lenda what he would change, and he tells them two things.

First, he will never assume a situation is safe again, and second he learned it's not up to him to judge God's plan.

"Everything that happened that day happened for a reason," he said, adding that a higher power was looking out for Murphy. "Brian has a story of survival. My story is about actions and what I did there."

Since the shooting, Lenda said the Oak Creek officers have all experienced individualized reactions—some better than others.

As for Lenda, he's been at peace with it. "I haven't lost a night's sleep over it. My view is that I confronted evil in the parking lot. I have no qualms about what happened."

The incident, however, reaffirmed to him the importance of training.

"After all these years of training, we finally got to stop one," Lenda said. "I look at all the active shooting training I've gone through, and hey, it paid off. The more you sweat in training, the less you bleed in combat."

In the year following the incident, Lenda and Murphy collected many prestigious awards. They received the Hometown Hero Award from the State Assembly, they won the 2013 co-Oak Creek Citizens of the Year, and the International Association of Chiefs of Police honored them.

In May 2013, Lenda, Murphy, and the six other responding Oak Creek police officers received the National Association of Police Organizations

TOP COPS Award. President Barack Obama honored the officers, among the more than forty national law enforcement officers to win the award, in a White House Rose Garden ceremony.

Also in May, the Wisconsin Professional Police Association honored Lenda and Murphy with the Award for Valor. The other responding officers, John Finco, Kelly Romel, Derick Slamka, Dean Kleinhans, Michael Schultz, and Julie Grauberger won the Certificate of Merit.

The next month Lenda was honored at the National Patrol Rifle Conference and Competition in Detroit, where he won the 2013 Chudwin Award for Patrol Rifle Excellence.

"It is what it is," he said of receiving the awards. "We do what we do because of who we are."

Wisconsin Mass Shootings

The Oak Creek Sikh Temple shooting on August 5, 2012, that left seven dead, including gunman Wade Michael Page, is among six mass shootings to occur in Wisconsin since 2004. The other five are as follows:

1. November 21, 2004: Hmong immigrant Chai Soua Vang, thirty-five, fatally shot six people and wounded two others while deer hunting east of Birchwood in northern Wisconsin. He was sentenced to life in prison.
2. March 12, 2005: Terry Michael Ratzmann shot and killed seven people and hurt four others at a Living Church of God service at the Sheraton Hotel in the Milwaukee suburb of Brookfield. The forty-four year old then committed suicide.
3. June 9, 2007: Ambrosio Analco, twenty-three, fatally shot his twin infant boys, his estranged wife, her sister, and a friend in the southeastern city of Delavan before turning the gun on himself.
4. October 7, 2007: Off-duty Forest County Sheriff's Deputy Tyler James Peterson shot and killed six people and hurt one at his ex-girlfriend's apartment in the northern city of Crandon. The victims were teenagers who were his high school friends and classmates. The twenty year old then took his own life.
5. October 21, 2012: Radcliffe Haughton, forty-five, fatally shot his estranged wife and two other women and wounded four others at the Azana Salon and Spa in Brookfield. He subsequently killed himself. The shooting rampage took place less than half a mile from the one at the Sheraton Hotel (see following chapter).

—Information from "Wisconsin's history of mass shootings," Today's TMJ4, December 14, 2012, and "Killings mark 5th mass murder in state since 2004," *Milwaukee Journal Sentinel*, August 6, 2012.

2

Better be Ready for that Call

Salon shooter asked taxi driver's advice

Associated Press

MILWAUKEE

A man who shot his estranged wife and six others before killing himself at a Wisconsin salon asked a taxi driver on the way there for marital advice, according to police reports released Friday.

Radcliffe Haughton told taxi driver Jesse Thomas on Oct. 21 that he suspected his wife was cheating on him and he had bought a gun, according to the reports.

Haughton asked Thomas "what he would have done if this was his wife," according to police reports. Thomas told him he would do nothing because it "wasn't worth it," police quoted the driver.

Details of the moments before Haughton fatally shot his estranged 42-year-old wife, Zina, and two others at Azana Salon & Spa in Brookfield are among the hundreds of pages of police reports released Friday. The department also released 911 calls, photos, security video from nearby businesses and squad video.

Thomas noted to police that Haughton was wearing a fatigue jacket and fatigue-colored backpack when he picked Haughton up. Haughton told the driver that he suspected his wife was cheating and he was behind on bills and lost his job.

Reports also said Haughton told Thomas he was going to have lunch with his new girlfriend who began work at 11 a.m. at Azana. They initially drove past the spa and he did not see the car he was looking for, the report said, so Haughton bought Thomas lunch at a nearby Burger King drive-thru. Thomas told investigators that Haughton appeared very nervous.

They drove by again and Haughton saw the car and instructed the driver to take him to the rear of the building. The report says Radcliffe gave him a $20 tip but he tore it because he was shaking. Thomas watched him put the hood of his jacket up and carry the backpack inside.

Zina Haughton, a hair stylist at the spa, had just greeted her 11 a.m. client, Elizabeth Brunner, the report said, and while she was getting Brunner coffee, Brunner saw Radcliffe Haughton come in.

"He had a revolver in his hand pointed straight in the air," she told police. She said Haughton pointed the gun at the employees behind the reception desk and yelled "Get down! Get down! Everybody get down!"

Brunner laid on the floor and heard Zina Haughton calmly talking to her angry husband. She heard her say, "It's okay, sir, these are good people here," as well as "What do you want?" and "This is a peaceful place."

She told police he grabbed his wife by her right arm and pulled her into another room caliber semi-automatic handgun the day before from a private individual.

Court records show Haughton had terrorized his wife for years, including threatening to throw acid on her face, dousing her car with tomato juice and slashing her vehicle's tires.

Three days before the spa shooting, Zina Haughton obtained a restraining order. She wrote in her request for the order that her husband had accused her of cheating and had threatened to kill her if she ever left him.

Radcliffe Haughton's friend Jeffrey Simmons told police that on Oct. 16 while they were riding in a car together he had overheard Haughton's phone conversation with his father, in which he said, "If I had a gun, I would shoot her." Simmons said he tried to calm him down.

Haughton also later told him "She's not the only one I'm going to get," according to police reports, which also said Simmons told them Haughton had made statements about "sitting on a hill"

A high-pitched *"weeeeeee"* sound escaped from the sprinkler system as it sprayed frigid water on him. The alarm system unleashed a blaring buzz. All the while Train's "Meet Virginia" played on in the background.

Brookfield Officer Adam Behnke entered the Azana Salon and Spa with the mindset of encountering the armed suspect and eliminating the threat. He was fully intent on squeezing the trigger, but all these environmental factors really messed with his psyche.

The bloody water splashed over his boots as he and Waukesha County Deputies Michael Doud and Juan Rodriguez made a loop around the main level with their weapons drawn. Right away Behnke spotted three women on the floor behind the receptionist desk. Two of them were undoubtedly deceased; the other was playing dead.

"Police! Police! Police!" Behnke shouted.

In searching for the suspected shooter—a man decked out in camouflage carrying a backpack—Behnke felt like he was leading the two deputies on a suicide mission.

———

Behnke, a nearly ten-year veteran assigned to third shift, ordinarily wouldn't even have been at work that day, October 21, 2012. He had switched to first shift though, so he could sleep that night before ironically attending an active shooter training the next day.

In another uncanny twist, Behnke started off that calm fall Sunday morning by telling his coworker, Anthony Kader, as they loaded their gear into the squad cars, "You better be ready for that call today. We're going to have a big one."

Looking back, Behnke doesn't know what made him say that. Maybe it was luck; maybe it was someone watching out for cops. Whatever it was, he somehow correctly sensed what was to come a few hours later.

The shots fired report came in a little after eleven a.m. at a place that normally represents serenity and tranquility: the Azana Salon and Spa.

On October 21, 2012, Radcliffe Haughton entered the Azana Salon and Spa in Brookfield, where he fatally shot three women, including his estranged wife, and wounded four others before subsequently killing himself (photo by Hilary Dickinson).

Behnke and Brookfield Officer Eric Bills were both just down the street sitting in the parking lot of the Midway Hotel & Suites. They sped down the affluent Milwaukee suburb's busy Moorland Road and arrived within thirty seconds, making them first on scene.

Behnke pulled up in front of the two-story Azana behind a parked car pulling a boat. Two duck hunters, ironically also wearing camouflage, stood next to the car.

"A guy with a gun just shot up the place," one of them told Behnke, pointing toward the spa. They had just been alerted to the shooting by a screaming woman who had dashed out of the spa and across traffic to the Brookfield Square mall across the street.

Behnke got out of his squad car, grabbed his rifle, and rushed toward the spa.

That's when he spotted a man round the corner, running away from the building. Behnke knew he must be the shooter.

He began to chase the suspect, but he lost sight of him when the suspect bolted back around the building. Bills, who parked behind the nearby golf course, spotted him go back inside and lock the door.

Behnke ran behind a brick wall concealing a dumpster to make arrangements with other officers to meet him there before they made entry into the building.

He and Bills still didn't know what was going on until an uninjured woman rushed out from the same door that the suspect had locked and ran to Bills. She told him a man had a handgun and had shot several people. He had plenty of ammunition, she added.

From his position about fifty feet from the building, Behnke glimpsed the suspect open some window shades and peer down at them from the Azana's second floor. His immediate thought was that the man would start firing at them with a rifle.

Behnke radioed in the suspect's location, as more women—some bloodied, others barefoot and clad in bathrobes—poured out of the exits and headed toward the numerous officers now arriving.

Behnke specifically remembers observing Frank Riederer, a calm, mellow Brookfield officer, make two or three trips transporting victims in his squad car to an area for the paramedics to retrieve them.

With it just after eleven on a weekend morning in the busy commercial area surrounding the spa, the police locked down the mall, the Westmoor Country Club, and the McDonald's next door.

It just so happened that Elm Grove Sergeant Ryan Unger was in the drive-through lane of the fast-food restaurant when officers first began responding to the call and successfully got everyone to leave without any questions asked.

Meanwhile, a 911 caller stated that the building was filling up with smoke, activating the fire alarms and sprinklers.

Behnke detected a burning odor moments later, once Doud and Rodriguez arrived.

After advising dispatch he smelled smoke, Doud smirked. "That's from my engine and tires," he told Behnke, citing how fast he raced to the scene.

They then decided to go inside the spa, making them the first three to enter.

The possibility of a fire didn't register with Behnke. He was too concerned with the prospect of a gunman lying in wait.

———

Less than a year after the Azana shooting, discussing what had happened that day and how it affected him is still somewhat difficult for Behnke. He's only talked about it at length to his wife, fishing buddy, and younger brother who's also a police officer, but that's it.

"It's always on my mind in some aspects," he said. "It sticks with you."

There are certain details, for instance, that he has not forgotten, such as how he couldn't believe how small one of the victims made herself as she hid under a window sill.

She gave him a thumbs-up to signal she was okay and another one when he asked her if she could move. He then told her to run to McDonald's where the police were staging the victims.

Another victim lying nearby on the floor heard him yelling "Police!" She briefly looked up at him before resuming to play dead.

Police reportedly rescued nineteen women from the spa, including women who fled from the upper level and another group of women huddled together in a bathroom. Out of fear of the suspect finding them, Behnke said the latter pressed buttons on their cell phones to signal to the dispatcher that they were okay.

In addition to the two deceased women he saw behind the reception desk,

Behnke also spotted a third one, later identified as the target in the shooting, lying by a stylist chair.

While he's not numb to seeing dead bodies, Behnke admitted that some of the sensation of the sight has been removed for him. Despite his almost ten-year law enforcement career primarily in the quiet, affluent suburb of Brookfield, Behnke had already been involved in another mass shooting.

In 2005, Terry Michael Ratzmann walked into a Living Church of God service at the Sheraton Hotel less than half a mile from the Azana and started shooting. He killed seven people that day and wounded four others before turning the gun on himself.

Behnke, twenty-five years old then, was among the first four officers, including Riederer, to respond. The loudness is what Behnke remembers most about the aftermath of the shooting. Everyone was screaming and crying. There were more people shot than there were cops on scene.

He calls that situation a "different animal" than the Brookfield one.

While the three women were dead in the latter and there was nothing he could do for them, the victims were still alive in the former, talking and pleading out for help. The officers had to triage the patients, and Behnke recalls the difficultly in having to tell them, "I'll get to you next." Also, the police knew the shooter was dead in the hotel massacre, but in the spa shooting the assailant was alive as far as they knew and still somewhere inside.

While Behnke and the others moved through the first level checking closets and locking down the stairwells, he was looking through what his boss likens to a "toilet paper tube." He was so focused that he didn't even know Sergeant Mark Tushaus and Kader had come inside the spa.

As more and more officers arrived, they pressed on, moving up into the second level of the Azana where they expected to find the suspect.

Besides the piercing cold water soaking the officers, the red-tinted water puddling up around their boots, and the loud noises assaulting their ears, they were also hindered by the wet ceiling tiles collapsing, which when dropped made gunshot noises and splashed bloody water in their faces. Behnke said that the officers grabbed towels from the massage rooms they cleared to wipe themselves off.

Inside one of those massage rooms on the second level, the one reportedly named "Bliss," is where police—with the help of a robot from the Milwaukee County Sheriff's Office—ultimately found the suspect dead of a self-inflicted gunshot to the head. He was in the same room from which Behnke saw him looking out the window.

———

The shooter was identified as Radcliffe Haughton, a forty-five-year-old Brown Deer man, who entered the Azana Salon and Spa that morning bent on killing his estranged wife, Zina Haughton, a stylist who worked there. Along with Zina, forty-two, he also killed two other women: receptionist Cary Robuck, thirty-five, of Racine, and stylist Maelyn Lind, thirty-eight, from Oconomowoc. Four additional women were wounded.

At the conclusion of the investigation, police learned that Haughton had used a makeshift explosive device made from a glass spaghetti sauce jar filled with gas to start a fire on the second floor. The suppression system extinguished the fire almost immediately.

In the aftermath of the shooting, the media widely reported the domestic disputes that had occurred between Haughton, a former marine, and Zina, which included threatening to throw acid in her face and to kill her if she ever left him, dumping tomato juice on her car, and most recently slashing her car tires. Three days before the shooting Zina had obtained a four-year restraining order against him, a copy of which police reportedly found stuffed in his pocket after he killed himself.

He was also ordered to turn over his guns and prohibited from buying a gun from a dealer, but he reportedly bought a gun from a private individual the day before the shooting. Behnke, who had been relieved and replaced by tactical officers by the time they discovered Haughton, calls him a coward.

"He had some marital problems. Everyone in the world has marital problems, and he takes it out on the nicest people you could imagine," Behnke said. "We're trained to go into something like that, but they're just trying to get their hair or nails done and then all of a sudden hell breaks loose. I have unbelievable respect for them."

The victims were selfless, he added, as they stuck by each other holed up in the rooms of the Azana, telling each other they'd be okay and that they'd get through it.

In fact, Behnke was struck by how everyone came together that day, from the Elmbrook Memorial Hospital emergency room doctor who voluntarily called his nurses and doctors in early so they'd be ready to help, to the two dozen officers from six agencies who set aside their safety to protect the victims and to assist their brothers and sisters in blue.

"It's amazing how you've got one asshole who walks into the place and shoots it up, but all the other good that goes on," he said.

Behnke recalls the nine Wauwatosa cops who responded in what felt like "the blink of an eye."

They had been eating lunch when the call came in, but the dispatcher reported it as calmly as if the call were a dog at large. The officers took one more bite before the magnitude of the situation clicked. Then they immediately rushed off, including one who hopped on his motorcycle and arrived on scene with a pickle still on his face.

Behnke didn't realize it at the time, nor would anything have been funny during the incident anyway, but now he looks back and laughs about it.

He also remembers the sense of relief that he felt when a nearly seven-foot-tall officer wearing a green uniform showed up. He thought that he was someone named Craig from another department whom he knew from SWAT. It was nice to see a familiar face, and the fast, hectic pace of the situation inside the spa slowed down for him.

Behnke called him Craig three times before the officer finally replied, "My name ain't Craig." He in fact was a Waukesha County Sheriff's Department tactical officer who Behnke still doesn't know to this day.

Though he turned out not to be his friend Craig, that incident highlighted to Behnke the significance of the brotherhood that cops have with each other and how they can be calmed when their fellow officers begin to show up.

In total, twenty-five officers from Brookfield, Elm Grove, Wauwatosa, the village of Pewaukee, the Wisconsin State Patrol, and the Waukesha County Sheriff's Department initially responded to the shooting.

As the incident unfolded, hundreds of officers from agencies including West Allis, New Berlin, Menomonee Falls, and the town of Brookfield came, as well as the FBI, Secret Service, and, according to Behnke, every federal agency short of immigration.

"It's amazing that when you really need help, cops flood in to help," he said. "It redefined the whole brotherhood for me. These guys put aside their safety and whatever their patches say and do what needs to be done."

———

Behnke finally got back to the police department at nine that evening. Before returning home to his wife and two-year-old daughter, he unwound with Kader for the next two hours cleaning their guns. (Kader, by the way, is still "pissed" at Behnke for eerily telling him that morning to be ready for that big call.)

Despite the danger Behnke and the others were in that day inside the Azana, he didn't think about it in the moment.

As they kicked open doors—any of which could have confronted them with the armed suspect—all he thought was, *Onto the next room. Let's find this guy.*

It took the next two or three days for the adrenaline to subside, but it was at that point that he finally realized how much he and the others were at risk.

"You're just thankful that what could have happened didn't," he said.

For instance, Haughton could easily have shot at them down the open spiral staircase in the center of the salon.

Behnke, who thinks Haughton doubled back inside the Azana because he spotted Brookfield Officer Julie Stubblefield, doesn't know what he would have done if Haughton had kept running. Perhaps he would have escaped or tried to shoot the woman who darted out into the street and stopped the duck hunters—she was later identified as Haughton's own stepdaughter. Whatever his motive, Behnke thinks he had some sort of agenda.

Though he hasn't had difficulties sleeping or driving past the Azana, he did experience one unsettling aftereffect.

In the spring following the shooting, he was transported back inside the spa during a family vacation to the Wisconsin Dells when buckets of water dumped onto him.

He brought his daughter, with whom he had been playing, over to his wife while he stepped aside and collected himself for a few minutes.

"I'm having a fun time with her and then I start thinking about the water," he recalled. "That's not fair to my kid, so you put all that aside and try to make sure she's still having fun."

On a less serious note, "Meet Virginia," a song he used to like, is also now ruined for him.

Behnke, however, credits running, faith, and the opportunity to confide in a couple of good buddies in helping him work through his emotions.

Still, the ordeal did yield some positives. For example, it helped put into perspective what is and isn't a big deal, it made him appreciate training even more, and it further reinstated that police officers have to be ready for anything.

"When people call for the police to show up they expect you to solve the problem," he said. "Whether it's someone stole their lawn mower or some guy's shooting up the place, you're the answer to that problem. It's a good reminder that you need to act and get it done."

———

In recognition of his role in the response of the shooting, Behnke received the Meritorious Award from the Wisconsin Professional Police Association, as did Doud and Rodriguez, the Waukesha County deputies who along with Behnke were the first three to enter the Azana.

In addition, the Brookfield Police Department presented the Meritorious Service Award to Behnke and the other twenty-four initial responding officers. They are: Tushaus, Riederer, Bills, Kader, Stubblefield, Officer Russell Prusak and Officer Dennis Alreuter from the Brookfield Police Department; Unger, Officer Sandra Brown, and Officer Philip Doney from the Elm Grove Police Department; Doud, Rodriguez, and Deputy Robert Faith from the Waukesha County Sheriff's Department; Sergeant Jeffrey Farina, Sergeant Brian Zalewski, Detective Paula Roberson, Detective David Hoppe, Officer Theodore Engelken, Officer Patrick Kaine, Officer Gary Raymond, Officer Randy Simon, and Officer Luke Vetter from the Wauwatosa Police Department; Trooper Steven Lindman from the Wisconsin State Patrol; and Officer Peter Latona from the village of Pewaukee Police Department.

Since the shooting, Behnke also won a Distinguished Service Award from the Brookfield Jaycees for his overall body of work.

Domestic Violence Homicide
in Wisconsin in 2012

Number of domestic violence homicide incidents	38
Victims of domestic violence homicide (excluding by legal intervention)	48
Homicide incidents with two or more victims	5
Homicide incidents with perpetrator suicide	4
Total deaths (victim and perpetrator)	52
Female victims	31
Male victims	17
Female perpetrators	5
Male perpetrators	35

◆ The most common age range of female victims was eighteen to twenty-nine, while the most common age range of male victims was under eighteen.
◆ The most common age range of perpetrators was thirty to forty-nine for women. Eighteen to twenty-nine and thirty to forty-nine were equally common age ranges for male perpetrators.
◆ Caucasian was the most prevalent race for female and male victims.
◆ The most prevalent race for female perpetrators was African American and Caucasian for male perpetrators.
◆ Shootings were the most common method of killing.
◆ When the perpetrator was a man, the victim was most often a current female partner.
◆ When the perpetrator was a woman, the victim was most often a current male partner.

—Information compiled from the 2011 & 2012 Wisconsin Domestic Violence Homicide Report from The Wisconsin Coalition Against Domestic Violence, published in September 2013.

HIGH-RISK CALLS

"Shoot him! Shoot him! What are you waiting for?"
—Retired Madison Officer Jean Papalia

3

In the Bumblebee Room

MEDALS OF VALOR

Police Department honors officers and civilians who took action in Red Caboose crisis.

By Nathan Leaf
Wisconsin State Journal

Even as they became the first civilians to receive the highest honor the Madison Police Department gives, Gary Dosemagen and Wendy Rakower couldn't help but deflect the praise.

Dosemagen, Rakower and three Madison police officers were presented Thursday night with the department's Medal of Valor at an awards ceremony honoring their actions during a March 9 incident in which a suicidal man with two meat cleavers entered the Red Caboose Day Care Center on Williamson Street.

"These are our heroes," Dosemagen said, speaking for himself and Rakower, after asking Red Caboose employees at the ceremony to stand and be recognized by the crowd of more than 200 at the Monona Terrace. "I had confidence in all of them that they would protect the children."

Dosemagen, an employee of Red Caboose, struggled with Gregory Velasquez, 39, in the center and was injured but made it to a nearby store to get help. Velasquez then threat-

Photos by Leah L. Jones – State Journal

Wisconsin State Journal

A vivid red glob marred the otherwise spotless tile floor of the day-care center's kitchen, matching the spray of blood on the wall. An unhooked phone receiver bobbed up and down.

"Did we miss him? What's going on?" said Madison Officer Phillip Yahnke to Officers Jean Papalia and Shane Pueschner.

They had just arrived at the Red Caboose Day Care Center, 654 Williamson Street. A man armed with a knife was said to be threatening staff and children, but so far they saw no suspect or kids inside the silent day care.

"Police! Come out!" they yelled, walking down the hall past the kitchen.

The door to what is called the "Turtle Room" burst open, and a woman Papalia knew named Olga bounded out. She stopped short and trembled, her eyes wide.

"Jean! Jean! They're in the Bumblebee Room. They have my Tati," she said desperately, referring to her daughter.

"Olga, what's going on?" Papalia asked.

"They're all in the Bumblebee Room!" she answered, pointing down the hallway.

One of four rooms in the day-care center, along with the Turtle Room, the Elephant Room, and the Grasshopper Room, the Bumblebee Room is designated for the youngest children.

"Don't worry. I'll get her back," Papalia said calmly, despite knowing that that could be a promise she may be unable to keep.

With their guns drawn, the officers moved through the narrow hallway of the day care kicking open doors to empty rooms until a closed door belonging to what turned out to be the Bumblebee Room confronted them. In the upper third of the wooden door, a man peered out from a six-by-twenty-four-inch window, his face drawn into a snarl of rage.

They knew it was him.

Pueschner made eye contact with the suspect, a man who appeared to be in his late thirties, before kicking the door open. The suspect backed out of the way, and Pueschner and Yahnke stepped onto the threshold, pointing their guns at him. Behind them, Papalia raised herself on her tiptoes to peer between their shoulders.

Out of their peripheral vision, the officers glimpsed day care owner Wendy Rakower trapped between the doorframe and a stack of milk cartons. Unbeknownst to them, she had been standing slightly to the left of the doorway when Pueschner busted in the door. She had just dialed 911, but when the door swung back it had knocked the phone out of her hand before she had a chance to speak. The abandoned phone lay on the floor recording the whole situation that was to come.

"Police! Drop the weapon! Drop the weapon!"

Until then, the officers expected the suspect to be armed with a knife, but they now saw he had a meat cleaver. He held it in his right hand extended upward over his head, a determined look on his face.

"I want to talk. Listen. I want to talk. I'm serious," he told the officers.

The suspect stood six feet from them and about two steps from the dozen or so children aged one to four, whimpering and squirming in the corner. They lay on top of each other in a heap under an elevated playhouse surrounded by three or four adults who threw their bodies over them like a human shield. One boy wormed out of the pack in an attempt to escape only to get stuck back into the pile while others buried their faces in the carpet.

"It's all right. The police are here. They'll take the bad man away," one of the adults cooed to the children. They focused on keeping them as still and quiet as possible.

"Drop the weapon!" the officers ordered.

BEEP BEEP BEEP BEEP BEEP!

Broadcasted from the officers' body microphones, the alert tones went off again as dispatch advised of an injured man at the Gateway Plaza next to the Red Caboose.

"Give me a freaking break," Papalia mumbled.

Ignoring the alert tone, the officers continued fruitlessly yelling at the suspect to drop the weapon.

Rakower, meanwhile, remained trapped behind the door, but she had no fear nor did she cower. In fact, just moments before the police arrived she bravely strode into the Bumblebee Room to try to reason with the suspect. He didn't cooperate with her then or with the police now. So far he had disregarded about a dozen commands to drop the cleaver.

"Shoot him! Shoot him! What are you waiting for?" Papalia screamed at last.

Pueschner hesitated, believing the suspect would drop the weapon any second now like they always do.

But that's not what happened.

With the meat cleaver still gripped firmly in hand, the man said in an even voice with no hint of frenzy, "I'm not scared. I'm going to do this. I want this to be over. She's going to be dead, and I'm going to be dead."

He took a step toward Rakower.

BANG! BANG!

Pueschner fired twice in succession, and Yahnke followed.

The man spun backward in a pirouette motion, tumbling and twisting. They fired at him until he collapsed.

In all, Pueschner got off five rounds, Yahnke three. Six hit the suspect, and investigators later dug the other two out of the wall.

"He made us shoot him in front of the kids. They're gonna need counseling for this," Yahnke said aloud, while thoughts scrambled inside his head. *We just shot somebody. A justifiable homicide, yes, but we just killed somebody. This isn't happening. It's nine, ten in the morning. This is Madison.*

"Phil, it was a good shoot. It was a good shoot. Let's handcuff him," Pueschner said. Although to him it seemed like ten minutes had gone by, not more than ninety seconds passed from the time they entered the threshold to the moment they shot him.

Yahnke rolled the man onto his stomach and cuffed his wrists behind him.

"Well, we might as well find out who we just shot," Pueschner said.

Yahnke pulled out his wallet, slid out the driver's license, and read "Gregory Velasquez."

"We just shot my sexual assault suspect!" he exclaimed.

A week before the shooting, Velasquez allegedly abducted his estranged girlfriend and forced her to drive them to the east part of Madison. There he instructed her to park her Honda hatchback in a gloomy, abandoned lumberyard, and reportedly raped her twice in the back of the car. The woman promised him that she wouldn't call the police for twelve hours. During that time period she told him to flee to Chicago.

Police had not yet located Velasquez, but now here he lay on the floor bleeding out. His eyes were fixed and his breathing labored. Pueschner grabbed a child's blanket lying nearby and used that to apply pressure on his chest wounds while he waited for the paramedics. He wanted him to stay alive at least until they arrived.

Velasquez took a last gasp, and his eyes rolled up. Pueschner knew that he was dead.

————

Partly due to the 911 recording of the incident and an eight-page suicide note titled "Why I need to self-destruct" stuffed in Velasquez's shirt pocket, the district attorney ruled it a justifiable homicide by five p.m. the same day of the shooting, March 9, 2004.

The suspect, whom the officers didn't realize was actually armed with two meat cleavers, had no vendetta against Rakower or anyone at the day care. Instead, he chose the Red Caboose as a "soft target." He knew putting small children in physical danger would generate an immediate and lethal response from the police. They would have no other choice but to kill him, and that's exactly what he wanted.

During the incident, Velasquez did hurt one person: Gary Dosemagen.

When the teacher confronted Velasquez as he entered the day care, Velasquez slashed his arm with a meat cleaver. The blood officers found on the kitchen floor belonged to Dosemagen, and he was the injured man at the Gateway Plaza seeking help that prompted the alert tones during the incident.

———

Yahnke, then a sixteen-year veteran, spent the two days after the shooting at home tinkering with his model trains and trying to feel normal. As he walked the eight blocks in the predawn dark to the police station on the day he returned, he thought to himself, *It's too early. I'm coming back too soon. People won't look at me the same. I killed someone, and I will never be the same. How do I face them?*

Not only did coworkers support Yahnke, Papalia, and Pueschner, peers across the state and nation commended them as well. The officers received the Madison Police Department's Medal of Valor, the Meritorious Award from the Wisconsin Professional Police Association, and the national TOP COPS Award. They accepted the latter award at a ceremony hosted by *America's Most Wanted's* John Walsh in Washington, D.C. Yahnke and Pueschner also won the Everyday Heroes Award from the Madison Chapter of the American Red Cross.

Still, everyone did not support their actions. After the shooting, Yahnke in particular found himself frustrated with the reaction from the many local citizens who were floored that they shot and killed Velasquez.

"I'm just shocked Madison cops shot him. What is this—Los Angeles?" one person wrote in a letter to the editor of the *Wisconsin State Journal.*

"We told him twelve to eighteen times to drop it [the weapon], but the public thinks we just went swish bang," Yahnke said.

Community members also questioned Papalia at the community meetings that she attended as a neighborhood officer. She suspected that the public's disapproval had to do with their reluctance to accept officers as the only people justified to shoot. That is not something, however, that weighs lightly on officers.

"It's a fact we think about all the time," said Papalia, then an eighteen-year veteran. "We think about it whenever we put on our gun belts."

One can't be an officer, according to Papalia, and not realize that they may one day have to use it. Rather than say, "Oh please don't let it happen to me," they say, "If it happens, let it be so clear, so necessary, so unquestionable."

———

In the day care incident, nothing could have been clearer to Papalia about the need to use deadly force.

"I would have killed him instantly," Papalia said. "Mothers and children are a bad combination. He wouldn't have gotten any words out of his mouth."

Eight years after the shooting, she said she harbors no regrets and it does not upset her. "I believe we were all there for a reason. There is no joy in seeing someone die, but so powerful was the need to protect the innocent," she said.

Before Papalia went to work the day of the day care incident, her then three-year-old daughter crawled into bed with her and together they snoozed a bit longer.

"The joy of a kid warm from bed—their hair is a mess, they are still groggy, they smell like sleep and fabric softener," she said. "There should be a fragrance called 'sleeping child' and mothers would snap it up. On that day, I made sure that more than twenty-five other moms and dads got to smell that grand perfume for another day ... but for the strength and courage of Phil and Shane, there would be dead children—dead kids ages one to four—can you think of anything more unresolvable than dead toddlers?"

Papalia knows it is okay with the universe because eight years later on her last day of work before retirement in 2012 she happened to see Olga drive by with her daughter, Tatiana, in the front seat next to her.

It was Olga who had told Papalia that they were in the Bumblebee Room that fateful day and asked her to save her Tati.

"Olga went home with Tati that day," Papalia said. "Seeing them together that last day of work, it was how it was supposed to be."

———

Yahnke also is at peace with the shooting, saying eight years later that he never gave his actions a second thought nor has he ever struggled with flashbacks or nightmares.

"Do I wish he died in a prison infirmary rather than in the classroom of that day care? Yes. But I understand he was a tormented man," Yahnke said. "I don't hate him. Maybe I should, but life's too short to hold grudges. Sometimes I have survivor's guilt because of friends who unraveled after shootings, and I'm still here and still married and I'm still a productive member of the department. I wonder why I'm still here and they're not. They were so messed up over their shootings that the only way they could get better was not to be a police officer anymore, but I'm still here. So as odd as it may be, I feel survivor's guilt over that, but I don't look back. I don't dwell on it or think about it every day."

———

The shooting affected Pueschner differently.

"I tell recruits that the easiest thing was to pull the trigger," he said eight years later. "It was the aftereffect that for me turned out to be the hard thing."

A week after the shooting, the Catholic-raised officer sought absolution from a priest. Afterward he believed he could move on from the shooting, but within weeks his wife could see the shooting still bothered him. He became withdrawn, agitated, and short with their two daughters, and she witnessed him experiencing nightmares, breathing heavily, and calling out. He initially rebuffed her concerns and asserted that she was reading too much into things.

"It turned out she was right, and I was wrong," said Pueschner, then a twenty-one-year veteran.

About six months after the incident—during which time he had intrusive thoughts about the shooting and swore he heard the sounds of children crying one night at the gym—Pueschner began counseling for post-traumatic stress disorder.

"I had a hard time with the idea [PTSD] because it [the shooting] happened very fast and it was over very fast," Pueschner said. "I always looked at the troops from Vietnam as being victims of PTSD, and I didn't think I was worthy of that term because of the relative lack of exposure I had."

Pueschner gradually began to come to terms with his PTSD once he started counseling sessions and realized that the loss of control he experienced during the shooting was what upset him.

"Cops are control freaks," Pueschner explained. "If they're not born that way, they become one because their whole job is to gain and maintain control in situations."

Pueschner determined that he had lost control at two points during the incident: when it became clear Velasquez had no intention of dropping the weapon and when he died before the paramedics arrived.

"Once I got my head around that and saw that this was bothering me more than I thought, it led me to getting better," Pueschner said.

Conducting presentations for recruit classes and area police departments about the shooting and his PTSD also played a role in his recovery. The more he talked about the incident and relived it, the more therapeutic it became for him.

"By facing it and not burying it, you gain control," Pueschner explained.

Pueschner gradually overcame his PTSD and reached a point a couple of years later when he stopped thinking about the shooting on a consistent basis.

Around this time, however, his youngest daughter began showing signs of vicarious post-traumatic stress disorder. Whereas his older daughter cried and got out all of her emotions at once, his then seven-year-old kept it in and acted like it didn't bother her. Over the next year or two, however, she became more emotional. Then one day she spilled milk on the floor and burst into tears. She eventually explained to her mother that she feared if she made mistakes her dad would be upset with her and become preoccupied at work and get hurt.

Pueschner took her to counseling as well and learned that it is very common for children to experience vicarious PTSD. After six months of sessions on her own and with Pueschner, she has been fine ever since.

Looking back on the shooting, Pueschner, who retired in 2013, said, "I'm not mad at him. I don't know if I want to say I take pity on him, but I do feel bad for him because he was in such a bad position personally that he felt he had to commit suicide. I don't feel bad for him for assaulting his girlfriend and traumatizing kids and civilians."

Although most of the children had their faces buried in the carpet the instant the officers fired, Pueschner said several of them endured nightmares and had to see therapists. He, Yahnke, and Papalia had an opportunity to visit with the children and their parents at a thank you picnic, where they each received framed awards depicting handprints of the children superimposed on the Red Caboose logo.

"Velasquez did a smart thing as far as picking the day care as a target because society has such an ingrained desire to protect our young. Using them as the threat, he knew he was going to get the response he desired," Pueschner said.

The officers will never know what Velasquez would have done if they hadn't shown up when they did.

"If we wouldn't have shot him, he probably would've harmed Wendy," Pueschner said. "He did cut up Gary pretty good so he had the ability to do that. Whether or not he would attack a child I don't know, but he knew he wouldn't have gotten to that point."

Suicide by Cop

Suicide by cop (SBC) is a method of suicide that occurs when a subject engages in threatening behavior in an attempt to be killed by law enforcement.

In a recent study, researchers studied 707 officer-involved shootings at North American police departments.

Below are some of their findings:

Subjects
+ The mean age of all SBC subjects was thirty-five.
+ They are likely male (95%), Caucasian (41%), single (37%), not a parent (36%), and not employed (54%).
+ 62% had a confirmed or probable mental health history.
+ 16% had a prior known suicide attempt, and 4% had attempted SBC on a prior occasion.
+ 36% of SBC subjects were under the influence of alcohol at the time of the incident.

Incidents
+ 81% of the incidents were spontaneous, 17% were planned, and 3% were unknown.
+ 72% of SBC incidents were over in an hour or less, 62% within thirty minutes, 41% in fifteen minutes or less, and 29% within ten minutes.
+ 46% of the incidents occurred at a residence, 38% in a public or open-air environment, and 11% at a business.
+ SBC subjects were armed with weapons during 80% of the incidents, while 19% feigned or simulated weapon possession.
+ Of those who were armed, 60% possessed a firearm, which was loaded and operational 86% of the time.
+ 48% of those who possessed a firearm fired their weapon at the police.
+ The three most prevalent police service calls in SBC cases were domestic violence/family-related disturbances (15%), observed events (14%), and person with a gun reports (11%).

Outcome
+ 51% of the SBC subjects, 4% of civilians, and 1% of cops were killed during the encounter.
+ 40% of the SBC subjects, 12% of civilians, and 16% of cops were injured during the encounter.
+ 7% of SBC subjects committed suicide during the encounter.

♦ 43% of the SBC subjects who survived the incident were arrested, 25% were arrested and convicted of a crime, 7% went to a mental health system, and 26% were unknown.

— Information compiled from "Suicide by Cop Among Officer-Involved Shooting Cases," by Kris Mohandie, Ph.D.; J. Reid Meloy, Ph.D., A.B.P.P.; and Peter I. Collins, M.C.A., M.D., F.R.C.P.(C) published by the American Academy of Forensic Sciences in 2009.

4

Aftermath

La Crosse Tribune

75¢ >> Serving the region since 1904   **THURSDAY, April 8, 2010**   >> lacrossetribune.com

'The suspect's intent was to kill'

By ANNE JUNGEN
ajungen@lacrossetribune.com

Scott Krome had parked his pickup truck on a cul-de-sac to get a better view of a burning town of Hamilton home March 29 when a stranger opened the driver's side door.

"He goes, 'What is going on here?' He scared the hell out of me," Krome said. "Then he said, 'You should probably get out of here!'"

The man reeked of gasoline

and looked disheveled and scared, like "he knew he was in trouble," Krome said.

He asked for a ride. Panicked, Krome agreed.

But as the man climbed into the passenger seat, Krome saw a friend come out of a nearby home and sprinted away, watching the truck over his shoulder.

He saw the man walk toward a 2006 silver Cadillac sedan, also parked on the cul-de-sac.

"Then he disappeared into the backyard," Krome said. "I heard

Keith Marchbanks moved quickly toward officer James Page, raising the knife, as the officer backpedaled and fired one shot from 7 to 10 feet away, the investigation report stated.

voices going, 'Get down, get down, get down.'"

Then, a gunshot.

Onalaska police officer James Page hit Keith Marchbanks once in the upper abdomen after Marchbanks came at him with a butcher knife outside N5243 Hidden River Road, according to

reports.

Marchbanks, 45, also reportedly stabbed his 43-year-old estranged wife in the chest and thigh before confronting police.

The new details emerged Wednesday as the La Crosse Police Department released its investigation report into the

shooting. Marchbanks remains hospitalized; his condition is not being released.

Page and La Crosse County sheriff's Deputy Daniel Baudek heard Marchbanks' daughters, ages 12 and 21, screaming from behind the door of a locked basement room as smoke from an attached garage fire billowed into the home.

Earlier, the older daughter told her mother to "just go get

See **SUSPECT**, A9

A man stabbed his estranged wife and was now at large.

The daughter called 911 and then barricaded herself in a basement bedroom with her younger sister.

The incident happened in the town of Hamilton near the La Crosse River. It was out of his jurisdiction, but Onalaska Officer James Page volunteered to help knowing the La Crosse County Sheriff's Department would need assistance and he was only five miles away.

"There's reports the house may be on fire," dispatch informed Page just as he approached the driveway to the rural, blue one-story home.

Dispatch was right.

Page pulled into the driveway and immediately saw black smoke billowing from the two-car attached garage and flames shooting out of the windows. The gunshot-like sounds of car tires exploding and windows blowing out pierced the late evening silence as the bright full moon glowed overhead.

He jumped from his car and bolted around the front of the house looking for a way into the exposed basement where the daughters were barricaded. When he found a door, he kicked it in without hesitation.

La Crosse County Deputy Daniel Baudek arrived as Page entered the basement. With guns drawn, the two began searching for the children and the suspect, a black man in his forties. All the while, smoke filtered down the basement steps.

Baudek twisted the knob of a bedroom door and was greeted by the girls' muffled screams. He tried opening it, but it wouldn't budge.

"Deputy Baudek with the La Crosse County Sheriff's Department. Open the door and come out."

The girls neither responded nor came out because, as the officers later learned, they were terrified it was their drunken father, Keith Marchbanks, trying to get in.

The then forty-five-year-old Marchbanks had shown up earlier that evening with an open beer in his hand. He wanted to talk to his twenty-one-year-old daughter even though she had previously told him that she didn't want to see him. He told her that he was going on a trip, shook her hand, and gave her a hug.

Then he walked over to where his wife was sitting in a chair and pulled a paring knife from his jacket. "This is for you," he snarled. He tapped her on the nose with the tip of the knife, accusing her of lying and breaking up their family.

"You did this, you did this," he sneered at her.

Marchbanks silenced her response by choking her until his daughter cried out, "Dad, Dad stop!"

Ignoring her, he stabbed his wife once in the left side of her chest and again in her left leg. He jabbed the knife at her a third time, but missed.

The daughter pleaded for him to stop and said she'd talk to him. He followed her into the kitchen still clutching the paring knife. She backed away, watching cautiously as he cleaned the blood off the weapon. He set it on the counter and exchanged it for a fifteen-inch knife from the butcher's block.

"Mom run! He's got another knife! Get out of the house!"

Despite not wanting to leave her daughters behind, the woman escaped through the front door and ran to a neighbor's house.

Rather than chase after her, Marchbanks went out the door leading to the garage while the daughter stepped out the front door to make sure her mother was okay. While calling 911, she spotted her father outside standing by the garage smoking a cigarette. They made eye contact, and she fled back into the house, locking the front door and the door to the garage.

Within seconds he was at the door, trying to break in. He first rammed it with his shoulder; then he tried drilling through the knob with a tool.

Obeying the 911 dispatcher's instruction to hide, the girl grabbed her twelve-year-old sister and they barricaded themselves in the basement bedroom where Page and Baudek were now, attempting to get in.

"We're the police. The house is on fire. You need to come out now!"

Baudek kicked and shouldered the solid oak door. When the door bowed enough, Page held out his badge, illuminating it with his flashlight to identify himself.

Still screaming, the girls moved the bed and dresser away from the door and bounded out. They ran past Page, and Baudek swiftly handed them off to an officer waiting outside the house.

Page and Baudek then cleared the rest of the basement looking for the suspect and climbed the stairs to the main level. The officers, coughing and struggling to breathe in the black smoke rapidly consuming the house, searched the family room, the kitchen, the bathroom. Still no suspect. It became harder and harder to breathe, especially for the asthmatic Page. The officers discovered a trio of black Labrador retrievers, but there was no sign of the suspect.

"You have to get out of the house—now!" the county sergeant told them over the radio after a few minutes.

Satisfied that the suspect was not in the house, Page scooped up one of the dogs and exited through the front door with Baudek. At some point in the chaos, the other two dogs got out on their own.

The danger was not over though.

"He could be in there," Page said, pointing to a nearby detached garage, "we need to clear it."

"Let's move the squads first," Baudek said, nodding to their cars. Both were parked dangerously close to the blazing attached garage.

Just as the officers split apart, Page spotted him.

The six-foot-tall suspect, wearing a bloodstained white T-shirt, emerged from between the garages and locked eyes with Page.

Page stood about forty feet away in the center of the driveway, directly in Marchbanks' sightline.

He swiftly moved toward Page, carrying the knife in his right hand. The tip was stained with blood. It was later believed that Marchbanks unintentionally cut himself with the knife when jumping a chain-link fence in the backyard.

"Get on the ground!" Page yelled, redrawing his gun.

"Ain't fucking happening," the suspect replied, spit flying from his mouth.

Baudek, now noticing the suspect but not the knife, pulled out his Taser and shouted "Police! Stop!"

Marchbanks paid no attention to Baudek, remaining fixated on Page instead.

"On the ground!" Page screamed.

"Ain't fucking happening!"

He raised the knife up by his head and stormed toward Page.

As the officer backpedaled down the slope of the driveway, time slowed down. He stared back into Marchbanks' eyes. There was an intensity there that he had never seen in his twenty-two years experience in law enforcement. It was almost like looking into his soul. He had no doubt that Marchbanks was going to kill him.

Now just seven feet away, he had ignored some six commands to get on the ground and to drop the knife. He was now out of chances.

Baudek deployed his Taser just as Page pulled the trigger.

The Taser probe struck Marchbanks in the chest and stomach. The round penetrated his abdomen.

The knife fell out of his hand as he dropped to the driveway with a thud. He laid mumbling incoherently on his back with his hands on his chest.

"Don't move! Don't move!" the officers yelled, running over to him.

"We need an ambulance now. Shots fired!" Baudek bellowed into the radio.

Marchbank's eyes rolled back, and he reeked of booze. The officers handcuffed him above the head and dragged him twenty feet from the raging garage fire. When Page cut his T-shirt off, he initially thought the bullet missed. He didn't see any gunshot wounds resembling the way Hollywood portrays them. Then he noticed blood and tissue oozing out from the entry wound two inches under his heart. He knew the bullet had struck him.

To Page, the encounter felt like sixty seconds when in actuality only five or six seconds had elapsed. He didn't remember redrawing his gun. He didn't remember aiming.

Just a little pop. That was it.

———

The March 29, 2010, shooting left Keith Marchbanks paralyzed from the waist down. He pleaded guilty to two counts of second-degree reckless endangerment with use of a dangerous weapon, two counts of first-degree reckless endangerment, and arson. After an emotional testimony where the family spoke of their immense fear of their former patriarch and Page discussed the negative effects on his own life following the incident, Marchbanks received a twenty-two-year prison sentence.

"I was stunned. Everyone thought he was going to get five to seven years," Page said. "It was a good day for my family, his family, and me." The mother recovered from her stab wounds, and Page still keeps in touch with her and one of her daughters. The family even invited him to the oldest daughter's college graduation.

A week after the shooting, the district attorney's office ruled that Page was justified in using deadly force. Initially, he felt fine—even good—after the shooting. He knew his training took over and he did what he was supposed to do.

But once things settled down, reality set in. He had shot someone.

In Onalaska, a town of about twenty thousand, an officer-involved shooting is rare. The last time a cop from the twenty-officer department shot someone was in 1988. "It's a big deal around here," he said. "I'm from here. I grew up here. Everyone knows who I am. You feel like everyone's talking about you."

Page went on a pre-planned vacation for a few days following the incident, during which time he noticed changes in himself. He became hyper-vigilant, struggled to sleep, and went through phases of over-eating and not eating. He didn't feel as though he was a good barometer of his feelings and asked a few cops at the department to keep an eye on him and to let him know if they noticed anything different about him. They never said anything, but over time he felt himself becoming a pressure cooker.

A couple of months later, Page participated in a bicycle race and for the first time since the shooting had an uninterrupted opportunity to reflect on all the ways it had affected his life: How he couldn't sleep. How comments were made to his kids. How people made insensitive remarks about why he would try to kill someone. The more the intrusive thoughts whirled around in his head, the angrier he became and the harder he pedaled. He rode faster and faster until he finally started to cry.

Page continued to be upset when a woman outbid him by a dollar in a silent auction held after the race. Her grin infuriated him. He kept in his anger, but soon after he snapped when he received a complaint at work. The caller rattled on, talking about how his dad, a former detective, would have handled the case, until Page burst out, "Well then have your fucking dad do the fucking report himself!"

The union president sitting next to Page in the patrol room grabbed the phone. Page broke down crying and couldn't stop. He and the assistant chief decided that he should go home early that day. It was seven months later when he returned to duty.

Page was diagnosed with post-traumatic stress disorder during his time away, and once a week he drove fifty miles each way to visit a counselor specializing in treating troops returning from Iraq.

"It was difficult because cops don't talk about their feelings," he said. "But I knew that if I didn't do something I'd be out of this line of work."

According to Page, 80 percent of police officers involved in a shooting either commit suicide or are out of work willingly or unwillingly within five years.

"I knew for my career and my family that I needed to do something," he said.

In total, Page saw the counselor for about seven or eight months. Part of his recovery involved looking at an image of Marchbanks wearing the bloody shirt and gripping the butcher knife. The more he stared at the image, the more desensitized Page eventually became.

"There's no doubt that the aftermath of a shooting is much, much worse than the shooting itself," said Page, who continues to talk to his counselor every couple of months to make sure his emotions are still in check. "It's something you plan for and train for, but when it happens you have no idea what's coming. It hits you like a train."

It made him realize his own mortality, and the thought of his five sons growing up without a father scared the hell out of him.

"I let him [Marchbanks] get way too close to me," he said, noting that officers are allowed to shoot from a much greater distance. "It's difficult to put into words how everything affected me, what affected me, and why I ended up with PTSD. That was building for a number of years, and this was the breaking point for me. After that many years, I saw a lot of things people don't see or don't want to know about. It was a building thing."

Page now conducts speaking engagements across the state, relaying his experience with post-traumatic stress disorder and its effects on cops.

"My goal is to get other officers to speak up and admit that these calls affect us," he said. "I'm not saying everyone has PTSD, but the potential is there and they need to know the warning signs and the treatments before it happens to them. If they go into it blind like I did, it's like trying to find a way through a maze."

In addition to helping others, Page's speaking engagements have proven therapeutic. "I used to have really intrusive thoughts about this incident," he said. "Now I just think about it when I want, and that's a good thing. It's not constantly on my mind like it used to be."

In recognition of Page's and Baudek's actions, they received the Award for Valor from the Wisconsin Professional Police Association and the U.S. Justice Department's Congressional Badge of Bravery. They were the first law enforcement officials in the nation to win the latter award. Page also won the Medal of Honor from the Onalaska Police Department.

"When we were responding to this call and going through it, we didn't even think about any of that," he said. "It [the award] seems unnecessary, but I greatly appreciate it. We were just doing what we had been trained for years to do."

Post-traumatic Stress Disorder in Law Enforcement

Approximately 15 percent of first-responders on average suffer from post-traumatic stress disorder (PTSD), according to Dr. Craig D. Childs, a licensed psychologist from Tyre and Childs Public Safety Consultation in Delafield, Wisconsin.

Here Childs answers some general questions about PTSD as it pertains to law enforcement officers.

What is post-traumatic stress disorder?

PTSD is a complex condition that can develop in anyone exposed to a traumatic event. To meet diagnostic criteria, the condition must last for more than one month and cause significant distress or impairment at home, work, or other areas of social functioning.

What are the symptoms of PTSD?

Symptoms can be broken down into three clusters:

1. Involuntary re-experiencing of the event(s): intrusive thoughts, nightmares, or flashbacks
2. Avoidance or numbing behaviors: avoiding thoughts, feelings, places, or people that are a reminder of the event as well as detachment from friends and family
3. Persistent signs of increased physical arousal: sleep problems, irritability, concentration problems, and exaggerated startle response

To meet diagnostic criteria for PTSD, an officer must exhibit one or more behaviors from each of the three clusters. Symptoms often occur within three months after a traumatic event. After such an incident, officers are distracted by everything going on around them (i.e. the investigation, getting flooded with calls of support from coworkers, family, and friends). Thus, it is often not until an officer gets back to work and resumes his/her daily lifestyle that the symptoms may start to appear.

Why are law enforcement officers likely to develop PTSD?

Officers are more likely than the general population to develop PTSD because of the very nature of their employment. They experience traumatic events at a higher rate than the normal population, and every single workday in the life of an officer carries the potential for danger. "Very few individuals consider their mortality on a daily basis, but officers must consider this on every single call," said Childs, adding that they must practice good officer safety on even routine traffic stops. "This type of vigilance leaves an officer constantly on guard for potential threats. It is physically and emotionally exhausting for the officer to operate this way for years on end."

While not all officers will face a dramatic, life-threatening event, most officers will experience multiple "low level" traumatic events, which often go unnoticed and untreated. Events such as getting beat up while breaking up a bar fight or getting confronted with a knife leave officers feeling vulnerable; but, because no physical harm is done, the officer is typically sent back to work without treatment or support.

"Years of exposure to events like this can have a cumulative effect and can lead to the development of PTSD symptoms over time," Childs said. "At the very least, years of cumulative stress makes an officer more likely to develop PTSD following a more dramatic, individual event than the average officer."

How can a law enforcement officer recover from PTSD?
Recovery from PTSD is most likely when the officer is treated by a qualified professional, preferably soon after the development of symptoms. These professionals should have an understanding of evidence-based therapies for PTSD in addition to an understanding of law enforcement.

Officers will not often seek out counseling, especially when they do not believe that the provider understands law enforcement. Officers that receive treatment from qualified professionals stand a good chance of recovering and returning to duty.

Is there any way to prevent PTSD from developing?
Education can help, but there is no way to completely prevent PTSD. Understanding the signs and symptoms of PTSD, however, can help individuals to identify whether their behaviors are typical or whether they should pursue treatment.

5

March 18

Oneida County officer fired fatal shot during confrontation

BY DAILY NEWS STAFF

Authorities say the officer who fatally injured a Michigan man early Friday morning was an Oneida County deputy.

According to Lincoln County Sheriff Tom Koth no members of the Lincoln County Sheriff's Department fired their weapons during the incident.

Matthew Fisher, 18, of Calumet, Michigan was killed at approximately 1:40 a.m. Friday after he lead Oneida and Lincoln County deputies on a chase. The chase began after an Oneida County deputy observed Fisher acting suspiciously outside of a Woodruff gas station. Fisher left that scene and headed south into Lincoln County, near the town of Bradley, where he began to have car trouble.

Authorities say Fisher got out of his car holding a sawed off shotgun and threatened deputies. He was fatally shot after he refused to drop his weapon.

The Merrill Police Department is assisting as the lead investigating law enforcement agency in this matter.

Koth, interim Oneida County Sheriff John Sweeney, and investigators from the Merrill Police Department are scheduled to meet Monday to discuss the progress of the investigation. A debriefing session was also held Sunday at the Tomahawk City Hall for members of various agencies that were involved in the shooting.

This is the second fatal police shooting in two months involving Oneida County deputies. On February 12, three Oneida County officers fired on and killed a town of Pelican man who had been wielding a gun.

An inquest into that death is being planned by the Oneida County District Attorney's office.

Rhinelander Daily News (now The Northwoods River News)

B rad Fogerty pulled his rifle out of his squad car's gun rack and set it on his lap.

The Oneida County deputy sheriff received the call of the chase while he sat in his parked squad car in the lot of his former elementary school a block from his parent's house. It was March 18, 2005. With his rifle now situated, he took off in search of the suspect, an alleged drunk teenager who fled from a gas station in a run-down Jeep Cherokee.

From his location on the east side of Rhinelander, Fogerty was about fifteen miles south of the deputy who initiated the pursuit. The latter drove eighty-five to ninety miles per hour southbound on Highway 51 through the towns of Minocqua and Woodruff trailing the suspect until he ultimately lost sight of him.

It took Fogerty about ten minutes to get from Highway 8 onto Highway 51. He was now five miles south of the suspect and the closest of all the deputies that had responded. He swiftly sped through the dark night, one of the few solitary cars on the road.

Near the county line of Oneida and Lincoln, Fogerty pulled his squad over onto the snowy side of the road. He planned to set up road spikes, but it was too late. Before he could get out of his car, a pair of headlights belonging to the jeep appeared.

When it zipped past him he whipped his squad around and set off after it.

After one long minute, he spotted the jeep's taillights. He trailed close behind, the two zooming down the lonely highway at around seventy miles per hour.

The chase went on like that for a few minutes until big white clouds of smoke billowed out from the jeep, swirling toward Fogerty. He knew the jeep would die any minute.

"This is going to end real quick," he said over the radio. "Get me some help."

The nearest deputy was about six miles away.

The smoke intensified and within a minute the jeep slowly pulled over just south of Highway 8. The jeep chugged to a stop just after passing a road sign reading *Hospital Exit 231.*

Fogerty stopped about seventy feet behind it and, with his .223 rifle already in hand, got out of his squad. He knew a Lincoln County deputy was almost there.

The suspect simultaneously emerged from the jeep, illuminated by the headlights of a passing car. He took one step toward Fogerty, raising his left hand high in the air. While the latter motion conveyed a message of surrender, the object in his other hand proved otherwise. Standing in the steady glare of the squad's headlights, the suspect gripped in his right hand a .22 semi-automatic rifle pointed toward the ground. It was whittled into a pistol grip with the barrel sawed off in order to conceal it.

"Drop the gun!" Fogerty yelled. "Drop the gun!"

The suspect looked at Fogerty with a blank expression, remaining focused on him despite the arrival of two Lincoln County deputies. One stood to the left of Fogerty; the other came up behind him on the right side of his squad car. Fogerty didn't notice the deputy to his right until later.

"Drop the gun!" Fogerty yelled. He commanded the teenager to drop the gun fifteen to twenty times, but when the suspect manipulated the hammer of the gun he knew it was time. He started to give him one final command when the suspect started to level his gun at Fogerty.

Fogerty fired five times from 66.7 feet away. The first three shots came out automatically, and he fired two additional shots after that.

The suspect tried to brace his fall, but he dropped to the ground, flat on his stomach with his hands outstretched in front of him.

Fogerty prepared to fire again as the suspect's right hand moved toward the gun he'd dropped, but the motion abruptly stopped. Fogerty knew he had struck him too many times to be getting up again.

The moment of shock the deputy initially felt lasted less than a second, as powerful black smoke suddenly rose from the front of the jeep. It was on fire.

He briefly hesitated. He would have normally waited for the rest of his unit to arrive before approaching the suspect, but the fear of an explosion forced him to attend to him right away. Knowing his sergeant and partner were at least on the way, he rushed over to the suspect with his gun aimed at him, followed by the two Lincoln County deputies. It wasn't until then that Fogerty noticed the deputy on his right, later telling him, "I'm glad you're a good guy because I definitely had no idea you were there."

Under the protection of the deputy on the left, Fogerty and the other deputy inspected the motionless suspect.

"Handcuff him," Fogerty instructed the latter, glancing at the growing fire.

Another deputy arrived and peered into the car to see if anyone else was inside. Two more deputies came next, all the while the ominous dark smoke billowed from the jeep. It gushed around the edges of the hood and smelled like burning plastic and oil.

With no portable radio capabilities, Fogerty ran back to his squad car and announced over the radio, "Shots fired! Suspect down!"

Ultimately a dozen cops responded, some of them holding guard over the suspect while others examined the car. One retrieved an extinguisher, but that proved useless. The acrid smoke now mushroomed from the wheel wells and rippled across the ground.

Fogerty and his partner each grabbed the suspect by his arms and dragged him away from the fire, just as the black smelly smoke gave way to the eruption of vivid orange flames. The jeep was now fully engulfed.

While deputies worked to extinguish the blaze, Fogerty turned his attention back to the suspect, whom they laid on the ground in front of his squad car. He was still and non-responsive. His partner—a former EMT—inspected the suspect's wounds. He was struck four times above the rib cage and once in the upper arm and side of his chest.

He appeared to be dead.

Moving away from the intense heat, the other deputies joined Fogerty and his partner by the front of his squad. They waited for an ambulance and rendered what little medical aid they could as the fire raged on ahead of them on the otherwise quiet, dark highway.

———

Initially Fogerty was angry.

"I was pissed off at this guy for pointing a gun at me," Fogerty recalled eight years later. "He made me shoot him, which is the last thing cops want to do."

Then Fogerty learned that the teenager may have had gang affiliations. Nothing ever came of that, but he initially worried about retaliation against his pregnant wife, family, and friends.

Next he started doubting himself.

Did he put both hands up in the air saying, "I'm giving up because my car's on fire?"

Did I just shoot someone who didn't have a gun in his hand?

Fogerty was unable to talk to the two Lincoln County deputies as they were all separated after the shooting at the nearby Tomahawk Police Department, but the next day his concerns were put to rest after the Merrill Police

Department investigators concluded that everything happened as he described it. The suspect—later determined to be eighteen-year-old Matthew Fisher—did not drop the gun, and he did point it right at him.

"Once I heard that it did happen the way I thought it happened, I was okay with it after that," Fogerty said. "I had no issues, and there's been no nightmares or flashbacks."

Fogerty credits the non-stop phone calls that he received from co-workers over the next four days.

"Every time someone would call, I'd go through it again and that helped because I'm not a big talker," he said. "But that forced me to talk about it."

Fogerty only experienced two lingering effects from the shooting.

The first took place a couple of weeks later when he heard a gunshot for the first time after the incident. Sergeant Randy Keller took him to the shooting range to get him acclimated to shooting again, and the sound of the shot caused him to shake for about thirty seconds.

The second effect happened a year after the shooting during a SWAT training when deputies strapped a bomb on top of a car and blew it up. The sound of the explosion, the sights of the smoke, and the smell of the burning car transported Fogerty back to that night on the highway. Again, the anxiety lasted about thirty seconds before he shook it off.

Fogerty struggled for a while about whether or not he waited too long to shoot; after all the deadly force requirements were there the moment the suspect stepped out of the car armed with the gun. He took consolation, however, in knowing that he did the right thing and that the "good guys" went home.

"I gave him every opportunity to not let it turn out that way, but I knew I was going home that night," he said. "I'm okay with it because I'm here now, and if I wouldn't have done what I did there's a high probability I might not be. I look at my son, whose seven now, and he wouldn't have ever known me."

The two Lincoln County deputies on scene with him both had less than a year of experience. Neither one of them reacted as quickly as Fogerty, a then seven-year veteran of the department who was also on the SWAT team.

"I'm still not convinced either one of them would have taken care of the situation, which would have turned out bad," said Fogerty, who believes he reverted back to his training. "It wasn't me pulling the trigger that night. It was [my firearms instructors] Randy [Keller] and Nate [Ouimette]."

Keller asked Fogerty to become a firearms instructor shortly after the shooting, a task the latter does not take lightly.

"Now it's my responsibility to get the rest of these guys ready," Fogerty said. "I'm hard on training and push them, but in the end they all understand why because you've got to be ready for your own March eighteen."

One of his biggest pieces of advice is to always have your gun ready when responding to a high-risk call or pursuit, as he did.

"If I had left my rifle in the rack, he would have beat me out of the car with that gun," Fogerty said. "That's something I now drill into the guys: If you think you might need it, get it out. If you don't end up needing it, throw it in the seat next to you and put it away later."

Technical schools use Fogerty's squad car dash-cam video of the shooting as a learning tool for police recruits, and Fogerty agreed to be featured in an episode on deadly police shootings on Court TV (now TruTv).

"I didn't ask for it to happen; I did all I could to prevent it, " said Fogerty, who won the Wisconsin Professional Police Association Award for Valor in 2006. "But it happened, and I did it [the show] in case another copper would see it and learn something from it."

Deadly Force Decision-Making

- Deadly force is defined as the intentional use of a firearm or other instrument, the use of which would result in a high probability of death.
    - ◊ An officer accidentally striking a person in the head with a baton because they ducked or fell would not be considered deadly force because it wasn't intentional. A baton strike to the knee area that inadvertently causes death due to a fractured bone slicing an artery, for example, is also not considered deadly force because that action was not likely to cause death.
- Subject behavior that justifies an officer's use of deadly force is defined as any behavior that an officer reasonably believes has caused or imminently threatens to cause death or great bodily harm to him/herself or another person.
    - ◊ The definition includes great bodily harm because an officer may respond to a given level of force with a higher one in order to control the situation.
- For a subject's threat to be considered imminent, it must meet three criteria:
    - ◊ *Intent:* Examples include pointing a weapon at the officer, stating an intention to kill him/her, rushing at him/her with a knife, etc.
    - ◊ *Weapon:* The subject must have a conventional or unconventional weapon capable of inflicting great bodily harm or death.
    - ◊ *Delivery System:* The subject must have a means of using the weapon to inflict harm. For example, a person armed with a baseball bat who stated his/her intention to kill an officer meets the criteria for imminent threat if he/she is standing ten feet away—not fifty yards away on the other side of a fence. The danger zones for weapons are:
        - ◊ Unarmed: less than ten feet
        - ◊ Club or edged weapon: less than twenty-one feet
        - ◊ Gun: in the line of sight unbroken by cover
- Referred to as *preclusion*, deadly force should be used as a last resort. Furthermore, an officer must be able to articulate that, if possible, he/she attempted to escalate through other modes and tactics and that all other options were closed.
- Once an officer determines that a threat meets the deadly force response requirements, three *target requirements* must be met:
    - ◊ Target acquisition: An officer has acquired an actual target to shoot at. One cannot fire blindly in the direction of a sound, for example, because he/she may endanger others.

◊ Target identification: An officer has identified his/her target as the source of the imminent threat.

◊ Target isolation: An officer can shoot at his/her target without danger of harming innocent people. The one exception to the requirement is called the *greater danger exception*, which allows an officer to shoot without target isolation if the consequence of not stopping the threat would be worse than the possibility of hitting an innocent person.

♦ An officer's judgment in a deadly force situation is based on the totality of circumstances known at the time. For example, an officer is justified in using deadly force if a suspect pointed a pistol at him/her with the clear intent to shoot even if it turns out later the suspect's gun was not loaded.

♦ The purpose for using deadly force is to stop a threat. When the threat stops, the officer must stop shooting. His/her judgment as to whether the threat has stopped, however, is based on his/her reasonable perception of the totality of the circumstances at the time.

—Information provided by the Wisconsin Department of Justice's Training and Standards Bureau.

6

A Lifetime of Respect

Vernon Broadcaster

Grenades, gunfire rock rural Viola

Tactics allow authorities to avoid injuries

by Matt Johnson

Law officers attempting to arrest a rural Viola man last Thursday had to withstand rifle fire and explosions from about 15 improvised hand grenades.

The Vernon County Sheriff's Department, which was acting in mutual aid of the Richland County Sheriff's Department, had 12 tactical team officers at the scene when Robert Bayliss, 60, was apprehended after he was subdued by non-lethal bean-bag rounds. Vernon County Sheriff Gene Cary said the fact that officers were able to escape injury and also arrest Bayliss unharmed was a combination of having the proper equipment, training and a good plan.

"We do a lot of training and sometimes it's so much you wonder if we'll ever use it," Cary said. "But yesterday I became convinced training saved lives."

On Monday, March 31, Richland County officers attempted to serve papers to Bayliss at his home on Co. G about two miles from Viola. When they approached his residence, they were fired upon.

The Richland County Sheriff's Department then sought mutual aid from Vernon and La Crosse counties. While they kept surveillance on Bayliss' residence, they formed a plan to arrest him.

That plan included using La Crosse County's Bear Cat

See *'Gunfire'* page A-2

Robert Bayliss

Bear Cat emerges with scars—Damage sustained by La Crosse County's armored rescue "Bear Cat" vehicle was evident after two raids on the residence of Robert Bayliss in rural Viola, Thursday. The vehicle was shot seven times. Bayliss was firing a high-powered rifle of unknown caliber. (Matt Johnson photo)

"We are going to be shot at. If you're uncomfortable with that tell me now."

Lieutenant Rodney Stearns, the SWAT team commander for the Eau Claire County Sheriff's Office, delivered this warning to his officers prior to engaging in a twelve-minute shootout involving about two hundred officers from nearly two dozen Wisconsin agencies and units.

The incident began three days earlier on March 31, 2008, in rural Richland County when deputies attempted to serve civil process papers for tax delinquency to Robert C. Bayliss, a man described by Stearns as a survivalist and non-believer in government entities. Deputies had made several previous attempts to serve Bayliss, but each time proved unsuccessful, as the then sixty year old always came to the door with a holstered gun, his temperament worsening each time.

Four uniformed deputies decided on this particular afternoon to approach him from a field next to his eighteen-acre property off County Highway G near Viola in an attempt to prevent further escalation. The situation they feared became a reality when Bayliss shot at them multiple times with a high-powered rifle loaded with a type of ammunition designed to penetrate ballistic armor known as "cop killers." In the words of Stearns, Bayliss "knew what he was doing."

Unharmed, the deputies retreated, but the confrontation was not over. This was a full-on operation now that Bayliss shot at law enforcement officers.

The police knew that they would not be able to arrest Bayliss the next time he left the house because he was holed up inside of it and hadn't left for months. Furthermore, they knew that they needed an armored vehicle because there was no way to near his secluded hilltop house unnoticed, especially since the surrounding trees were all bare. Bayliss was sure to spot and shoot at any entering police vehicles with his superior viewpoint.

Over the next two days, the Richland County Sheriff's Department formulated a plan to peacefully resolve the situation. Authorities obtained arrest and search warrants, increased police presence in the area with the help of the Vernon County Sheriff's Department, and requested assistance from the Richland County Special Response Team, the Vernon County and La Crosse County tactical teams, and the Wisconsin State Patrol Fixed Wing that would provide air support.

In the early morning hours of April 3, Richland County authorities secured the area and snipers lay ready. Then at nine a.m. the La Crosse County Emergency Response Team headed toward Bayliss' residence in its bulletproof vehicle, the Ballistic Engineered Armored Response Counter Attack Truck, or "BearCat."

Bayliss, said to be armed with about seventy weapons in his house, immediately opened fire from a second floor window, compromising the windshield of the BearCat. The La Crosse team retreated to the end of the driveway at the bottom of the hill, and police ordered Bayliss to surrender via the public address system. He refused, and it became clear to authorities that more resources were needed.

It was at this point that Stearns became involved. The authorities requested the Eau Claire County SWAT team's assistance along with that of the Sauk County Emergency Response Team, the Kenosha Air One helicopter, and the Dane County Tactical Response Team. Like La Crosse, the Eau Claire County and Dane County tactical teams each had a BearCat.

Stearns immediately responded, bringing with him half a dozen SWAT team members and a medic. They drove the entire hour and fifteen minutes from Eau Claire to Richland County with lights flashing and sirens blaring, prepared to enter a dangerous and potentially deadly battle.

Stearns met with the sheriffs from Richland, Eau Claire, and Vernon Counties around noon, and they devised a new strategy. The three BearCats from La Crosse, Dane, and Eau Claire would converge on Bayliss' property and pump tear gas into his house until he was forced to come out. While Bayliss distracted himself shooting at one vehicle, another would fire back.

Meanwhile the police continued to speak to Bayliss via the public address system during the day, encouraging him to surrender peacefully. He neither surrendered nor communicated with them.

By the time late afternoon arrived, the police were ready to engage in what they rightly predicted would be one of the largest shootouts ever in Wisconsin.

Stearns, a then twenty-eight-year veteran, climbed into the driver's seat of the Eau Claire BearCat while his team braced themselves to shoot from the six-inch holes, called ports. Another member responsible for reloading the weapons positioned himself in the middle of the vehicle, and a medic prepared to provide first-line care in the event of injuries.

Just before five p.m., the three BearCats ascended the hill leading to Bayliss' dwelling. It was so small that Stearns thought it looked like two shacks stacked on top of each other. Following a muddy trail, he struggled to navigate through the myriad trash and abandoned vehicles and trailers. Given all the junk scattered on Bayliss' property, Stearns thought it would appear to most people as an uninhabited area.

When Stearns crested the hill, the shots he anticipated rang out as Bayliss fired at them from the second story of his house about thirty-five feet away. The rounds pinged off the BearCat like rocks hitting a tin can. His team fought back, returning fire and pumping chemicals into the house. A home-made grenade exploded behind the BearCat before Bayliss hurled another, this time detonating on the fender wall of the vehicle.

Nothing stopped Bayliss, a sharpshooter, from his attack because as Stearns later discovered he hid behind a three-and-a-half by two-and-half foot wide steel plate, the same material from which BearCats are constructed. He also learned after the incident that Bayliss put a plastic bag over his head to protect himself from the chemical munitions, but of course that did no good.

Despite the outside warfare, the ambiance inside the BearCat was un-ruffled as the team remained focused on what to do next. Officers dutifully fired rounds and chemicals, periodically handing back a gun and shouting,

"Reload! Reload!" They warned of incoming grenades and ducked, and they made announcements over the mild radio transmissions.

Stearns' adrenaline raced and his heart pumped. Even though he knew that the BearCat was designed to keep them safe, as the team commander, he still feared for his teams' safety. He knew Bayliss would fire at them, but he didn't expect him to shoot so many lethal rounds at them.

What he describes as a "wild barrage of gunfight" only came to an end when the house inexplicably caught on fire. Escaping the smoke and flames, Bayliss climbed out through a second story window onto a makeshift ladder armed with a small handgun on his side.

"Drop the weapon! Drop the weapon!" the police ordered.

He refused, and the Eau Claire team blasted him with five beanbag rounds until he dropped the pistol. The police took him into custody after a brief struggle while the house he had holed himself up in burned to the ground. The rounds and ammunition cooking inside the blazing building, in addition to the possibility of explosives in or around Bayliss' house, made it impossible for the firefighters to enter.

During the eternity that was those twelve minutes, Bayliss threw three homemade grenades and fired at least a hundred rounds, busting out the windows of Eau Claire's BearCat. The teams in the BearCats returned two to three hundred rounds and pumped about thirty-five rounds of chemical munitions into the house. With the exception of some chemicals getting into officers' eyes, no one was injured thanks to the BearCats. Bayliss, other than some pain from the beanbag rounds striking his thighs, was uninjured as well.

"This vehicle is what allowed these law enforcement officers to go home and hug their wives and bounce their children on their knees that night," Stearns said. "If it hadn't been for the BearCat, we would not be here."

The purchase of the armored vehicle a few years earlier caused a lot of controversy in Eau Claire with many thinking the sheriff's office was becoming too militaristic, but Stearns said this incident proved to citizens just how necessary BearCats are for tactical teams.

"Maybe people are starting to see that we don't live in such a safe world," he said. "They want to believe we do, but there's a line of what you believe and what actually exists."

The words "rescue vehicle" were initially plastered on the BearCat, but after the standoff Stearns peeled that off and relabeled it "SWAT." "I figured we earned the respect," he said.

Eau Claire County Lieutenant Rodney Stearns brought Eau Claire's BearCat (short for Ballistic Engineered Armored Response Counter Attack Truck) to the incident with Robert C. Bayliss. During the twelve-minute shootout, the BearCat was struck three times (photo provided by Rodney Stearns).

The BearCat was struck three times during the shootout. Next to one of the areas where it got hit Stearns placed a six-by-six-inch emblem reading, "In memory of Richland County armed stand-off 4-3-2008. With appreciation to the Sheriff's Departments of Vernon County, La Crosse County, Dane County, Eau Claire County, and Sauk County. S.W.A.T. Twelve Minutes of hell ... a lifetime of respect!"

In addition to the recognition they gave each other, the Wisconsin Association of SWAT Personnel awarded the

Next to one of the three places the BearCat was struck during the shootout, Eau Claire County Lieutenant Rodney Stearns placed this six-by-six-inch emblem (photo provided by Rodney Stearns).

2008 SWAT Team of the Year Award to the six teams from Eau Claire, Dane, La Crosse, Richland, Sauk, and Vernon. For the first time in the association's history the award was given to multiple teams involved in a single event.

The Eau Claire team members also received a special recognition award at the sheriff's office's annual banquet in early 2009. The Richland County sheriff, the Wisconsin Emergency Management director, and the regional team coordinator of the Office of Justice Assistance attended the banquet to present the awards.

When the case went to trial a year after the standoff, Bayliss told a jury that he shot at them because they trespassed on his land. During the trial he represented himself, referred to himself in third person, and refused to recognize the court or judge. He even referred to the BearCats as "Weinermobiles," according to Stearns. The jury found him guilty on thirteen of seventeen charges, including four counts of attempted first degree intentional homicide, and he was sentenced to forty-eight years in prison.

The incident with Bayliss proved to be a reality check for Stearns of how dangerous it is to work in law enforcement.

"It brings you closer to your family, and you become very defensive about what you do," he said. "You look at people and wonder how they dare criticize [the police] when these guys are the only ones willing to take on an incident like this and not bat an eye."

Members of the SWAT team who didn't have their pager on when the call came in for Eau Claire to respond were upset, according to Stearns. "They should've been thankful, but they're not because something in their blood tells them they are supposed to respond to a call of need—not away from it. Most times society doesn't understand that this is what law enforcement officers are made of. We were in a territory we didn't know, protecting a community we didn't know, but we were called upon to help and that's how we are."

After the incident, Stearns led a closed-room discussion with his team to give everyone the opportunity to talk openly about what happened.

"They vented. They said what was bothering them and what they were thinking about during all of this," he said. "You think of the strangest things during an incident as horrific as this, like, 'Why didn't I take my daughter when she was nine to that game she wanted to go to?' You think of your family almost immediately because that's who stands by you every time."

The team also thanked each other for ensuring that they all got themselves home that night.

"It's not a game that you won, but you feel somewhat elated that the incident took place the way it did," Stearns said. "You ask yourself one question: would you feel the same when you walked away had this guy died in this battle, or are you elated because this incident was huge and everyone lived? Would that have changed if this guy died? That's a tough one."

BearCat Basics

Eau Claire County Lieutenant Rodney Stearns credits the agency's BearCat for saving his team members' lives during the 2008 standoff in Richland County.

But what exactly is a BearCat?

It is an armored vehicle whose name is short for Ballistic Engineered Armored Response Counter-Attack Truck made by Lenco Industries, Inc. in Massachusetts. The Eau Claire County Sheriff's Office purchased the $186,000 vehicle in 2003 with a federal Homeland Security grant.

The BearCat is used about twenty to twenty-five times a year in high-risk situations such as taking an armed suspect into custody or rescuing injured officers or citizens. Besides Eau Claire, it is available to other law enforcement agencies with the northwest Emergency Police Services and occasionally outside this region when additional BearCats are requested.

The BearCat features:
+ Half-inch steel armor plates
+ Bulletproof windows
+ Blast fragmentation resistant floors
+ Specially designed gun ports
+ Roof hatches with rotating turrets
+ Gun mounts
+ Gear storage
+ A ram on the front to bust open doors
+ A speaker system for communication efforts
+ Biological and nuclear detection devices
+ FLIR (Forward Looking Infrared Radars)

—Information provided by Eau Claire County Lieutenant Rodney Stearns.

7

You Just Never Know

Police say suspect just kept coming

He "was like a bucking bronco," says the officer who shot him on Williamson Street.

By Ed Treleven
Wisconsin State Journal

Despite gunshot wounds to his abdomen, both thighs and a wrist, a man calling himself David Lopez Jr. "was like a bucking bronco" as Madison police struggled to handcuff him, the police sergeant who shot Lopez said.

"After I fired the fourth shot, he was still going at it," Sgt. Karen Krahn told a Madison police detective investigating the shooting of Lopez, 28, whose true identity police have not yet confirmed. "It's like the shots didn't do anything at all."

In all, it took more than six officers to get the 5-foot-8-inch, 200-pound Lopez into an ambulance.

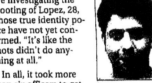

Lopez

The comments were included in a detailed criminal complaint filed Friday that charged Lopez with nine felonies related to an incident early Monday in the 900 block of Williamson Street. Lopez allegedly fought with and sexually assaulted a woman before fighting police who attempted to arrest him.

Lopez was charged with second-degree sexual assault, false imprisonment, attempting to disarm a police officer, driving a stolen vehicle, battery to a police officer, two counts of battery, two counts of resisting police and two counts of misdemeanor bail jumping.

Dane County District Attorney Brian Blanchard said that after reviewing the case, he saw nothing criminal about the use of deadly force by Krahn.

"Sgt. Krahn was faced by a situation where she had no option but to use lethal force," he said. "I don't consider it a close case in any sense."

The criminal complaint hints that cocaine found in Lopez's system might have played a role in his behavior. In a statement to police at UW Hospital, Lopez said he was once very addicted to cocaine but had been clean for two years until Sunday night.

According to the complaint:

The woman told police the incident began about 4:15 a.m. after she and Lopez had a long and intense talk at her apartment. Lopez refused to leave.

Please see SHOOTING, Page A9

Wisconsin State Journal

I n mere minutes she went from taking her meal break to fearing for her life. The incident happened on June 14, 2004, at about four-thirty a.m. Madison Sergeant Karen Krahn sat in her parked squad car eating and catching up on reports when dispatch advised of a woman screaming for help from her backyard.

"Dispatch assign me to that," said Krahn, assuming the call had to do with a domestic situation.

She would normally let officers handle those types of calls, but a victim shouting for help outside at that time of night gave her the sense that it required a supervisor's attention.

Being about a mile-and-a-half from the scene, Krahn headed over to Williamson Street, a major road running through Madison. The incident was reported in the nine hundred block, an area comprised of mostly turn-of-the-century houses and a smattering of small businesses. Along the way, dispatch continued to receive calls about the screaming woman.

Officer Rhonda Jackson arrived on scene first, less than a minute after the call was dispatched.

"I got them. They're in the backyard," she called out over the radio. Before dispatch could respond, she added in a heightened tone, "Now they're in the street!"

As Krahn rounded the corner onto Williamson, she saw a police car taking off ahead of her and silhouettes of people in the road.

"He's taking my squad! He's stealing my squad!" Jackson yelled.

Flipping on the lights and sirens, Krahn took off after the stolen police car. As she zipped past Jackson, she locked eyes with her and pressed her hand against the window as if to say, "I've got this."

Krahn noticed Jackson's messy hair and rumpled uniform. She didn't appear injured, but Krahn could tell she had been in an altercation. She learned later that after Jackson arrived she witnessed the suspect dragging a woman across the street by her hair. When she confronted him, he let the woman go and squared off with Jackson. She deployed her Taser, but because all but one probe fell out, it only worked momentarily. He got her on the ground, straddled her, and began striking her. After she Tased him a second time, he got off of her but that deployment didn't affect him either. He ran toward Jackson's car and hopped into the driver's seat.

Krahn was now right behind the suspect, the two reaching speeds of about fifty to fifty-five miles per hour down the residential street. Trailing the suspect as he drove erratically down the centerline of the road, she considered all that could go wrong: He had access to Jackson's shotgun. He could listen to their radio traffic. Not to mention that none of the officers would know which vehicle he was driving because they were all in marked police cars.

After about a block-and-a-half, Officer Joel Holum drove toward them from the opposite direction. He pulled over to the curb to avoid a collision, stopping about thirty feet behind a large terrace tree.

As he approached Holum, the suspect jerked the car to the left in an effort to hit the officer. He over-steered and crashed into the tree at about fifty miles per hour. The front of the vehicle caved in, causing the airbags to deploy. The force of the impact lifted the rear of the squad and pivoted it, positioning it parallel to the terrace.

Krahn stopped her squad and radioed in their location. From where she sat, she could see the man flailing his arms about. She assumed that he had been significantly injured. Shifting into rescue mode, she made a wide arc around the damaged vehicle, stopping about thirty to forty feet in front of it.

With her headlights directed on the suspect, she rushed over to him and knocked once on the window. The man, a Hispanic in his early twenties with collar-length, wavy hair, wore an angry expression and looked at her with large, intense eyes. She could see that he wasn't injured, but before she had a chance to say anything he began reaching down toward the floor of the car, presumably for a weapon.

"Show me your hands!" Krahn yelled, backing away and drawing her gun. He continued reaching, and she ordered him again to show his hands, but to no avail.

Krahn tucked her handgun back into the holster on her right hip and pulled on the door to get the suspect to open it. She wondered if the door might be jammed shut from the impact and that's why he wasn't already out. When she lifted the handle it clicked open, and he violently tried to get out. Knowing she needed to control how he exited and not the other way around, she pushed in the door against his efforts to push it out. She didn't see Holum anywhere, but she expected him to show up any second. Together they could get him out of the car and into custody.

Krahn quickly realized, however, that plan wasn't going to work. While she's not a weak woman, she could tell that he was stronger. She used every bit of her five-foot-four, a hundred-fifty pounds to keep that door closed, but she knew she would ultimately lose the battle.

He finally pushed his way out, and she stepped back. She didn't want to fight with him. She would let him escape for now and go after him when the other officers arrived. She moved toward the front of the cruiser so that he wouldn't feel cornered. She wanted him to run.

When he climbed out of the squad, however, the six-foot-tall, two hundred pound man came after her.

"Get on the ground! Get on the ground!" she ordered, drawing her gun and backpedaling away from him.

He ran at her, his arms spinning in a windmill motion, yelling "BAM BAM BAM, POLICE, BAM BAM BAM!" in a thick accent.

What is he talking about?

She looked for a weapon in his hands, but didn't see any.

He came at Krahn in, what felt like to her, slow motion. He stepped closer. And closer. He reached for the barrel of her gun, coming within three to four inches of it.

The next step he takes he's going to snatch it, and if he does, I'm dead.

After all, he'd already proven to her that he's capable of anything. He stole a squad car. He didn't run when she gave him the chance. If he grabbed her gun, she knew it wasn't because he wanted a souvenir. He would use it.

She had no other option. She had to shoot.

BANG!

Krahn somehow slipped to the pavement and shot again as she fell.

She scooted on her back, using her legs to fend him off. He continued to swing his arms in the air yelling, "DIE! DIE, POLICE, DIE!"

Suddenly a few drops sprinkled her skin; but, in the predawn darkness, she didn't immediately identify the source.

Then she spotted his bloody hand whipping at her.

I hope he doesn't have HIV.

While using her left leg to push him away and her right leg to kick at him, she fired a third shot.

No reaction.

He continued swinging his arms at her, trying to hit her.

Despite firing three shots, the suspect didn't flinch or react at all.

Am I shooting blanks?

With her foot pressed against his hip she fired a fourth shot at almost point blank range at his midsection. The blast of air from the muzzle zoomed past her foot, leading her to believe she'd blown it off.

Officers later told her that the shots sounded like BANG! Pause. BANG! Pause. BANG! Pause. BANG! Pause. Though she fired the shots within seconds of each other, the encounter felt like an eternity to Krahn.

After the fourth shot—less than ten seconds after the suspect surged from the vehicle—Holum arrived.

"Sarge, let me get in there," he said.

Holum made a running tackle, knocking the suspect to the ground as Krahn attempted to restrain him. She tried to holster her gun so she could use both hands but discovered her gun belt had shifted and her holster was now in the small of her back.

With her gun still in her right hand, she continued using her left to help Holum subdue the suspect, now flat on his back. It wasn't until the suspect grabbed onto her gun that her brain caught up, allowing her to pull her gun belt around so she could holster it.

More officers arrived and joined in the struggle. Laying on his stomach in a pool of blood, the suspect blabbered and foamed at the mouth like a wild animal. One moment he'd stop and relax and the next he'd be furiously fighting again. During the quiet episodes Krahn feared he was dying. Even though he had tried to kill her, no officer wants the burden of taking a life.

Ultimately it took seven officers to restrain and handcuff him. While in the ambulance, he continued to fight and bite at the air, aiming for the paramedics. After the five-minute ride to the hospital, a football player-sized officer who helped control the suspect in the ambulance told Krahn his forearm shook from the physical exertion of trying to keep the suspect's head down.

The man was treated at the hospital for four gun shot wounds: one in his hand, two in his abdomen, and one in his upper thigh.

The district attorney's office cleared Krahn of the shooting a few days after the incident.

The suspect, who she said was mentally unstable and high on cocaine the night of the shooting, was charged with three counts of battery, one count of false imprisonment, one count of disarming a peace officer, one count of taking and driving a vehicle without owner's consent, one count of battery to law officers/firefighters, and two counts of resisting or obstructing an officer. According to Krahn, he later told authorities that he fought her because he believed he was an Angel of God and had to kill her.

The man, Carlos Toledo-Rubio (alias David Lopez Jr.), was found guilty of the charges but not guilty due to mental disease or defect and was committed to Mendota Mental Health Institute for nineteen-and-a-half years. After approximately three years of treatment, doctors determined that he had regained his sanity, and he was released and deported to Mexico.

Krahn knew without a doubt that she made the right decision to shoot him, and she has always been at peace with her decision. Initially, she worried that other cops wouldn't believe her about what happened that night, but considering that so many officers witnessed him fighting like a bucking bronco after having been shot four times, she knew she had everyone's support.

Friends and family often asked if she feared returning to work following the shooting, but she always said no. She felt confident that her training would kick in when needed and she would react the right way. Police always wonder if they'll be able to pass the ultimate test, and Krahn felt gratified knowing that she did. If anything, she felt more confident returning to work after the shooting.

For her actions that night, Krahn received the Wisconsin Professional Police Association Meritorious Award and an award from the Wisconsin Association of Women Police.

"You just think you did your job, and you get an award for it," said Krahn, who at the time of the shooting had been an officer for nine years and a sergeant for two. "You don't think of yourself as brave. You just do what you do."

This is not to say that the shooting did not affect her.

Over time, the incident led Krahn and her domestic partner to discuss how quickly things can happen in life and how they needed to live more in the moment. They led a frugal life, always preoccupied with saving money for the future, but this experience encouraged them to do things they previously only dreamed of, such as buying a lake cottage.

"It's given us a lot of enjoyment, and it's one of the best things we ever did," Krahn said of the purchase. "We've had a lot of good, peaceful times up there with friends."

In the years following the shooting, she also put her experience to good use by speaking to recruits, giving them a step-by-step account of how she felt and what she thought during and after the incident.

"It really helps put them in that situation," she said. "TV's not reality, and you can only do so much training. You have to mentally make it as real as you can and rehearse it in your mind."

Shootings are traumatic, life-changing experiences that take a long time to digest. For Krahn, she often thought she had come to terms with it, only to discover she hadn't. Five years passed before she could get through a day without thinking of the shooting. Then one day she realized she hadn't thought about it the day before.

"You just don't know when life is going to be taken," she said. "I was just taking a moment to unwind and eat when this happened, so you just never know."

———

Sergeant Karen Krahn died in May 2013 following a battle with cancer. Shortly before her death, Madison Police Chief Noble Wray presented her with the department's first Courageous Service Award.

*Officer Rhonda Jackson is a pseudonym as requested by the officer for privacy's sake.

Women Police in Wisconsin

Women make up about 20 percent of Wisconsin's law enforcement community according to figures provided by the Wisconsin Department of Justice's Training & Standards Bureau.

Officer by Assignment	Male	Female	Total
Tribal Law Enforcement	71	10	81
Law Enforcement	10,570	1,467	12,037
Jail Officer	1,309	869	2,178
Secure Juvenile Detention	89	48	137
Law and Jail	1,448	340	1,788
Law and SJD	1	0	1
Law, Jail, and SJD	6	1	7
Jail and SJD	98	74	172
Total Active, Primary, and Certified	13,592	2,809	16,401

Furthermore, there are over 20 female law enforcement officers overseeing Wisconsin police departments and sheriff's offices according to the 2014 Wisconsin Law Enforcement Directory maintained by the Training & Standards Bureau. They are as follows:

1. Arcadia Chief Diana Anderson
2. Argyle Chief Hayley Saalsaa
3. Brillion and Reedsville Chief Jo Ann Mignon
4. Chippewa Falls Chief Wendy Stelter
5. Coleman Chief Ida Soletske
6. Dodge County Sheriff Patricia Ninmann
7. Edgar Chief Jeanette Stankowski
8. Endeavor Chief Jennifer Beckett
9. Menomonee Falls Chief Anna Ruzinski
10. New Auburn Marshal Tosha Reetz
11. Oakfield Chief Renee Schuster
12. Pierce County Sheriff Nancy Hove

13. Ridgeway Officer in Charge Sarah Havens
14. Shiocton Chief Kristine Brownson
15. South Milwaukee Chief Ann Wellens
16. St. Croix Falls Chief Erin Murphy
17. Thorp Chief Sharon Verges
18. UW-Madison Chief Susan Riseling
19. UW-Stout Chief Lisa Walter
20. Whitewater Chief Lisa Otterbacher
21. Wonewoc Chief Julie Ott
22. Woodville Chief Lori Hetfeld

8

Shot Out

"Why do you listen to the radio? You're not on patrol," his coworkers would scrutinize him.

As a detective at the Waukesha County Sheriff's Department, Paul Renkas didn't have to listen to the radio, but he did so because he wanted to be aware of what was happening.

On the afternoon of February 4, 2002, the fourteen-year veteran was glad he did.

He sat in his cubicle in the detective bureau working when at about noon the Waukesha Police Department issued an attempt to locate a potentially suicidal suspect. The forty-year-old man named Brian Lamb was said to be divorced, out of work, and an alcoholic. In addition to trying to kill himself twice in the past, earlier that day Lamb sent an email to a friend in Texas threatening to commit the "Big S."

Twenty minutes later two deputies found Lamb parked in a Ford Explorer at the dead end of a road near Vernon Marsh, a five thousand acre wildlife preserve in the eastern part of the county. Pulling their squads up to the front end of Lamb's car, they signaled for him to get out of the vehicle. He refused. What's more is that the deputies discovered Lamb was drinking and armed with a gun.

More police were called to the scene, including a K-9 officer and a negotiator. Lamb would flash his car lights and roll his window up and down to acknowledge the negotiator's commands, but he refused to exit the vehicle and give up. He remained peaceful until a half hour later when he suddenly fired a shot out the window.

Still listening to the radio, Renkas—a sniper for the SWAT team—decided to head out to the scene, passing the internal affairs detective on his way out.

"I hope I don't get involved in a shooting," Renkas told him. "I've got a SWAT conference tonight."

———

Shortly after Renkas left the department, the rest of the SWAT team got called out in response to the shot fired.

The police on scene meanwhile discovered that two deputies who had taken perimeter positions were now not answering their radios. Fearing that they were injured when Lamb fired the shot, two other deputies went out in search of their missing comrades in what Renkas called the "golden hour." A term used by law enforcement and the military, it describes the precious one hour time period that one has to get an injured person to a hospital for the best chance of survival.

When Renkas arrived on scene—the same time as his sniper partner, Jim Materna—he learned the unresponsive deputies were perfectly safe. Neither were hit by Lamb's bullet; they had just left their radios in the prisoner van.

With that harrowing incident over, Renkas and Materna grabbed their gear and looked around, discussing where to set up their position, otherwise known as a hide. Other than a house a hundred yards away to the southeast, they were surrounded by endless acres of marshland to the north and west.

Renkas wanted to go farther back; Materna wanted to go closer. They settled on Materna's choice when the K-9 officer said he wanted them to provide cover to the deputies closer to the scene.

The two snipers set up underneath the bumper of a squad car forty-two yards away from Lamb's vehicle. It was cold—just twenty-one degrees. Renkas looked through the scope at the suspect. From the chest up, he could see that Lamb had a mustache and wore a black stocking cap and camouflage jacket.

Renkas and Materna planned to take turns lying on the snow and ice while monitoring Lamb, switching on and off every twelve to fifteen minutes. While the one positioned at the rifle would focus solely on that job, the other was responsible for various tasks like moral support, wind estimation, and time keeping. When the twelve to fifteen minutes had passed, he would shout "Time!"

Through the scope of the rifle, Renkas and Materna intimately observed Lamb for the next two hours. They saw him laugh; watched him sob; witnessed him talking to himself; observed him drinking beer and smoking cigarettes.

(They would find out later that Lamb had a blood alcohol content more than three times the legal limit.)

The sun slowly sank and the temperature steadily dropped—down to fourteen degrees. As a TV news helicopter flew overhead, the thirty or so deputies on scene were prepared to wait until Lamb gave up or passed out from drinking.

Then at three-thirty Lamb got out of the car just as Materna yelled "Time!" It was his turn on the sniper rifle, but it was too late to switch.

Renkas was the one at the rifle. The one to fearfully watch as Lamb held the shotgun up under his chin.

You son of a bitch. You're going to make me watch this through a magnified scope, Renkas thought. He dialed the scope back to give him some distance but still managed to glimpse a grimace on Lamb's face as he prepared to pull the trigger.

"Less lethal! Now!"

The SWAT commander's order echoed out into the stillness. Not wanting to break their cover from thirty-seven yards behind Lamb, the less lethal team hesitated.

"Now!" the commander barked again.

With the speed and intensity of a ninety mile-per-hour fastball pitch, the deputies stepped out from their barrier of trees and one of them fired six rounds at Lamb. Renkas watched the plastic projectiles flying through the air like bumblebees before striking him in the wrist, elbow, buttocks, and below the kidney.

Lamb, mostly unfazed, moved toward the less lethal team, prompting the K-9 officer to release his dog. Lamb ignored the animal and leveled his shotgun at the deputies.

Without any hesitation, Renkas fired.

In that moment everything slowed down for him. He could almost feel the firing pin striking the primer.

"Shot out!" Materna yelled.

Renkas—who didn't even hear the round go off—prepared to take another shot, but discovered it was unnecessary. Lamb dropped straight down and fell forward on his hands and knees. *Down like a sack of potatoes,* the detective thought.

———

"Go in the van and warm up," Materna told Renkas. "I got your gear."

Renkas climbed into the vehicle and tried to call his wife, but he was shaking too hard from the adrenaline and the cold to dial the number. Materna sat across from him watching him struggle, and Renkas couldn't help but feel embarrassed.

"Do you need some help with that?" Materna asked, reaching forward for the cell phone.

He dialed it and then stepped outside to give his partner some privacy.

"Hon ..." Renkas said when his wife picked up.

"What?"

They had been in a big fight about some household chore, and she was now giving him the cold shoulder.

"I don't know how to tell you this," he continued. "But I was involved in a shooting. I'm not going to be home for a while."

Before she answered, there was a drawn-out pause.

"Well I don't know how to tell you this, but the girls never came home from school."

"I'm going to call your brother. I can't come home and deal with this right now."

He knew he needed to take care of the post-shoot procedures before he could go home. He felt nervous and helpless.

Renkas hung up and called his brother-in-law, a captain for the Waukesha Police Department. He assured Renkas that he'd find his daughters and gave him the phone number of a Milwaukee attorney who could represent him in the shooting incident. The attorney advised him to write down everything exactly how it happened, but the important thing was to skip a line between sentences as he guaranteed Renkas that more details would come back to him in the hours and days to come.

Just before Renkas left the crime scene, the internal affairs detective arrived, smiling and shaking his head at the thought of what Renkas had told him earlier that day.

———

Later that evening Renkas found out that his daughters were safe—they went to a friend's house after school without telling anyone—and he and Materna attended the SWAT conference. The conference continued the next day when the guest speaker was Lieutenant Colonel Dave Grossman, an army ranger and former West Point psychology professor.

During a book signing following his speech, Materna grabbed Renkas by the arm and yanked him up to the front of the line.

"Colonel, my partner shot someone last night."

Grossman stopped what he was doing. He looked up, set his pen down, and shook Renkas' hand.

"Are you okay? I want to hear all about it. Call me," he told him.

He gave Renkas his home phone number in Arkansas, signed a copy of his book, and handed it to Renkas before continuing the book signing.

———

"HOORAH, how are you doing my fellow warrior?" Grossman said energetically when Renkas called him a couple days later.

In the coming days and weeks, Grossman proved to be a great source for Renkas, helping him work through his post-shooting confusion. For instance, Renkas realized when writing his report that he was uncertain which finger Lamb put on the trigger when he held the gun up to his chin.

He thought it was the left index finger, yet he recalled Lamb using his right hand to drink and smoke.

"Why am I going crazy?" Renkas asked Grossman. He worried it wouldn't look good to the jury if he was wrong about such a crucial detail.

"You're not going crazy," the colonel reassured him. He explained to him that he was correct in that Lamb would have put his left index finger on the trigger because when committing suicide the person will use their dominant hand to control the muzzle.

The distance from which he had shot was another detail Renkas struggled to determine. He thought he shot from forty-two yards away, which he did, but he second-guessed himself because he remembered being close to a mailbox on the south side of the road another twenty yards back. Grossman, however, helped him realize his time sequence was off because it was when he sat in the van following the shooting that he saw the mailbox.

Renkas completed his post-shooting statement with the help of attorney Stephen Glynn, but his confidence was destroyed when the union attorney took one look at it and said, "I could easily blow holes through this."

Then he was hit with another surprise when the district attorney asked, "Have you ever had sexual relations with Brian Lamb's ex-wife?"

Unbeknownst to Renkas, Lamb's ex-wife up until recently had worked as a police dispatcher. He knew her, but he never put the two last names together. His son also knew Lamb's son as they went to school together. One day Lamb's son brought in a newspaper containing an article about the shooting.

"Was this your dad that killed my dad?" he asked Renkas' son.

His son didn't say anything and walked away, and Renkas said that there was no hostility between the boys despite the situation.

The district attorney ultimately ruled the homicide justifiable, but the experience taught Renkas to be prepared for anything.

"I had a certain point of anger toward Brian Lamb for making me [shoot him] and for making my life more complicated," Renkas said, a decade after the incident. "Lamb released his pain by death, however, I will take his pain to my grave."

———

Several weeks after he was cleared Renkas discovered that his attorney did not charge him. It was pro bono because he appreciates the work of law enforcement officers, the attorney said.

Renkas, however, didn't want anything for free. Nor did he want the next officer involved in a shooting to expect the same treatment only to be charged.

His attorney conceded and gave him a bill, which the county ended up paying.

At that time, the state law mandated that if the actions of a law enforcement officer, EMT, paramedic, or firefighter involved in a deadly force incident were found to be lawful, the county or municipality may pay his or her legal fees. Renkas testified four times before state legislators whom ultimately reworded "*may*" to "*shall*."

———

In the years following the shooting, Renkas—now a lieutenant—went on to serve on the American Sniper Association's post-shooting program and to conduct presentations to law enforcement officers across the country on his experiences after the shooting.

"I want them to know that they're not the only ones to go through this," he said of other officers who have been involved in shootings. "I can tell them that everything they are experiencing is normal and that they did the right thing."

During his presentations, Renkas discusses a variety of issues, such as mistakes he and his team made during the incident and what they could have done differently. He tells them about the legal and financial preparations an officer involved in a shooting must make, and he talks about the questions and concerns an officer may face when it comes to religion.

Shortly after the shooting a relative pulled out the Bible and told Renkas' three children—ages eleven, ten, and eight—that their dad would go to hell for murdering someone and that they would never see him again.

"I explained to my kids that there are very evil people out there, and sometimes they hold innocent people at bay," he said, adding that his children also spoke to the sheriff department's psychologist. "Sometimes the only thing they [evil people] understand is violence, and in extreme situations you have to use violence to stop them because there's no other way."

Grossman also helped Renkas to better understand the situation by going through Bible verses with him. For example, Exodus 20:13 "You shall not murder" helped to show Renkas that a difference exists between murdering and killing.

Renkas emphasizes that concept to officers during his presentations. He also explains to them that sometimes they have to take a life to save lives and also that the suspect dictates the outcome. Most importantly, don't carry your weapon never expecting to use it, he warns them.

Renkas advises officers how they can physically prepare themselves and what physical and emotional responses they should expect after a shooting (see the accompanying fact sheet on page 76 for more details). Following the shooting, he primarily experienced stomach pain, anger, and irritability. He also found himself preoccupied with the event, rewinding the incident over and over again in his mind.

In the event of a shooting, Renkas tells officers that they should make a plan on how to inform their families. This is something that he himself wishes he had been better prepared for.

One of his daughters asked him, "Did you kill him or did he kill himself?" Unsure of how to explain the situation to her and too preoccupied with other matters, Renkas ignored her question. He felt guilt over that for many years until they at last spoke about the incident and she forgave him.

In addition to talking to one's family about the shooting, Renkas said officers should debrief with all of their colleagues involved in the incident. Not only does it give everyone the opportunity to discuss ways to improve, it also offers the chance to talk about their emotions and guilt.

In Renka's case, the K-9 handler took blame because his K-9 was supposed to have grabbed Lamb when he turned toward the deputies, which would have prevented Renkas from having to shoot. Materna, who gives Renkas a card every year on the anniversary of the shooting, also felt guilt because it was supposed to be his turn on the rifle when Lamb got out of the car.

Debriefing is also a time to show appreciation to each other. Renkas recalls meeting the wife of the deputy who fired the less lethal ammunition at

Lamb. She ran up to Renkas and, without waiting for an introduction, hugged him and thanked him for saving her husband's life.

Renkas still thinks of the shooting often because he has a photograph of himself on scene that day on his office wall.

"It's a gentle reminder that it could happen again, and that I need to be ready."

Before and After a Shooting

Following his officer-involved shooting, Waukesha County Lieutenant Paul Renkas conducts presentations across the nation discussing how officers can prepare themselves and what to expect after a shooting. Here are some of his discussion points:

Physical preparations
♦ Know your physical limits
♦ Get plenty of sleep
♦ Hydrate
♦ Avoid eating junk food
♦ Control your breathing and heart rate by inhaling for a count of four and exhaling for a count of four
   The normal heart rate is 60 to 80 beats per minute. As a heart rate increases, the body experiences a number of changes:
   ◊ 115 bpm—fine motor skills deteriorate
   ◊ 145 bpm—complex motor skills deteriorate
   ◊ 175 bpm—cognitive processing deteriorates, tunnel vision, loss of depth perception, loss of near vision, vasoconstriction (reduced bleeding), and auditory exclusion
   ◊ Above 175 bpm—fight or flight response, submissive behavior, voiding of bladder and bowels, and performing at the highest level due to adrenaline

Post-shooting emotions
♦ Anger
♦ Irritability
♦ Preoccupation with the event
♦ Second-guessing one's actions during the incident
♦ Numbness
♦ Shock
♦ Isolation
♦ Alienation
♦ Memory impairment
♦ Happiness over survival

Post-shooting physical reactions
- Hypertension
- Stomach pain
- Restless sleep patterns
- Trembling
- Nausea
- Thirst
- Nightmares
- Chills
- Dizziness
- Diarrhea

Renkas adds that it's normal for officers to experience some of these emotional and physical responses, all of them, or none of them.

HOMICIDES

*"I think some people are just inherently bad.
They just have a dark hole in their heart."*

—Rock County Sheriff Robert Spoden

9

Innocence Lost

Borelli guilty of murder

By MARIA LOCKWOOD
Daily Telegram Staff Writer

Twelve jurors found Jason Richard Borelli guilty of first-degree intentional homicide within 90 minutes after they began deliberating at noon today.

"You are not to search for doubt," Douglas County Circuit Court Judge Michael Lucci told the jurors. "You are to search for the truth."

Borelli, 32, Superior, faced the charge for the Jan. 7 stabbing death of Leah Gustafson in her apartment at 1910 John Ave. She was found dying in her apartment, a samurai sword believed by police to be the murder weapon beside her. A trail of evidence led officers across the street to Borelli's residence, 1901 John Ave.

In March, Borelli pleaded not guilty by reason of mental disease or defect.

A twist was thrown into the deliberations by Chief Public Defender J. Patrick O'Neill, who represents Borelli. If the 12 jurors can't unanimously agree on the first-degree intentional homicide charge, they were told to consider whether Borelli is guilty of second-degree intentional homicide, a class B felony that carries a maximum penalty of 60 years. The penalty for first-degree homicide is life imprisonment.

Turn to **TRIAL, A3**

FILE PHOTO BY JED CARLSON / DAILY TELEGRAM PHOTOGRAPHER

Superior Police Department investigators search for evidence related to the Leah Gustafson near the defendant's residence last winter.

Superior Telegram

An unknown visitor rang the doorbell of a young woman living alone in an apartment in Superior. Although it was a little after four-thirty in the morning, Brandi was up visiting with her friend, Henry, and ignored whoever stood outside her apartment building.

She assumed the person left and continued talking to Henry until about ten minutes later, when she heard Leah from across the hall open her door. Footsteps teetered down the hallway and then her neighbor's door shut.

Within minutes she heard loud noises erupt from Leah's apartment. At first she thought Leah was having sex. Then came slapping sounds and pounding.

"Help me, help me, help me!" Leah screamed.

Brandi grabbed her cell phone and ran to her friend's door with Henry right behind her.

"Leah! Leah!" she hollered, banging on the door.

When she didn't answer, Brandi dialed 911, her fingers shaking.

"Somebody's getting beat! I need the police to come here now!" She spoke loudly hoping to scare the intruder away.

With 911 still on the line, she and Henry went back to her apartment to wait for help, leaving her front door open. Moments later Henry glimpsed a man dressed in black run out of Leah's apartment and down the stairs.

"I'm going to go check on her," Henry said. "Try to get a good look at the guy."

From her front window, Brandi saw a short, stocky man wearing a black stocking cap, black jacket, and black pants with white stripes. She watched him run from her building toward a house across the street.

"Brandi, she's been stabbed!" Henry yelled from Leah's apartment.

She rushed back to Leah's ordinarily tidy apartment, which was now trashed. Her friend lay face down, her back covered in blood.

"Go outside and wait for the police," Henry told her. He didn't want her to see her friend dying.

Brandi scurried down the steps and out the door as the police arrived.

"He went toward that house," she panted, pointing across the street. "A man dressed in black."

———

Within minutes of the stabbing and the suspect's escape, an officer searching outside the apartment building discovered what appeared to be bloodstains on a sidewalk next to a dark-colored Minnesota Vikings baseball cap. More red smears were found on a doorknob of a nearby residence.

Superior Officers Michelle Lear and John Heinen showed the damning evidence to their sergeant, Nicholas Alexander. He looked around, observing that the trail of bloodstains ended at the door. They appeared to start from the direction of the apartment building across the street—the one where the stabbing reportedly just took place.

As Alexander and the two officers examined the red smears on the door, they were joined by Officer Todd Maas, who had been attending to the victim with another officer.

"It doesn't look good," he told them. "I don't think she's going to survive."

Alexander, fearing that the suspect could be inside this house endangering more innocent people or destroying evidence, made the decision to enter.

"We're going to go in and remove anybody inside," Alexander instructed his officers. "We'll secure the residence and then freeze the scene while we wait for a search warrant."

Before they did, however, he requested radio silence. He knew they were likely to be confronted by an armed subject, and he wanted the airwaves free if he and his officers needed to call for help.

Heinen kicked the door open, and he, Mass, Lear, and Officer Patrick Carey rushed into the house behind Alexander.

"Police! Police!" Alexander shouted.

He continued to announce their presence as he led the officers straight up a short set of stairs. He scanned an unoccupied kitchen on the left and climbed another set of stairs. Upon reaching the landing, Alexander saw several closed doors on the next level. He would later learn that these bedrooms were rented out to various occupants.

"Carey, come up here with me," Alexander said.

While the others waited on the landing, the two reached the top of the stairs where they saw another closed door and an open door to the left of it. The latter looked like a dimly lit bedroom.

With Carey covering Alexander's back, the sergeant moved toward the bedroom. As he crossed the threshold, the jiggling of the door handle on the closed door on his right caught his attention. He quickly checked the bedroom, saw no one, and then turned back toward the hallway in time to see a man exit the closed room.

"Police! Get on the ground!" Alexander ordered, pointing his gun at the startled man.

Alexander looked him up and down. The man wore no clothes other than a pair of blue boxer shorts. Fresh scrapes and cuts marred his face, and redness surrounded his eyes. His skin was shiny and wet as if he had recently showered. Alexander was surprised to see that the man wasn't armed.

"Police! Get on the ground!" he repeated.

Gripping his gun with his right hand, Alexander grabbed the man's right shoulder and directed him down to the floor. Alexander placed his left knee in the center of the man's back, forced him to the floor, and ordered him to put his hands behind his back.

"What did I do, what did I do? I didn't do anything!"

As Carey handcuffed him, Alexander noticed the man's shorts appeared to be stained with blood, and abrasions, scratches, and cuts covered his back and shoulder.

He knew he didn't cause these injuries when he decentralized him nor did the man complain of any pain.

"It's clear," Heinen said, stepping out of the bathroom that the man had come from. "The tub is wet."

Heinen went on to clear the nearby bedroom where he found a pair of shoes with what looked like blood on them.

"Get him out of the house," Alexander said. "We need to clear the rest of the building. Announce your presence and if no one comes to the doors, force them open. Remove anyone you find, but don't search for any evidence yet."

He and the officers spent the next five minutes clearing the three floors of the house and basement, forcing open most of the locked doors. Along the way they found three more occupants whom they escorted outside and placed into separate squad cars. Unlike the man who came out of the bathroom, however, these three men were groggy and confused. They also didn't have any signs of injury or blood on them.

Alexander and Heinen were the last to exit the house, leaving it secure and frozen until they could go back in with a search warrant.

Just as Alexander stepped outside, officer Thor Trone approached him.

"She's been called," Trone said.

The victim was pronounced dead, and the medical examiner was on the way.

"Take him to the police department," Alexander told Carey. "Don't ask him any questions and wait for a detective."

Alexander knew that the man who had come out of the bathroom was their homicide suspect.

———

The man arrested for the January 7, 2006, murder of twenty-nine-year-old Leah Gustafson was Jason Borelli. The thirty-one-year-old man had a history of domestic abuse, battery, and violations of restraining and harassment orders.

Though a clear motive was never learned, Alexander believes that Borelli came over to Leah's apartment building to see Brandi, who had a friendship with him. He thinks Leah answered the door, but doubts she invited him inside because there was nothing to indicate that Borelli was anything more to Leah than just an acquaintance. Borelli perhaps followed her into her apartment before she had a chance to close the door.

Alexander believes Borelli became angered when a sexual advance went unrequited, leading him to attack her. He hit her over the head with an ashtray and ultimately grabbed a sword displayed on Leah's wall and stabbed her to death.

The autopsy revealed that Leah sustained numerous bruises to her throat and both arms and hands; eleven wounds/cuts to the back of her head; puncture wounds to the middle of her back, upper left and right shoulder area; three puncture wounds to the right lung and right side of the heart; hemorrhages to her throat, eyes, chin, and nose; and an abrasion on her right hip area. A Samurai-type sword with sheath, an ashtray, and a porcelain candleholder were identified as the weapons. Leah had been strangled, bludgeoned, and stabbed.

Borelli pleaded not guilty by reason of mental disease or defect, but a jury found him guilty of first-degree intentional homicide. He was sentenced to life in prison. A state appeals court later upheld the sentence.

"Leah just struck me as an innocent young girl who was finally out on her own, living in an apartment and starting to explore life," Alexander said, seven years after the incident. "She truly is a classic victim in the sense that she was a completely innocent bystander in the wrong place at the wrong time."

Alexander and the officers on his team the night of the homicide each received the Meritorious Conduct Ribbon from the Superior Police Department in recognition of their exemplary police work tracking Borelli to his home and stopping him from destroying evidence. Although Alexander is proud of their actions that night, he said it was bittersweet receiving an award for something so tragic.

"I remember her [Leah's] father approaching me sometime during the trial and thanking me," he said. "Here's a guy who lost his daughter, and he's thanking me. It's just an odd feeling that he felt the need to say thank you, even though you're there for the trial of the death of his child. But he was thankful we did our jobs, and it gave him some closure that the person responsible was brought to justice."

Alexander, now deputy chief, recalls the immense responsibility he felt the night of the homicide.

"It was very stressful," he said. "When you're a night shift sergeant you're like the president because you're the highest ranking person awake in the city.

I know that the mistakes that get made in law enforcement can end up with bad people acquitted, so I remember feeling the pressure that we had to do this right and our actions needed to be justified."

Though the then-eight-year veteran had investigated homicides before in the northwestern Wisconsin city of Superior, this was the first one he had dealt with as a supervisor that had to make decisions. What's more is that since this was an active incident—opposed to one where the deceased body was found sometime after the homicide took place—he had to make decisions even quicker.

For the first time in six years he had smoked a cigarette that morning to get some relief and to calm his nerves. He was confident he had detained the right person, but he still wanted some additional information to assure himself that he had made the right decision.

Alexander got that reaffirmation when he woke up later that day after his shift. In addition to the bloody shoes Heinen had seen in the bedroom, police officers recovered bloodstained clothing stashed in the bathroom vanity. The clothing matched that of the suspect's description. They also found a white towel smeared with blood on the floor and bloodstained keys in Borelli's bedroom.

Alexander doubts that neither he nor anyone else on his team that night will ever be involved in another case as significant as this one and with such a successful outcome.

Still, he can't help but wish that they would have gotten to Leah's apartment thirty seconds sooner.

"Unfortunately that just wasn't in the cards," said Alexander, who still tears up talking about the murder. "We were there in under sixty seconds. There's no way we could have gotten there sooner. There was really no way to prevent it, but we still feel bad. We're there to protect and serve, and we wish we could have saved her."

Use of Force

Use of Force is the generic term used whenever the police have to strike, hit, use OC (pepper) spray, a Taser, or even shoot a person in order to gain physical compliance of him or her, or to stop a resistive subject, according to Superior Deputy Chief Nicholas Alexander.

Below, Alexander details the Use of Force Continuum, otherwise simply known as force options:

1. **Presence**, referring to the physical presence of an officer in uniform as well as standing in a way that commands authority.
2. **Dialogue**, which means using one's voice and communication skills to gain compliance. It could be an officer smooth-talking a person into compliance or it could be loud and direct commands meant to startle a person such as, "STOP! Police ... show me your hands!"
3. **Empty Hand Controls or Passive Countermeasures**. These are hands-on techniques and include many options:
   - *Escort-type holds* that police use to help walk a person in the direction they want, often called compression or compliance holds.
   - *Pressure points*, which are nerve bundles that when pressed properly create pain, thereby usually causing a resistant person to comply.
   - *Decentralizations*, techniques used to take a person safely from a standing position to a prone position on the ground. The techniques are designed to control the person's descent and to protect him or her from injury whenever possible. Once on the ground the subject is stabilized and ideally handcuffed. The idea with decentralizing is that it is usually easier to control a resistive person when they are on the ground versus in a standing position.
4. **Active Countermeasures**, which include strikes—more commonly known as punches and kicks—as well as the use of pepper spray, Tasers, and baton strikes.
5. **Deadly Force**, an option reserved for when an imminent threat of death or great bodily harm exists and no other options would be practical to stop it.

10

On the Eighth Day

Killer gets life times 3

Sentenced for slaying mother, teens in 2007

By Hilary Dickinson
hdickinson@beloitdailynews.com

JANESVILLE — The convicted sex offender found guilty of a triple homicide received three life sentences on Tuesday in Rock County Court.

James Koepp, 51, of Janesville was found guilty in February of stabbing and strangling his neighbor and her two teenage children in their mobile home south of Janesville in January of 2007.

Koepp will serve the remainder of his life in state prison where he has no chance of parole, according to Rock County Sheriff Robert Spoden.

He was also sentenced to pay restitution to the state's Victim/Witness program, which paid for the family's funerals.

"It's great to finally see it done, and the work our detectives did paid off," Spoden said. "Finally the family can move on and those three innocent people can rest in peace."

Koepp's sentencing marked the end of a high-profile murder case that captured the county's attention for three years.

In January, the case came to trial and Koepp was found guilty a week later of three counts of first-degree intentional homicide in the deaths of 38-year-old Danyetta Lentz, her 17-year-old daughter, Nicole, and her 14-year-old son, Scott.

The ordeal started on the morning of Jan. 12, 2007 when the bodies of the Lentz family were discovered in their mobile home by Danyetta's father, Russel Lucht.

It was determined that Nicole had been stabbed four times in the back and strangled, Scott had been stabbed six times and strangled, and Danyetta had been strangled and stabbed 23 times. Fifteen wounds came after she was already dead.

District Attorney David O'Leary said the victims' DNA on Koepp's clothes and his DNA under Lentz and Nicole's fingernails was what convinced jurors that Koepp was responsible for the murders.

Koepp's attorney, Walter Isaacson, argued during the trial that the murders resulted from a robbery that took place in the Lentz residence. He also said Koepp only visited the residence prior to the murder to discuss a recent sexual encounter that allegedly occurred between himself and Danyetta.

Originally, however, O'Leary said Koepp denied visiting the residence the night before the murder. Eventually, he admitted he was there to talk to Danyetta about the alleged affair, which O'Leary said proved to be a motive for the murders.

Koepp became the key murder suspect after Nicole's boyfriend

Please see **KILLER** P. 2A

H e was rejected, embarrassed, and worried. After making a move on the seventeen-year-old girl who lived in the trailer next door, he walked over to the family's home to explain the situation to her mother.

It didn't work out like he thought though.

"You son of a bitch! I'm going to call the police!" Danyetta threatened.

He couldn't have that. He didn't want the police involved. He panicked, and he strangled Danyetta in the bedroom where they had been talking. Her kids, Nicole and Scott, were in the family room doing homework, but their headphones muffled out the frantic sounds of their mother's screams. She eventually collapsed and stopped moving. He thought she was dead.

Now he had to kill them all.

He came out of the bedroom and grabbed Nicole from behind. He strangled her, too, and next went after Scott.

Suddenly, Danyetta staggered out of the bedroom.

She ferociously fought with him, digging her fingernails into his skin. He ultimately overpowered them all, and, as they lay motionless on the ground, he removed their socks and slipped them onto his hands like gloves. Then he brutally stabbed them all to death. To ensure that they were dead, he placed smiling stuffed animals on each of their legs. If the toys shifted by the time he returned to clean up the crime scene, he'd know they weren't dead and his job wasn't done.

The stuff animals didn't move an inch.

They were all dead.

That's Robert Spoden's theory of what happened the evening of January 11, 2007—the night James Koepp killed the Lentz family. Though he didn't have any evidence and the defense and prosecution teams would later cite an affair with the mother, Spoden speculated that Koepp was at the family's home that night to talk to Danyetta about an advance he had made on Nicole.

Regardless of why he was there, the triple homicide of the impoverished, divorced mother and her two teenage children is to date the worst crime in the south central county of Rock, and it happened on Spoden's eighth day in office as sheriff.

———

The then nineteen-year veteran found out about the crime early the following morning when he was in briefing, reviewing films of allegedly neglected horses.

What he was about to hear would hold the same level of significance to him as learning about the assassination of John F. Kennedy, the Challenger Space Shuttle disaster, and 9/11.

"Have you been listening to the radio?" a deputy asked, referring to the police scanner.

"No. Why? What's going on?" Spoden asked.

"They found three bodies at Jacobs Mobile Home Park."

When the deputy said it didn't appear to be carbon monoxide poisoning, Spoden's next thought was a murder/suicide.

He climbed into his black, unmarked car and drove south from the sheriff's office in Janesville down U.S. Highway 51. Starting off narrow, the road winds through parts of the city before widening into a rural highway surrounded by fields.

Once in Rock Township, Spoden arrived at the rundown Jacobs Mobile Home Park. He pulled up to a white trailer surrounded by yellow crime scene tape. Passing the deputies milling around outside searching for evidence, he walked up the small, wooden front porch and instantly spotted Nicole, whose lifeless body was just inside the door next to a steak knife with a bent blade and a knife handle. She had been stabbed four times in the back and strangled. Fourteen-year-old Scott lay next to her surrounded in a pool of blood, a large knife embedded in his chest. He had been stabbed six times and strangled. Danyetta, thirty-eight, was found partially clothed in a hall leading to the back of the trailer. She had been strangled and stabbed twenty-three times. Fifteen of the wounds likely came after she was already dead. Around the victims were open, disheveled drawers and scattered clothes. The trailer was trashed.

While taking in the gruesome scene, Spoden couldn't help but notice the cheerful Christmas decorations still hanging up, a three-quarters eaten frozen pizza on the kitchen counter, and Nicole's birthday balloons bobbing around the trailer.

Bound and determined to ensure that the investigation would be properly conducted, Spoden immediately pulled everyone out of the trailer after the initial walk-through and taped it up, only allowing access to detectives and state crime lab technicians, the latter of which he hoped would collect crucial DNA evidence to link to a suspect. They spent about sixteen hours processing the scene and were not finished until two a.m.

Next, Spoden knew he had a responsibility to inform the public.

"It really became for me a moment where I felt I had to reassure the community because I knew people would be scared and have fear it could happen to anybody," Spoden said four years later. "When I addressed the media, I wanted to give an air of calm and a commitment that I would do whatever it took to make sure we bring justice to the family and to use every resource we have—and we did."

The investigation moved rapidly, and it wasn't long before a person of interest was identified.

That person was James Koepp, a neighbor in the trailer park that had previously been sentenced to ten years in prison for sexually assaulting two women at a substance abuse center in 1983.

"We realized that Koepp could easily be involved in this," Spoden explained. "It's a pretty isolated trailer park, the victims were typical people that didn't live a high-risk lifestyle, and people just don't randomly get off [Highway] 51 and go murder a family. Someone knew them and had a connection to them."

Upon questioning, police caught the then forty-seven year old in a couple of lies. Then on the evening that he was supposed to come in for a scheduled interview, he didn't show up. Police discovered him driving drunk on Highway 51 and a high-speed pursuit ensued, during which time Koepp called his brother, rambling and making statements about killing himself.

Spoden, who authorized his deputies to cross state lines and to use whatever means necessary to catch him, likened monitoring the radio traffic during the chase to listening to a sports game.

"It was like, 'Come on, come on guys,' and then 'yes we got him and no one's hurt. We won.'"

Koepp was arrested and subsequently sentenced to four years in prison for operating while under the influence as a third offense and first-degree recklessly endangering safety.

While Spoden felt there was sufficient evidence to charge him with three counts of first-degree intentional homicide, the district attorney did not.

"I'd say, 'I disagree with you, but you got to do what you got to do—as long as he's not on the street,'" Spoden said. "The DA's view was not to hurry and to build a good case."

The media meanwhile pummeled Spoden with questions, asserting that his case was falling apart and expressing doubt about whether or not he caught the right guy.

This was frustrating for Spoden because he knew all along that Koepp was the killer and he had a strong case, but he couldn't present the evidence for fear of jeopardizing the case.

Finally, one year to the day that the family was killed, Koepp was charged with three counts of first-degree intentional homicide. The evidence against him included all three of the victims' blood on the pants and shirt he had worn on the night of the murders.

"He gave us that clothing, which I still don't know why he did," Spoden said.

Also, Koepp's DNA was found on the ends of the ligature used to strangle the victims, on the scrub brush he used to clean the blood off his hands, and underneath the fingernails of Danyetta and Nicole.

Other evidence against Koepp included his own words.

While in prison, Spoden said that Koepp admitted to a cellmate that he had committed the murders. He even told the cellmate that the family ate pizza that evening and that Danyetta fought for her children. Only someone who was in that trailer the night of the murders would know such details, according to Spoden.

So why would Koepp confess to his cellmate?

"It's very hard for people to keep a secret," Spoden said. "Whether it's Watergate or any other big crime, people can't keep quiet about what they've been involved in. It's a natural instinct."

Spoden's other theory for why Koepp admitted to the murders to his cellmate was because he was physically a small man and wanted to build himself up to keep himself from getting assaulted in prison.

Koepp was not the only one who implicated himself in the murders.

Nicole also identified him as the killer.

After dinner that fateful night, she had been talking to her boyfriend on the phone when he heard a man's voice and asked who was there.

"Our neighbor, Jim," Nicole said.

"Her doing that really gave us a lot of help," Spoden said. "It really did."

Finally, the case went to trial in January of 2010.

Every day Spoden sat in the first row of the courtroom where Koepp attempted to engage in stare-downs with him.

"I have never spoken to him and never will speak to him because he doesn't deserve any kind of attention from me," Spoden said. "I wouldn't lower myself to speak to him. The people I wanted to talk to were the victims' family. They deserved the attention and for people to care and interact with them. He deserved nothing. I have nothing but disgust for him."

During the trial the defense team and the district attorney both cited an alleged affair between Danyetta and Koepp as the reason why he was at the Lentz home that January evening.

Koepp's attorneys alleged that he visited the residence prior to the murder to discuss a recent close sexual encounter that allegedly occurred between himself and Danyetta. They said that the married man felt embarrassed and guilty and wanted to explain to Danyetta why he was avoiding her. He left shortly afterward without telling her though, according to the lawyers, because her children were there.

The district attorney, however, said that the alleged affair proved to be a motive for the murders because Koepp was reportedly worried that Danyetta would tell his wife about it.

The district attorney also played a taped interview with detectives for the jury to demonstrate how Koepp kept changing his story. For example, Koepp initially denied that he was at the Lentz home the night of the murder. Then he admitted he was there but just to talk and then left. Finally, he confessed that he was there to talk to Danyetta about their alleged affair.

The defense team refuted Koepp's role in the murders, claiming the family was murdered during a robbery that they alleged took place at the Lentz home sometime between ten at night and three in the morning, after Koepp left.

Regardless of the defense's theory, Spoden said he never wavered in his belief that Koepp would be convicted. In fact, he had the same sense of confidence from the day Koepp was taken into custody on January 17, 2007, to the day of the guilty verdicts on February 2, 2010.

"We had a huge amount of DNA evidence, and the DA did a fantastic job. It took less than three hours to come back with a guilty verdict," Spoden said. "I thought of that case every day, and I felt I owed them [the victims] a measurement of justice for what happened to them. I went to that trial every day and had such a sense of relief and satisfaction when the jury came back and said, 'Guilty, guilty, guilty.'"

Not only was Koepp rightfully pronounced as the killer, Spoden said that the Rock County Sheriff's Office was at last vindicated after three years of public and media scrutiny.

Koepp received three life sentences with no parole. A state appeals court upheld the convictions in 2012.

"They were relatively very simple people with not a lot of money, but that mom worked her butt off every day for those kids and did everything she could for them," Spoden said of the Lentz family. "When we looked at that crime scene, we could tell she fought very hard for her children and tried to keep them protected from the monster he was—and he really was a monster."

Murderers like Koepp affirm Spoden's belief that there are truly evil people in this world.

"I think some people are just inherently bad," he said. "They just have a dark hole in their heart. Whether it was through events in life or they were just born that way I don't know, but I believe they make a conscious decision to be bad, to minimize what they do, and to try to blame the victim and the circumstances. It's never their fault."

He believes Koepp, who pleaded not guilty, will deny committing the murders for the rest of his life.

Looking back at that case, Spoden remembers it as a very stressful time that reinforced to him the amount of responsibility he has as sheriff.

"I realized that this was a different realm of responsibility than I had in the past and that I was responsible for making sure people got justice in their lives and they have their day in court," he said. "I have a responsibility to assure citizens that I will do everything I can to keep them safe."

Besides the Koepp murder occurring in his first year of office, 2007 also saw a high-profile bank robbery that resulted in a high-speed chase and massive manhunt, a record number of SWAT calls, and a domestic incident that resulted in a deputy fatally shooting the suspect.

"It felt like baptism by fire that first year, but it was all worth it," Spoden said. "I would tell you it made me a different person than I was four years ago. I hope that I've grown and am a better sheriff. That whole first year it was a lot of really trying to follow your instincts and having faith in the people you surround yourself with."

Although Spoden no longer thinks about the Koepp murders every day as he did before the conviction, that doesn't mean he has forgotten about that mother who fought for her children up to the last minute.

"Even now I get choked up about it," he said. "They were just a decent family. It was tragic. It really was."

Early Wisconsin Sheriffs

The first sheriff in the state of Wisconsin was George Johnson, who served as the Brown County Sheriff from 1818–1829. Prior to becoming sheriff, he was the territorial sheriff of the Northwest Territory.

Brown County made history again in 1957 when it elected Wisconsin's first full-blooded Indian to the position of sheriff. Artley Skenandore served until 1960.

The first known Wisconsin law enforcement officer to be killed in the line of duty also happened to be a sheriff. Robert D. Lester, who served as the sheriff of Crawford County, was killed in 1844. He was paddling down a river in a canoe when he was shot and killed by an Indian whose intention was reportedly to rob Lester.

The position of sheriff dates back to as early as 600 B.C. as indicated by biblical references. Some believe that the United States of America is named after Richard Amerycke, who was the high sheriff of Bristol, England, when King Henry VII authorized John Cabot's voyage to seek the New World in 1497. Upon Cabot's return to England, he was paid his pension by Amerycke.

Today in Wisconsin, the sheriff is the chief law enforcement officer of each county and is elected every four years on a partisan ballot. The sheriffs' duties are to enforce the law in the county, take custody of the jail, attend the courts, and serve all processes. The sheriff is responsible to the electorate and can be removed from office by the governor, and then only for just cause.

—Information compiled from the Brown County Sheriff's Office website and the Officer Down Memorial Page.

11

The Walking Wounded

Hudson won't get new trial

STEPHEN VAN DYN HOVEN said he's glad area residents haven't forgotten his daughter, Shanna.

KENNETH HUDSON leaves Outagamie County Circuit Judge Harold Froehlich's courtroom Monday in Appleton. Froehlich denied Hudson's eight motions for a new trial in the June 25, 2000, murder of Shanna Van Dyn Hoven.

Outagamie judge denies all 8 motions

By Dan Wilson
Post-Crescent staff writer

Convicted killer Kenneth Hudson, 32, will not get a new trial for the murder of Shanna Van Dyn Hoven of Kaukauna, at least not yet.

"The motions are denied," said Outagamie County Circuit Judge Harold Froehlich Monday after hearing arguments from Hudson's attorney, Jonathan Smith, for a new trial based on pretrial publicity and Hudson's on-again, off-again legal representation.

Froehlich said he saw no reason to overturn any of his rulings made before

Van Dyn Hoven

ATTORNEY JONATHAN SMITH (left) and his client Kenneth Hudson listen to Outagamie County Circuit Court Judge Harold Froehlich's decision Monday. Smith said he will appeal Froehlich's decision denying a new trial.

and during the jury trial last March.

Hudson, formerly of Little Chute, is serving a life sentence without parole for the June 25, 2000, murder of 19-year-

old Van Dyn Hoven while she was jogging near her Kaukauna home. She was stabbed in what is believed to have been an abduction attempt.

Hudson maintained his

innocence throughout the trial. Most of the eight motions filed by Smith dealt with Hudson's legal representation. After the state Public Defender Office withdrew from his case because of a conflict of interest, Hudson went through two state-appointed attorneys.

Hudson was found guilty of first-degree murder, attempted first-degree murder, first-degree reckless endangerment and attempted kidnapping.

"I think the record speaks for itself," said Smith. "This person was not competent to act as his own counsel."

"You have to look at the trial as a whole," Froehlich said in explaining his ruling.

"The defense counsels

See TRIAL, C-3

Appleton Post-Crescent

Over two decades later he still thinks about the sixteen-year-old boy who slit his own throat and barely survived. He'll always remember the look of absolute horror on the boy's mother's face.

He also hasn't forgotten about the beautiful young woman with the troubled marriage who intentionally crashed her car, killing herself. Symbolically, her gleaming diamond wedding ring prominently stood out among the wreckage.

Kaukauna Chief John Manion has had many memorable calls throughout his nearly thirty-year career, but his biggest case came on June 25, 2000, when he was the assistant chief.

He was driving home from a family reunion west of Appleton with his wife and two young children when an Outagamie County squad car zoomed past him with its lights and sirens activated. About a mile away he heard the blaring of more sirens.

He knew something serious must be happening on that calm summer Sunday evening, and he wondered what it might be.

Once he arrived home an awaiting answering machine message told him.

A homicide had occurred, and he needed to come into the police department right away.

This was Manion's first homicide in which he would be in charge of the investigation.

Don't screw this up, he told himself.

He reminded himself to use all his training, move in chronological order, and take his time.

———

At the crime scene Manion found the victim lying on a backboard on the side of Plank Road covered with a sheet. Sticking out from the sheet was a pair of bloody blue and white running shoes and bloodstained white socks.

Later he would think about his own daughter who was twelve at the time, but at the moment he had a job at hand and his training taught him to treat the body as evidence.

Manion pulled the sheet back and looked at the young deceased woman with strawberry blonde hair pulled back into a ponytail. She wore bloodstained men's blue plaid boxer shorts and a blood-covered bra and white T-shirt. Her legs and inner thighs were smeared with blood; a puncture wound marred her stomach; and numerous bruises and abrasions covered her left leg. A horizontal linear pattern imprinted on one of the bruises led Manion to believe a tire had run over her.

Her body had been discovered just after police had responded to a high-speed chase originating from the crime scene. The same pursuit Manion had witnessed on his way home.

After the perpetrator nearly ran over a witness who heard a woman's screams and then found him standing over her body, he sped through Kaukauna, weaving through traffic and running red lights. Officers from Kaukauna, Fox Valley Metro, Grand Chute, and Outagamie County trailed him until they at last closed in on him fifteen miles later near the village of Hortonville.

Inside his truck police discovered a red-stained knife, a blood-soaked passenger seat, and clothing covered in blood. The driver, thirty-one-year-old Kenneth Hudson of Little Chute, was taken into custody at the scene at gunpoint. He had blood smeared on his feet, legs, torso, arms, and hands.

When Manion saw Hudson at the hospital later that evening, he lay hand-cuffed on a medical cart in a fetal position with his eyes closed. Hudson opened his eyes and watched Manion as he walked past, but when he caught the officer looking back at him he quickly shut his eyes.

"Watch him," Manion whispered to a guard.

Not only did he fear that Hudson may try to escape, he wanted to make sure he stayed quiet. The presumed family of the victim was seventy-five feet away. The suspect and family weren't aware of each other, and Manion wanted to keep it that way.

Nancy Van Dyn Hoven had called police earlier that evening to report that her nineteen-year-old daughter, Shanna, had not returned home from a jog. With Nancy and her husband, Steve, both too upset to make the identification, Shanna's aunt and uncle followed Manion into the x-ray room where the victim lay covered with a sheet up to her neck.

It was Shanna.

Her parents were clinging to the hope that she was the victim of a hit and run and that she was still alive. Now he had to go tell them that their daughter was not only dead, but murdered.

Trying to keep it together, Manion prepared himself to go deliver the news. He's delivered plenty of death notices in the past, but still his stomach churned. It's always an ugly part of the job.

———

The weekend of the murder, Hudson had been with his girlfriend at her property up north in Langlade County. He had invited his mother from Buffalo, New York, with whom he had a volatile relationship, to come along to show her how well he was doing in Wisconsin. He said that his mother hated him and often told him her "good" son died, referring to his brother.

They ended up arguing, and the mother and girlfriend left, leading an upset Hudson to consume approximately a dozen Valium Saturday and Sunday, some of which he mixed with alcohol.

He told Manion and Lieutenant Kevin Shepardson that he then drove around, but he had no memories of where or what he did. The next thing he remembered was that the police were chasing him.

When they asked about the woman he encountered on Plank Road and what had happened, he became nervous, only admitting to getting in a fight with an unknown person for a reason he couldn't recall.

"Is your mother the reason why you stabbed that girl?" Shepardson eventually asked.

"I didn't stab anyone," Hudson said. "Is this serious enough that I need a lawyer?"

"You need to make that decision yourself," Manion said.

"Do you think you need a lawyer?" Shepardson asked, after Hudson didn't respond.

"I don't know. I'm scared."

Manion told Hudson that they knew what happened on Plank Road and his involvement. "We just want your side of the story," he said.

"I got into an argument with a girl, and I think I stabbed [her]," Hudson relented.

He went on to tell them that he didn't know her, but he remembered talking to her. He didn't recall what she said to him, but they got into a confrontation. She was running, and he got out of his truck and moved around to the front passenger side.

"Is she dead?" he asked.

Manion and Shepardson ignored his question, instead only asking if he had tried to pull her into his truck.

"I think I tried to. She fought with me. She fought with me like my mother did up north," he said, sobbing. "All I wanted to do was give my mom a hug."

"Did you stab her?"

"I think so. I didn't want to hurt anyone. It wasn't my intention to hurt anyone."

He went on to admit that he had pushed her into the passenger side of the truck where he stabbed her.

"How many times did you stab her?" Manion asked.

"I don't remember. I got in my truck and left."

Hudson was ultimately booked on homicide-related charges and transported to the Outagamie County jail. During the ride he made the voluntary statements of, "Why did I stab her? I didn't want her to die. This is all because of my mother. I didn't even know her. Does Wisconsin have the death penalty? I wanna die. My dad and my brother are looking down on me right now and seeing what I've done."

———

Hudson was convicted of killing Shanna in 2001 and sentenced to life, but the case was not over—far from it.

He appealed a judgment of conviction for first-degree intentional homicide, attempted kidnapping, attempted first-degree intentional homicide, and first-degree reckless endangerment. Among the nine categories of arguments he presented, he accused police of framing him by throwing a cup of the victim's blood on him.

"He attacked my honesty, my character, and my ethics as a police officer," Manion said. "It's frustrating when someone challenges that, but police officers go through it every day."

Manion's irritations, however, were outweighed by the sympathy he felt for Shanna's family with whom he had developed a friendship over the years. They were the walking wounded as Manion termed it, reliving the nightmare at every hearing, and they needed peace.

The court hearings dragged on for ten years until a state appeals court in August 2011 rejected his plea for a new trial.

"Hudson caused the representation issues by his own conduct; none of the actual or alleged discovery violations had any practical effect on the outcome of [the] trial; the victim's blood was found on Hudson's hand, interior driver's door, and the seat of his truck; and Hudson's conspiracy defense was far-fetched," the court wrote.

Despite all of Hudson's appeals and requests for a new trial, Manion never second-guessed the work he and his officers had done.

"We caught him red-handed," said Manion, who, along with Shepardson, won an award for outstanding investigative work from the Outagamie District Attorney. "There was no disconnection between him and the victim and the knife in the car. I never want to say a case is open and shut, but this case is ironclad. There's never been a doubt in my mind, and he definitely is a candidate for the death penalty in my eyes. This particular case just opened my eyes to what humans can do to each other. That there's an animalistic instinct to people, and some people are just plain evil."

Murder in Wisconsin

From Milwaukee native Jeffrey Dahmer, who murdered seventeen men and boys between 1978 and 1991, to La Crosse-born Ed Gein, who reportedly served as the inspiration for *Psycho*, Wisconsin is home to some of the nation's most infamous killers.

According to the most recent statistics from the FBI, 169 murders were committed in Wisconsin in 2012, making it the twenty-third state with the most murders that year. Alabama had the lowest with two, while California had the most with 1,879. (See next page for a complete list of homicides by state.)

Of the 169 Wisconsin murders, 108 were committed with firearms. Eighty-five of the firearms were handguns, five were rifles, one was a shotgun, and seventeen were unknown firearms. Knives and other cutting instruments accounted for thirty of the other murders, and another ten resulted from the hands, fists, or feet. Other undefined weapons made up the last twenty-one homicides.

According to preliminary data provided by the FBI from January to June 2013, thirty-four murders were committed in Milwaukee in 2013, a city of 599,395 people, compared to thirty-seven in 2012. Madison, a city of 237,508 residents, saw two murders each in 2013 and 2012.

Note: The FBI does not collect data from Florida because the state doesn't use the FBI's guidelines in reporting certain information on homicides.

Murders by State in 2012

1. Alabama 2
2. Vermont 8
3. Hawaii 13
4. Wyoming 14
5. South Dakota 14
6. New Hampshire 14
7. North Dakota 16
8. Montana 22
9. Maine 25
10. Idaho 26
11. Alaska 29
12. Rhode Island 34
13. Iowa 44
14. Utah 49
15. Nebraska 52
16. Delaware 57
17. West Virginia 66
18. Oregon 81
19. Kansas 84
20. Minnesota 89
21. New Mexico 109
22. Nevada 116
23. Massachusetts 121
24. Connecticut 146
25. Colorado 160

26. Arkansas 166
27. Wisconsin 169
28. Mississippi 174
29. Kentucky 192
30. Washington 194
31. Oklahoma 212
32. Indiana 275
33. Virginia 314
34. Arizona 321
35. South Carolina 324
36. Maryland 365
37. New Jersey 385
38. Tennessee 387
39. Missouri 389
40. Ohio 410
41. Louisiana 455
42. North Carolina 470
43. Illinois 509
44. Georgia 541
45. New York 682
46. Michigan 682
47. Pennsylvania 684
48. Texas 1,141
49. California 1,879

ONE OF THEIR OWN

"It's gut-wrenching. My heart dropped.
It's the worst thing in the world."

—Retired Fond du Lac Chief
and Director of the Training
and Standards Bureau
Tony Barthuly

12

A Chief's Nightmare

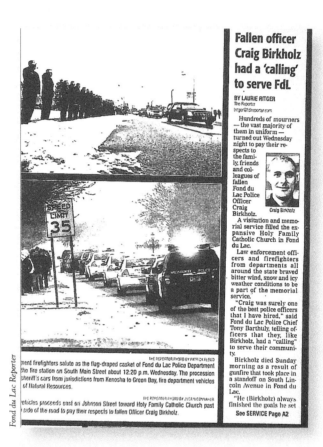

Fond du Lac Reporter

Fallen officer Craig Birkholz had a 'calling' to serve FdL

BY LAURIE RITGER
The Reporter
lritger@fdlreporter.com

Hundreds of mourners — the vast majority of them in uniform — turned out Wednesday night to pay their respects to the family, friends and colleagues of fallen Fond du Lac Police Officer Craig Birkholz.

Craig Birkholz

A visitation and memorial service filled the expansive Holy Family Catholic Church in Fond du Lac.

Law enforcement officers and firefighters from departments all around the state braved bitter wind, snow and icy weather conditions to be a part of the memorial service.

"Craig was surely one of the best police officers that I have hired," said Fond du Lac Police Chief Tony Barthuly, telling officers that they, like Birkholz, had a "calling" to serve their community.

Birkholz died Sunday morning as a result of gunfire that took place in a standoff on South Lincoln Avenue in Fond du Lac.

"He (Birkholz) always finished the goals he set

See SERVICE Page A2

THE REPORTER PHOTO BY PATRICK FLOOD
...ment firefighters salute as the flag-draped casket of Fond du Lac Police Department ...the fire station on South Main Street about 12:20 p.m. Wednesday. The procession ...sheriff's cars from jurisdictions from Kenosha to Green Bay, fire department vehicles of Natural Resources.

THE REPORTER PHOTO BY JUSTIN CONNAHER
...ehicles proceeds east on Johnson Street toward Holy Family Catholic Church past ...side of the road to pay their respects to fallen Officer Craig Birkholz.

F ond du Lac Chief Tony Barthuly felt gutted when he heard the news. It was the worst news a chief or sheriff can ever receive.

A shooting had happened early that morning, leaving one officer dead and another officer seriously wounded.

When Deputy Chief Kevin Lemke first called him around six-thirty that morning, March 20, 2011, to inform him of the shooting, no one had been reported injured at that point. Still, Barthuly was at his cabin an hour away and knew he needed to get back into town.

Lemke soon called again, this time telling him an officer had been struck. Then he called back and said another had been fatally shot.

"There's no words to explain it," Barthuly recalled. "It's gut-wrenching. My heart dropped. It's the worst thing in the world."

The fallen officer was Craig Birkholz, a two-year veteran of the department who had previously served in Iraq and Afghanistan. Barthuly immediately thought of the officer's family and wife, Ashley, whom he had recently married.

Meanwhile, the incident was not over. The suspect was continuing to shoot at officers. It felt like the longest drive of Barthuly's life getting back to Fond du Lac.

Once he arrived he met with the Fond du Lac County sheriff who agreed to have his agency handle the rest of the situation while Barthuly attended to other matters, such as notifying Ashley that her husband was dead. Deemed a hero by Barthuly, Birkholz had been shot twice while rushing to the aid of his fellow officers.

They were initially dispatched on that cold, snowy, rainy day to a duplex on South Lincoln Avenue at quarter to six that morning in response to a woman who reported that she had been sexually assaulted by her on-again, off-again boyfriend, thirty-year-old James Cruckson. He threatened that if she went to the police he would kill her, himself, and her six-year-old daughter, whom she had left in his custody while she was on vacation in Florida. She told police she thought the child was still at his house.

Officer Ryan Williams, Officer Zachary Schultz, and Captain Jon Gutzmann made entry into Cruckson's duplex just before six-thirty. They began to climb a dark, narrow staircase leading to the second floor when halfway up they were met by the bright glare of two muzzle flashes and the bangs of gunshots.

Williams was knocked back against Schultz, and the two tumbled down the stairs, coming to a stop on the landing. Gutzmann covered the stairwell with his firearm and pulled Schultz and Williams off the landing. Williams had been shot once in each shoulder and was bleeding, and Schultz injured his arm during the fall.

Gutzmann ordered Schultz to get Williams—barely able to stand on his feet—outside for medical attention before directing his attention back to Cruckson.

"Stop, you just shot a cop!" he yelled. "Where is the girl?"

"Fuck you, you're not getting her!"

A barrage of gunfire rang out from the second floor. Gutzmann tried to figure out where the gunfire was targeted and if the bullets might go through the floor, when Cruckson started hurling various items like boxes and a toilet down the stairs.

The objects lodged onto the landing, making it impossible to climb the stairwell without becoming an immediate target. Plus, one of the items hit what was believed to be a flashlight in the stairwell, turning it on and illuminating Gutzmann in the dark.

The captain sought refuge near the kitchen, where he waited to ensure that Cruckson's whereabouts remained known. Schultz and another officer, Becky Kollmann, joined him, and the three remained inside until they later escaped in an armored vehicle.

Meanwhile outside, Officer Dave Raddatz was the next to arrive. He parked a few houses south of Cruckson's home on the opposite side of the street and immediately realized his squad was getting sprayed with bullets.

He climbed through his squad car and got out on the passenger side, taking cover behind the right rear wheel and quarter panel. He was almost hit multiple times, and one bullet even traveled through the driver's side door and into the front seat.

Just moments after Raddatz called out that officers were taking fire, Birkholz arrived. He parked his squad on the north side of the scene facing the southeast corner of the intersection of Lincoln and Division Streets to match another squad angled on the southwest corner of that intersection. Birkholz grabbed his rifle and ran southbound along the west wall of a tavern parking lot in the dark, having no idea that Cruckson had an unobstructed view of him.

Cruckson fired once at him with a rifle from over fifty yards away, striking him in the abdomen below his bulletproof vest. Two seconds later another rifle shot was heard. This bullet hit Birkholz in the upper chest at the top of his vest. The bullet partially fragmented on the vest, but the major fragment continued downward into his torso.

Barthuly said either shot would have proved fatal.

Cruckson continued firing at sounds and objects outside his home. In total, he fired approximately forty-eight rounds—sixteen from a .308 hunting rifle, twenty-six from a .45 handgun, and six from a police tactical shotgun that Cruckson snagged when Williams was shot.

It wasn't until seven-forty that Raddatz, now safe behind a tree on the west side of the street, spotted Cruckson sticking a rifle out the window. The officer fired two shots at him, hitting him once in the finger.

Cruckson stopped shooting after that until just one more shot was heard. Cruckson was later found dead with his .45 caliber handgun near his hand and a self-inflicted gunshot wound to the head. The woman's daughter was ultimately found unharmed a few houses away with one of Cruckson's relatives.

Although the Fond du Lac Police Department usually uses chaplains to deliver death notifications, Barthuly knew he had to be the one to tell Ashley.

"This happened on my watch and under my command; I needed to be the one," he later said. "It was the most difficult thing I ever did to give her the news and to watch that disintegrate her. When I think about the devastation it had on her now, it makes me shake my head. It's just terrible someone had to go through this. A young lady who loved her husband and had all these dreams, and all that got taken from her. It's shameful now she doesn't have that."

Birkholz's parents in Kenosha were notified by the Kenosha Police Department. Barthuly, who later gave Birkholz's badge to his father, recalls going with them to view the body and telling his mother, "You know your son died a hero. He died running to help an officer who was shot."

Meanwhile, Williams was flown to a hospital in the Fox Valley, where it was uncertain if he would survive his critical injuries. Later on Barthuly learned William's K-9, Grendel, who was waiting in William's squad during the shooting, had also been critically injured.

"I made the decision that we'd do whatever it takes to try to save the K-9, too," Barthuly said. "I knew this dog was really important to Ryan and to the department. He was a team member."

Barthuly's officers were devastated at the loss of Birkholz and the uncertainty of Williams' and Grendel's survival.

"I could see it in their eyes that they had never experienced anything as tragic and horrific as losing a fellow police officer," Barthuly said. Plus, many of them witnessed him getting shot—murdered—and they had to leave his body lying on the cold concrete for what Barthuly estimated to be at least an hour until the scene stabilized and an armored vehicle could come to retrieve him.

A number of officers had also been shot at themselves. Barthuly remembers seeing Officer Brian Willis after the incident and noticing a knick on his face. He asked if he cut himself shaving, but he learned that Willis sustained the cut when a bullet flew through his squad window.

Barthuly likened the tragedy to watching his team fall off a pier and now needing help swimming to shore. He brought in counselors for them as well as for spouses, friends, and family members.

What didn't help matters was hearing several false rumors that Williams had died. Barthuly was immensely relieved when the surgeon called and said the surgery was successful and Williams was showing progress. Around the same time Grendel underwent blood transfusions and he, too, was stabilizing.

"It's funny that when Ryan had a good day, the dog had a good day," Barthuly remarked. "And when Ryan had a bad day, the dog had a bad day. It was almost freakish that he and the dog recovered the same way."

Barthuly visited Williams in the hospital a couple of days after the shooting and felt relief when Williams briefly opened his eyes and squeezed his hand. "That was enough for me," said Barthuly, who called Williams' recovery the best medicine the department could have had.

The surgeon's mission was to get Williams to Birkholz's funeral, to be held six days after the shooting. That goal was accomplished. A local car dealership lent the department a Cadillac SUV to safely and comfortably transport the wheelchair-bound Williams to the funeral in Kenosha.

"He looked weak and battered down, but where he got the strength and the power I'll never know," Barthuly said. "He had such a positive attitude."

The Wisconsin Law Enforcement Canine Handler Association sent thirty to forty K-9 officers to the funeral, where the handlers all saluted Williams. In addition to those officers, thousands of community members, military members, and law enforcement officers from across the country attended the funeral, which Barthuly described as meticulously planned.

"I wanted to make sure that Craig was honored in the fashion he deserved to be honored," he said. "I made one call to Chief John Morrissey in Kenosha, and he said, 'Tony, don't worry about a thing. I got it.' He and his team and the community paid tribute well to Craig."

Birkholz was one special person and police officer, according to Barthuly, who first met him during his job interview.

"Craig had one of those smiles that just light up the room," he said. "He was an individual you'd be proud to call your son. He was a hard worker and very positive. He always had that smile on his face, and when he talked about Ashley he just had a glow to him. He was so proud to get that interview, and he was just the nicest, most professional person you'd ever meet."

Birkholz ended all his emails with the message, "Stay strong, stay safe, stay positive," and Barthuly said those are the words he lived by.

He volunteered on the SWAT team, and he was always willing to help another person, especially another officer. He'd tell other cops that he wanted to be chief someday, and one of his goals was to go to the FBI Academy in Quantico, Virginia, and break the fitness records. Barthuly's certain that Birkholz, who was twenty-eight years old when he died, would have accomplished those feats.

"He had a lot going for him," Barthuly said. "A lot of class, a lot of charm, and a heart bigger than most."

Barthuly described Williams as intelligent, a hard worker, and very proud of his family.

"He's one of those guys you can never tell he can't do it because he'll prove you wrong," Barthuly said.

His successful recovery is one example of that.

Williams, who returned to work about a month after the shooting, transitioned from the wheelchair to walking to jogging to bike riding. He even started a bike race called The Birky Challenge, in honor of Birkholz. He decided the race would be sixty-seven miles in recognition of Birkholz's badge number.

Williams' goal was to get in shape for the first race to be held that June, not quite three months after the shooting, and he rode all sixty-seven miles.

"He wants to not only pay tribute to Craig but also set a good example of how you can survive tragedy," said Barthuly, adding that Williams has gone on to do numerous talks on the incident, becoming a role model on how to survive tragedy. Grendel also overcame adversity, as he has continued to work alongside his handler, Williams.

The Fond du Lac Police Department posthumously awarded Birkholz with the Medal of Honor and awarded Williams with the Medal of Honor and Purple Heart.

———

Barthuly retired from the Fond du Lac Police Department three months after the incident to take a new position as the director of the Wisconsin Department of Justice's Training and Standards Bureau, a job he had been in the process of pursuing when the shooting had occurred.

Although he found it difficult to leave his team behind, his worries were calmed by his successor, Chief William Lamb.

"Chief Lamb made a promise he'd take care of the team, and he's done that," Barthuly said. "I'm very proud of our team, and I'm very proud of how Chief Lamb has moved the department forward."

Since the shooting, Barthuly's mother died of cancer and his daughter was diagnosed with leukemia. These life-altering events taught him not to stress about the little things that happen in life.

"There's more to life than the little things we get upset about," Barthuly said. "These last two years have taught me to treat today like it's your last day, don't go to bed angry, and to help someone if you have the opportunity."

In Barthuly's new position, he is responsible for standardizing law enforcement training in the state, making sure officers receive the best training possible, and putting measures in place to take care of the wellness of officers.

"It's a tough job," Barthuly said of police work. "It's not a job—it's a calling. Police officers see the ugliest things in life, and it's important that we as a training community take care of our officers."

End of Watch

There have been 271 line-of-duty deaths in the state of Wisconsin. At 119 incidents, the most common type of fatality is from gunfire. The Milwaukee Police Department has experienced the most amount of deaths with 61 fatalities.

Below is a listing of line-of-duty deaths from the last twenty years.

Adams County Sheriff's Office
Deputy Michael Eron Shannon, March 7, 2003; gunfire

Bayfield County Sheriff's Department
Corporal Richard G. Parquette, Sept. 10, 1996; gunfire

Beloit Police Department
Patrol Officer Peter Arthur Larsen, Nov. 15, 1998; gunfire

Chippewa County Sheriff's Department
Deputy Jason Scott Zunker, Jan. 5, 2008; struck by vehicle

Crandon Police Department
Sergeant Todd Jeffrey Stamper, July 15, 2000; gunfire

Eau Claire County Sheriff's Office
Special Deputy Stephen Joseph Hahn, Feb. 16, 2006; automobile accident

Fond du Lac Police Department
Officer Craig Allen Birkholz, March 20, 2011; gunfire

Glendale Police Department
Officer Ronald Ennis Hedbany, Oct. 28, 1994; gunfire

Green Lake County Sheriff's Office
Deputy Bruce Allen Williams, Oct. 19, 2003; gunfire

Hobart/Lawrence Police Department
Officer Robert Galen Etter, Jr., July 22, 2002; vehicular assault
Officer Stephanie Rae Markins, July 22, 2002; vehicular assault

Kenosha County Sheriff's Department
Deputy Frank Fabiano, Jr., May 17, 2007; gunfire

Manitowoc Police Department
Patrolman Dale Robin TenHaken, Sept. 23, 1998; gunfire

Marathon County Sheriff's Department
Deputy Jeffrey Neil Sheets, May 21, 1994; gunfire

Marinette County Sheriff's Office
Deputy Edward R. Hoffman, May 26, 2000; heart attack

Milwaukee County Sheriff's Office
Deputy Sergio Aleman, July 31, 2012; automobile accident
Deputy Sung Hui Bang, Aug. 17, 2000; aircraft accident
Deputy Ralph Edward Zylka, Aug. 17, 2000; aircraft accident
Deputy David Michael Demos, Jan. 25, 1997; vehicular assault

Milwaukee Police Department
Officer Wendolyn Odell Tanner, Sept. 7, 1996; gunfire
Officer Michael A. Niehoff, Dec. 1, 1994; automobile accident
Officer William Arthur Robertson, Sept. 7, 1994; gunfire

Polk County Sheriff's Office
Deputy Mike Seversen, April 14, 2014; gunfire

Prescott Police Department
Patrol Officer Jackie Davis Ryden, Sept. 2, 2006; heart attack

Rice Lake Police Department
Patrolman Michael R. Baribeau, Dec. 19, 1995; gunfire

Sauk County Sheriff's Department
Deputy Richard Allan Weinke, April 5, 1998; automobile accident

Sawyer County Sheriff's Office
Deputy Michael Stanley Villiard, July 9, 1998; automobile accident

Sheboygan County Sheriff's Department
Lieutenant LeRoy Henry Nennig, Jr., Aug. 15, 2004; motorcycle accident

Town of Brookfield Police Department
Officer Donald Bishop, April 13, 2013; heart attack

Vilas County Sheriff's Department
Deputy Kory Elwyn Dahlvig, April 25, 2010; vehicular assault

Washington County Sheriff's Department
Deputy John Mark Schmitt, Sept. 7, 1998; automobile accident

Waukesha Police Department
Captain James Lutz, April 28, 1994; gunfire

Wauwatosa Police Department
Officer Jennifer Lynn Sebena, Dec. 24, 2012; gunfire

Winnebago County Sheriff's Office
Deputy Richard Meyer, Nov. 13, 2003; automobile accident

Wisconsin Department of Corrections
Captain Thomas M. Beahm, Aug. 17, 1994; automobile accident

Wisconsin Department of Justice—Division of Criminal Investigation
Special Agent Jay P. Balchunas, Nov. 5, 2004; gunfire

Wisconsin State Patrol
Trooper Jorge Ronald Dimas, June 14, 2009; automobile accident

—Information compiled from the Officer Down Memorial Page as of May 2014.

13

In the Wake of a Nightmare

J oseph Collins had been sick since Thursday. He got up on Sunday morning hoping he'd feel better, but he didn't.

Just before he went back to bed his phone rang.

The Two Rivers chief knew something was wrong. People don't normally call before seven in the morning on a weekend.

"Hello."

On the other end was his longtime good friend Tony Barthuly, the Fond du Lac chief of police.

"Joe, there's been a shooting. One officer is dead and another's down."

As the lead coordinator of Wisconsin's Law Enforcement Death Response Team, Collins immediately went into planning mode.

He first instructed Barthuly to assign someone from the police department as the liaison for the slain officer's family and then assured him he was on his way.

Within three minutes, the phone rang again. This time it was Barthuly's wife.

"You do know Tony wants you to come, right?" In the havoc of the situation, Barthuly—who himself was presently en route to Fond du Lac from his cabin an hour away—wasn't sure what he had asked him or what Collins told him.

The drive from Two Rivers—a small city along the shores of Lake Michigan—southwest to Fond du Lac typically takes a little over an hour. This particular journey, however, felt like a day and a half to Collins.

Along the way he stayed busy making several phone calls to fellow LEDR Team members, but in between calls he found himself lost in thought wondering how he would handle this situation—or if he even could. He was accustomed to responding to police departments in the aftermath of officer fatalities, but this situation was different. He and Barthuly had been friends for twenty-five years.

They had met as young police officers on their respective SWAT teams before going on to serve together on the board of the Association of SWAT Personnel-Wisconsin for thirteen years. Collins knew it's a chief's worst nightmare to learn that one of his or her officers has been killed in the line of duty, and he spent much of his drive contemplating how he would help his friend get through this.

When he arrived on the east side of Fond du Lac on Highway 23 he drove past a church, where a group of children running around in the parking lot caught his eye. They were having fun as kids should, completely unaware of what had just happened in another part of town. Not knowing that an officer was killed and another airlifted to the hospital. Oblivious to the fact that officers still surrounded the suspect's house, their lives in jeopardy.

At that moment it struck Collins why police officers do this job. They do it to protect people, like these children, so that they may have the ability to go about their lives on a day-to-day basis unharmed and free of fear.

To this day Collins reflects on this every time he drives past that church on his way into Fond du Lac.

———

Collins arrived around nine at the Fond du Lac Police Department, where he met with Barthuly and Deputy Chief Kevin Lemke. Within an hour they learned most of what had happened when that dreaded officer down call was transmitted.

At about six that morning—March 20, 2011—officers responded to a report of a sexual assault. The victim said the suspect was her on-again, off-again boyfriend, James Cruckson, and she believed he had her six-year-old daughter. Upon arrival, Cruckson fired at officers, striking Ryan Williams once in each shoulder.

Officer Craig Birkholz, who arrived moments later, was hit once in the abdomen below his bulletproof vest and again near the top of his vest.

The police didn't find out until later that Williams' K-9 partner, Grendel, had also been shot and that nearly every squad car on scene had been damaged by gunfire.

Now off-duty officers in addition to nearly every spouse and a few older children poured into the police department wanting to know what happened.

Although the situation at the house had not yet been resolved, Collins and the LEDR Team began conducting defusings (similar to debriefings) and one-on-one counseling sessions with officers—many of whom felt guilty for not getting to know Birkholz better. The married twenty-eight-year-old army veteran who served in Iraq and Afghanistan had worked as a Fond du Lac officer for just two years.

The LEDR Team met with at least twenty officers in the first few hours in addition to the police administration and staff, city manager, fire chief, and sheriff. Following those talks, Collins and the others spent much of the day preparing a press conference and determining what should and should not be said as to not impede the immense investigation.

They then scheduled a series of debriefings for the next day to provide information to various groups including supervisors, dispatchers, and spouses and significant others—the latter of whom began second-guessing their loved ones' decisions to become police officers.

"It may happen to any one of us because of the career choice, however, you don't expect it to happen to you or someone you work with," Collins said. "It was an emotional situation, and a lot of young families were now dealing with children not wanting their parents to go back to work."

Meanwhile, Fond du Lac, a city of forty-three thousand, still needed police service for its day-to-day calls. The North Fond du Lac Police Department, the Fond du Lac County Sheriff's Office, and the state patrol provided their services after the shooting, but due to limited staffing and resources more agencies were needed.

Collins called local fellow chiefs to ask for assistance with patrol duties, and the response he received every time was, "How many [officers] do you need? When do you need them? And what do they need to bring?"

Over the course of the upcoming week about sixty officers from over a dozen police agencies, including Neenah, Oshkosh, and Sheboygan, filled in for the Fond du Lac officers to allow them time to grieve and to attend Wednesday's memorial service in Fond du Lac and Saturday's funeral in Birkholz's hometown of Kenosha.

Collins, who oversaw the coordination of the services, was touched by the support from civilians and other law enforcement officers during that difficult time. For instance, somber flag-carrying citizens greeted Fond du Lac officers as they escorted the hearse to Kenosha, as did officers from other jurisdictions that joined in the procession.

Once Birkholz's body was prepared for the memorial service, the two officers escorted the hearse back to Fond du Lac, only this time they each rode with a partner due to the emotional experience they had driving to Kenosha.

The community continued to surprise Collins and the Fond du Lac Police. On the way to the memorial service they found blue ribbons tied around every pole and tree throughout the entire route from the police department to the church on the opposite side of town. Bystanders even held signs thanking Birkholz for his service.

Hundreds of civilians and cops alike attended the memorial service and thousands came to the funeral, including officers from all over the country and from the newly established state police honor guard association.

Once the more immediate pressing tasks of the week were resolved, Collins and others on the LEDR Team assisted with preparing future plans, such as how to honor Birkholz during the following year's National Police Week and determining what awards should be given to which officers to recognize their bravery, courage, and support. Over twenty individuals ultimately received recognition for their involvement during and after the shooting.

Collins, himself, did not go unnoticed. He received a Meritorious Service Award from Barthuly in recognition of his response to the department.

———

Among the approximately twenty-five incidents of officer fatalities that Collins has dealt with throughout his nine years on the LEDR Team, this one was the most complex in terms of the logistics and his emotions.

Not only is he close friends with Barthuly, he is friends with many at the Fond du Lac Police Department and at the time his daughter was an intern there.

Despite his first-hand involvement in handling officer fatalities, Collins said his role does not make him apprehensive about his own mortality on the job.

"It just makes me realize that we have to take care of our people physically, spiritually, and psychologically," said the twenty-eight-year veteran. "A lot of the public don't realize how much officers see and deal with on a day-to-day basis. We deal with the worst day that people may ever have in their lives, and people think that shouldn't impact us."

A fellow officer once told him, "We walk through the mud and are expected to come out clean on the other side."

"That's impossible," Collins said. "But we have to be able to deal with it and have it impact us for a time; then get rid of it and not have it deteriorate the quality of our lives. We do everything possible to make sure we bring in the best possible candidates as police officers, and we have to make sure we have the best retirement candidates when they're done with their jobs."

———◆———

The Wisconsin Law Enforcement
Death Response (LEDR) Team

Formed in 1999 by a group of law enforcement and affiliated professionals, the Wisconsin Law Enforcement Death Response (LEDR) Team provides assistance to agencies that experience a death, whether it is in the line of duty, off-duty, or suicide.

Chiefs and sheriffs are burdened with many responsibilities during these tragedies, and lack of timely action—or inaction—can have long-lasting consequences for the agency.

The LEDR Team's goal is to provide an objective view in making sure the family is served and every conceivable detail is covered. Some of the many tasks the team assists with include:

- Proper notification
- Peer counseling
- Critical incident debriefings
- Shift coverage
- Funeral preparations
- Benefit paperwork
- Officer memorials
- Survivor follow-up

The LEDR Team has assisted in over thirty incidents of officer fatalities since its inception. Other high profile incidents the LEDR Team has responded to include that of Vilas County Deputy Kory Dahlvig who was killed by a suspected drunk driver in 2010 (the charge was later dismissed) and Chippewa County Deputy Jason Zunker who was hit by a car while directing traffic in 2008.

The LEDR Team does not automatically help every agency that experiences a law enforcement death; an agency must contact the LEDR Team to request assistance.

—Information from the Wisconsin Law Enforcement Death Response Team website and Joseph Collins, the Two Rivers chief and lead coordinator of the LEDR Team.

———◆———

14

The Day Everything Changed

"He started running toward the tracks. He yelled. He told the woman to gun it, get over the railroad tracks. We could hear it, smell it. She gunned the thing. Her wheels turned and got stuck on the railroad track. The car flipped and faced the train. We could see the front tire spinning in the gravel on the side of the tracks itself."

Karen Grey-Hoehn, witness, on efforts to rescue a woman and child whose van was struck by a train

Heroic rescue; 2 hurt

Elm Grove police investigate a train and minivan crash Monday morning at Juneau Blvd. near Elm Grove Road. A woman and child in the van were unhurt, but a police officer and the woman's husband, who were trying to rescue them, were injured.

Train's impact injures officer freeing woman in van; her husband's also hit

By LINDA SPICE and MEG JONES
lspice@journalsentinel.com

Headed to the Elm Grove Memorial Day parade in bumper-to-bumper traffic, Monica Ensley-Partenfelder found herself and her 2-year-old son directly in the path of a 94-car freight train barreling toward them, whistle blaring.

What should have been a festive start to the holiday in-

to unhook the 2-year-old from a car seat.

He couldn't get him out.

The force of the impact created an explosive effect, hurling the minivan across the grass — crushed and collapsed. Much of the driver's side was gone.

The 2-year-old in the car seat was brought out, miraculously, uninjured.

Elm Grove train crash

Congestion before the Memorial Day parade in Elm Grove caused a train to collide with a minivan on Juneau Blvd. about 9:30 a.m. The husband of the woman driving the van and an Elm Grove police officer were injured while rescuing the woman and trying to rescue her child. The parade was canceled.

1 Traffic backup 2 Minivan 3 Officer and others 4 Minivan is

A hundred miles away, the Canadian Pacific freight train departed from Portage, Wisconsin. Headed for Bensenville, Illinois, it would first wind its way through the Milwaukee suburban village of Elm Grove.

Meanwhile, Officer John Krahn was at home getting ready for work. Today was the day of the 2009 Memorial Day parade, and the seventeen-year veteran of the Elm Grove Police Department would do traffic control from his usual post near the railroad tracks at Elm Grove Road and Juneau Boulevard.

Krahn and a nineteen-year-old boy in the police explorer program arrived at their post at nine-thirty that morning. Reaching into his pocket, the officer put on his Maui Jim sunglasses to ward off the already bright sun and explained their assignment to the police explorer. They would take turns stopping eastbound traffic to let other cars go through until quarter till ten when the roads would close.

"It's normally pretty uneventful. Not too much happens at the post," Krahn told him. Just as he said that, however, he heard the warning bell at the railroad crossing gates. About a hundred and fifty feet away he saw the crossing arms lower and the lights activate. Numerous cars were near the tracks, but he couldn't tell from his vantage point how clear it was.

"I'm going to go check this out," he told the police explorer. "I'll be right back."

He ran toward the railroad tracks and when he reached the crest of the hill he spotted a green Dodge Grand Caravan straddling the tracks. The train was a couple hundred yards away barreling toward them at forty to forty-five miles per hour.

"You got to get your car out of here now," Krahn shouted at the flustered woman through the open car window. The traffic congestion in front of and behind her prevented her from getting off the tracks.

He instructed her to drive off to the right, but when she did so, her right tire hooked onto the railroad tracks. He realized that there was no way she was going to be able to drive off the tracks. Not giving up, she hit the accelerator to give the car some gas. The van spun slightly clockwise facing the oncoming train. Its brakes screeched; its horn blared. Smoke and sparks zapped from the train wheels.

"Stop," Krahn yelled. "Get out of the car." He knew the collision was imminent.

She just looked at him, seemingly in shock.

"You need to get out of the car now! The train's coming!"

This Canadian Pacific freight train, which departed from Portage, Wisconsin, traveled through Elm Grove on its way to Bensenville, Illinois, during Elm Grove's annual Memorial Day parade (photo provided by the Elm Grove Police Department).

Still, she didn't respond.

Without a moment's hesitation, Krahn threw open the driver's door, yanked her out of the vehicle, and shoved her hard away from the railroad tracks.

They were safe. He felt himself relax.

That was until the woman cried out, "My baby's still in the car!"

Krahn couldn't walk away and leave the child. No one could survive the impact. He ran back to the sitting target that was the van and peered through the open driver's side door. A two-year-old boy stared back at him from the child seat in the back passenger side of the vehicle.

Krahn tried opening the back sliding door on the driver's side, but it was locked. His heart pounded as he frantically struggled to unlock it when a man suddenly appeared and began pulling on the door. Krahn reached into the car toward the rear driver's side door and manually unlocked the door.

The train was now just a couple hundred feet away, blaring its deafening horn. He decided in that moment that he was not going to walk away. He would stay there until he got the child out or until the train hit—whichever came first. Just as the door slid open and the man leaned inside reaching for the child, Krahn felt the impact of the train striking the van at forty-five miles per hour.

Krahn—conscious the whole time—was knocked eight feet into the air. He felt the momentum as he flew through the air, bouncing off the ground several times. He put his arms out in an attempt to stop himself until he finally came to rest sixty feet away in a grassy field south of the intersection. He lay on his right side grasping his left leg.

The other man landed in the grass just north of Krahn. The minivan, which sustained extensive frontal damage on the passenger side, crashed two- to three-hundred feet south of Juneau Boulevard in the field.

Elm Grove Officer John Krahn was struck by a train while attempting to remove a 23-month-old child from a minivan stuck on the train tracks. He since had to retire due to his injuries (photo provided by the Elm Grove Police Department).

Scattered among the wreckage were shattered glass, the other man's tennis shoes, one of Krahn's business cards and his broken Maui Jim sunglasses, a spare tire, a smashed headlight lens, and other debris. A large piece of the bumper area of the minivan was lodged under the front of the now-stopped train.

Krahn lay on the ground unable to move.

"Officer, are you okay?" a witness asked, kneeling next to him.

"There's a child in the car. I need you to go check on him," Krahn told him. He was certain the child had been killed, and he didn't want the mother to find him dead.

"I'll go check. Don't worry."

A minute later he returned assuring him, "He's fine. He doesn't appear hurt."

"What about the woman?" Krahn asked. He wasn't sure if he had pushed her far enough out of the way.

"She's fine, too. She's not injured."

Krahn heard the thundering of footsteps. He opened his eyes and looked up to see fellow officers standing over him, their eyes wide with concern.

They tried to calm him down, but he screamed in agony from the intense pain in his leg. He couldn't move it. He knew something was seriously wrong with it.

A few minutes later a doctor arrived.

"Am I going to die?" Krahn asked him fearfully.

"No, John you're not. You're going to be okay."

"Am I going to lose my leg?"

"John, I don't know."

Krahn wanted to get hold of his wife and eight-year-old daughter. He feared he was dying and wanted to say goodbye.

"John, John ... listen to me ... Flight for Life is on its way. You're going to be okay."

They cut off his boots, pants, and shirt and loaded him onto the helicopter headed for Froedtert Hospital in Milwaukee.

After the accident, Krahn was rushed to Froedtert Hospital in Milwaukee, where he spent the next two-and-a-half weeks in the hospital. He sustained a fractured pelvis, compound fractures to his left tibia and fibula, and four broken ribs, among other injuries (photo provided by the Elm Grove Police Department).

———

Krahn spent the next two-and-a-half weeks in the hospital, where he underwent five surgeries. He sustained a fractured pelvis, compound fractures to
his left tibia and fibia, four broken ribs, a sprained left ankle, a torn ACL in
his right knee, a broken shoulder blade, bruised lungs, and road rash. While
in the hospital he also developed compartment syndrome, which could have
resulted in the loss of his leg if not for an emergency surgery.

The man who tried to help Krahn get the child out was also transported
to Froedtert Hospital. He suffered a ruptured spleen, a transected pancreas,
multiple rib fractures, an aorta rupture, and a punctured lung. After the accident Krahn learned that this man was Scott Partenfelder, the woman's husband. He had been driving in front of her in an SUV with their other two
children. Like his wife, he had entered the railroad tracks and became stopped
when the Memorial Day Parade traffic came to a standstill. He, however, was
able to maneuver off the tracks onto a gravel shoulder area.

Both Krahn and Partenfelder suffered potentially fatal injuries. The child,
however, was completely unharmed. The child seat kept him safe. Krahn later
said it was actually fortunate the minivan's tire got hung up on the tracks and
the car spun when the woman accelerated. If it hadn't turned, the train would
have struck the side of the minivan where the child was sitting, undoubtedly
killing him.

———

During a press conference at the hospital, Krahn expressed his gratitude for
the "unbelievable support" he received from his family, friends, everyone at
the police department including Elm Grove Chief Jim Gage and Assistant
Chief Gus Moulas, employees from other Elm Grove departments, and the
staff at Froedtert Hospital.

He also cited the hundreds and hundreds of cards he received from his
D.A.R.E. students, from his brother officers across the state, and from citizens
he didn't even know. The community even threw a fundraiser shortly after he
was released from the hospital to assist with medical costs not covered by his
workers' compensation.

"I'm just happy to see people here," Krahn told Today's TMJ4, a local TV
news channel covering the fundraiser. "I've accomplished what I set out to do.
I made a difference as a person and as a police officer."

In addition to the accident and the fundraiser, the Milwaukee area media
took a keen interest in Krahn and his recovery. Nine months after the acci-

dent WISN 12 News checked in with him during a physical therapy session, where he grimaced in pain struggling to wade through a pool. At that time, just prior to his sixth surgery, he was still in too much pain and on too much medication to return to work.

"It's difficult," he said in the interview. "It's been going on for so long that there are the days you wake up, and you're like 'When is this going to end? When am I going to feel like I used to feel?'"

His heroic efforts, however, did not go unnoticed by his peers. Krahn earned over a dozen accolades, such as the Award for Valor from the Wisconsin Professional Police Association and the Officer of the Month title in December 2009 by the National Law Enforcement Officers Memorial Fund. In a video statement he made for *POLICE Magazine*, the media sponsor of the NLEOMF Officer of the Month Program, he said, "I've never considered myself to be a hero. I just did what I thought should be done at that time to help somebody who was in need of help. That's why I became a police officer."

———

Sadly, Krahn was not able to continue his career as a police officer after the accident.

He attempted to go back to work part-time on light duty, but the immense pain prohibited it. He even ended up back in the emergency room one night after a three-day stint at work. He filed for disability a year-and-a-half after the accident, around the time he spent two months at the Johns Hopkins Hospital in Baltimore for pain management. His last day of work as a police officer was April 29, 2012. He was forty-four years old.

"I was devastated. I had been a police officer for almost half my life," Krahn said. "The doctors encourage you and tell you if you work hard enough you can go back, so it created a conflict in me because I felt like a failure—like I wasn't trying hard enough. But then there were some doctors who said they didn't think I'd be able to go back to work."

———

Nearly four years after the accident, Krahn—who went on to have three more surgeries on his leg, making for a total of eight procedures—is still in pain every day. He gets around most of the time on a crutch, cane, or in some cases a wheelchair. He continues to receive treatment for post-traumatic stress disorder, he has not stopped going to physical therapy, and he is still plagued by nightmares. If he's lucky, he sleeps a couple hours a night.

Despite the persistent pain, the loss of the job he loved, and the acceptance of knowing he's never going to fully recover, Krahn is consoled by knowing that he did the right thing that day. When asked if he would do it all over again, he simply said, "Yeah. Without a doubt I would."

Line-of-duty Injuries

Below are the most common types of injuries sustained by officers, according to the National Institute of Justice, which cites a report titled *"Emergency Responder Injuries and Fatalities: An Analysis of Surveillance Data,"* published by the RAND Corporation in 2004.

Assault or violence: 27 percent

Physical stress and overexertion: 24.5 percent

Fall or jumping: 19 percent

Vehicle accidents: 16.5 percent

Struck by or contact with an object: 9.5 percent

Other causes: 2.4 percent

Fire and hazardous substances exposure: 2 percent

Struck by vehicles: 0.5 percent

RESCUES

---

*"I didn't know the guy, and I still haven't met him.
I'm just glad I was there to help him."*

—Milwaukee Officer Alberto Figueroa

15

"Angels Dressed Like Officers"

KENOSHA NEWS

Published: Wednesday, July 25, 2012Wednesday, July 25, 2012 | Publication: Kenosha News | Section: Local | Page: A3

Chief honors three for saving woman from July 5 fire

BY MATTHEW OLSON

molson@kenoshanews.com

Heroic acts at a house fire led Kenosha Police Chief John Morrissey to bestow medals of valor Tuesday — the first time he has done so since becoming chief.

Medals were presented to officers Tony Roberts, Kurt Zurcher and Martin Howard for their acts during a July 5 blaze in the 3900 block of 14th Avenue. Officer Daniel Bandi received a life-saving award.

Officers responded to the fire and found P.J. Hinrichs, who has multiple sclerosis, inside the burning house. Roberts, the first officer on the scene, started to take her out of the house. Zurcher and Howard then arrived and helped.

"We tell them not to run into burning buildings, but there is a time and a place where you get that courage, and this was that time and place," Morrissey said.

Morrissey said the effort involved great diversity in officer experience — Roberts is the second-most tenured patrol officer on the department and Howard was hired less than a year ago — and much cooperation and trust.

"Their teamwork was tremendous," Morrissey said.

Bandi helped Hinrichs' husband, Paul, out of the garage and found a safe place to take P.J. Hinrichs.

P.J. Hinrichs is still receiving treatment in Milwaukee for burns suffered in the fire, but Morrissey said he feels the officers' actions saved her life.

Paul Hinrichs thanked the officers — whom he referred to as "angels" — personally at Tuesday's meeting of the Police and Fire Commission, Morrissey said.

Morrissey said he has been fairly conservative in giving awards for service in the line of duty — and he has never given out the medal of valor before, the department's second-highest award — but felt these actions showed great bravery and courage.

"I'm extremely confident that these officers earned this recognition," Morrissey said. "It's meant to recognize when you go above and beyond the call of duty and when you are in imminent danger. They earned it, and they deserve the recognition."

A family was stuck inside a burning house in the middle of the night. The call to respond to the 3900 block of 14th Avenue came in about three a.m. on July 5, 2012.

This is crunch time, Kenosha Officer Martin Howard thought as he rushed to the residence with his partner, Kurt Zurcher. As a new officer just hired in September the year before, the twenty-five year old rode with Zurcher, a senior officer, as part of his field training.

When they arrived moments later they found the modest two-story house completely engulfed in flames. The extreme heat, the bright blazes, the cacophonous crackling—it was all indescribable to Howard. The fire department was not yet on scene, but he heard Officer Tony Roberts screaming from the back of the house for them to help.

"Tony's in the back. Tony's in the back," Howard hollered at Zurcher and Officer Daniel Bandi, who responded at the same time they did.

The three ran around the rear to the open attached garage where they found Roberts in the doorway leading into the house. Leaning forward, he was walking backward struggling to drag an unconscious woman in her fifties by her arms. Her husband and adult daughter frantically hovered around her, but if they said or did anything else, Howard was unaware. He was too focused on the woman and the fire.

Foreboding flames covered the three surrounding walls, inching closer and closer to them. Dark, increasingly heavy smoke sunk down on them, making it difficult to breathe. It grew hazy and scorching hot. Howard knew he could die. They had to get her out and go.

"Let's lift her. Let's get out!" he shouted.

Zurcher and Roberts each took an arm, and Howard picked up her legs. The woman was so badly burned that his hands slipped from her knees down to her ankles. Bandi followed them out, grabbing the husband, while the daughter, carrying a dog, walked out on her own.

The group escaped together and took safety in a nearby alley to wait for the paramedics. They rolled the woman on her right side in the recovery position and did the best they could to treat her. She was in and out of consciousness and in a lot of pain. Her husband, so overwhelmed, laid down in the grass and sprawled out his arms and legs. Howard turned to look at the house and discovered it was gone. Completely gone.

If they had arrived just a minute later, he was certain the mother would not have survived.

———

The woman, whom Howard later learned suffered from multiple sclerosis and was wheelchair-bound, sustained second-degree burns to approximately 55 percent of her body. As she was wheeled into the emergency room, Howard heard her repeatedly cry out in pain twenty to thirty times, "I'm burning, I'm burning, I'm burning." It was initially unclear whether or not she would live, but she survived. The husband suffered minor burns, and the daughter, aged twenty-two, was not injured.

Howard never heard the cause of the fire, but he thinks the culprit was a Fourth of July firecracker that hit the roof. The husband, Paul Hinrichs, woke up when the fire started and alerted his sleeping family. They tried to escape through the garage, but his wife's wheelchair gave out near the doorway. Hinrichs believed that she would have died if not for Howard and the other officers.

A month after the fire, Howard received the Kenosha Police Department's Medal of Valor, an award recognizing officers who performed an act displaying extreme courage while consciously facing imminent risk of great bodily harm. Zurcher and Roberts also were awarded the Medal of Valor, and Bandi received a Lifesaving Award.

During the award presentation, Hinrichs thanked the officers in a heartfelt speech.

"My wife has MS and can't walk," he said. "I looked up the word 'brave' in the dictionary, and the definition said 'possessing endurance and courage.' I then looked up 'courage,' and it said 'the power or quality of dealing with or facing danger, fear, pain, etc.' Then, I looked up the word 'heroic,' and it said 'bold, undertaking extreme measures,' and this is what these officers did. These angels, dressed like officers, came to our rescue that day. Without these officers, we would have buried my wife. I thank you, and I love you."

"It blew my mind that he called us angels. I was extremely, extremely honored," Howard said a few months after the presentation.

In addition to Hinrichs, twenty to thirty family members attended the presentation where they cried and hugged and thanked the officers. "It was one of the coolest things I've ever gotten to experience," Howard said. "They were a very nice and loving family."

Also during the presentation, Kenosha Chief John Morrissey commended the officers for disregarding their own personal safety by running into the house.

"They could have left the building due to the great danger to their own safety, but knowing all of them, I am sure leaving was never an option," Morrissey said.

According to Howard, it is against policy for officers to enter burning buildings because they don't have the proper equipment. Instead, officers are supposed to wait for the firefighters and make sure no one else enters the building.

Given the exigency of the situation, however, Howard and the others knew they had to go in. The woman would have been dead otherwise.

"For myself and Kurt there was no question because Tony was already there. We just ran in," he said. "But if he wasn't there, and I saw the lady, I would have made the same choice."

Howard's education and training had prepared him for dangerous situations, but he never expected to find himself involved in such an intense one so soon.

"I think it's a strange coincidence that I happened to be there this soon in my career, but I'm happy I got to go through that experience and I'm happy I was there to help get the lady out," said Howard, who along with Bandi, Zurcher, and Roberts, were later awarded the Certificate of Merit from the Wisconsin Professional Police Association.

Although the call served as a reality check to Howard of how dangerous his job can be, it assured him that he made the right choice to become a police officer.

"It reaffirmed that this is exactly what I want to do for my career," said Howard, the son of a Cook County, Illinois, judge. "I love people and being in the position where I can help people right on the front lines. If anything, this reaffirmed that this is what I want to do."

———◆———

10-70: Fire

Kenosha Officer Martin Howard, along with three other officers, risked their lives by running into a burning garage to pull out a disabled woman.

Responding to fires, known as 10-70 in police code, is not a rare occurrence for police officers.

In fact, Kenosha police officers responded to more than 1,500 fires over the last four years, according to Kenosha Captain Bradley Kemen.

> 2010: 354 calls
> 2011: 439 calls
> 2012: 411 calls
> 2013: 470 calls*

Although Howard and his fellow officers were commended for their actions due to the exigency of the situation, generally police should not enter a burning, smoking, or smoldering structure, according to the Kenosha Police Department's policy on fires.

Policy 41.9 of the department under the entering structures section states:

1. Generally an officer should not enter a burning, smoking, or smoldering structure. Rescue at a fire will usually be up to fire department personnel. They have the proper equipment, training, and expertise.
    a. If you decide to enter a burning, smoking, or smoldering structure, it shall be for the sole purpose of preservation of human life.
    b. Before entering a burning, smoking, or smoldering structure, you must consider your safety and the safety of others that may follow you.
    c. You must also consider that entering the structure may provide the necessary oxygen to cause the fire to increase or possibly cause an explosion.

Otherwise, some of the police responsibilities at a fire scene include: establishing a perimeter and preventing non-essential personnel and/or spectators from entering that perimeter; ensuring that all hydrants within the perimeter are accessible; conducting crowd control; rendering assistance to emergency medical personnel; and completing a police report in situations where the fire is suspicious or when there are serious injuries or death.

*The 2013 figure is approximate as the Kenosha Police Department changed its re-cord-keeping procedures pertaining to the number of fires to which police responded. The figure indicated reflects the number of responses by the Kenosha Fire Department for fire alarms or reported fires. As a general rule, however, the Kenosha Police Depart-ment responds to all fire calls for traffic assistance and other needs.

16

A Police Aide Called to Action

Off-duty police aide helps prevent suicide

Figueroa, 20, clung to man on overpass

By JESSE GARZA
jgarza@journalsentinel.com

A 20-year-old police aide on his way home from work intervened after seeing a suicidal man positioning himself for a leap from a freeway overpass.

It was about 4 p.m. Nov. 1 when Alberto Figueroa was riding his motorcycle on W. Lloyd St. near N. 47th St. and noticed the man climbing around a fence at the bridge over Highway 41.

What followed was a 40-minute drama in which Figueroa and police Officer Hector Claudio clung to the man's jacket until he was persuaded to return to safety.

"I didn't think of myself as a being a member of the Police Department at the time," Figueroa said Thursday. "I just acted as a citizen who saw someone needing help and I tried to help him."

After seeing the man climb around the chain link safety fence on the south side of the bridge, Figueroa parked his motorcycle, called 911 on his cellphone and approached the man from the sidewalk side.

"He was on the west end of the bridge. He said he was trying to get to the center of the bridge, over traffic, and that he controls his own life," Figueroa said. "I knew if he got over traffic he'd be in danger."

As the man made his way toward the southbound lanes of Highway 41, his leather jacket was brushing against the outside of the fence, Figueroa said.

"So when his left jacket pocket was touching the fence I grabbed it and held on as tight as I could."

About the same time Claudio had just started his shift and heard a call on his squad radio requesting assistance for a fellow officer.

Soon, Claudio was at the fence, opposite Figueroa, also clasping onto the 37-year-old man's jacket.

"He said he was done; life was over for him," Claudio said.

"I told him, I'm 38, and that I'm pretty sure I got some more years ahead of me and, good or bad, I'm going to take them."

With police blocking freeway traffic, Figueroa, Claudio and a police crisis negotiator continued talking with the man, and Milwaukee firefighters soon arrived and extended a ladder up to the overpass.

When Sgt. Michael Pelnar made his way onto the overpass next to Claudio, Claudio climbed up the fence and over to the man's right side so that he was "boxed in" between Claudio and the sergeant.

"Then he leaned back and let go of the fence, making it harder for us to maintain our grips," Claudio said.

With the help of the man's aunt, who happened to be driving past, Figueroa and Claudio continued talking to him until he finally allowed a firefighter to lead him down the ladder to safety.

"Police Aide Figueroa's actions were a game-changer," Claudio said. "He intervened."

Alberto Figueroa was driving home from work on his motorcycle one mild fall afternoon when he spotted a man climbing around the fence of a freeway overpass on Milwaukee's northwest side.

The twenty-year-old Milwaukee police aide immediately became suspicious. He knew there was nowhere underneath the Lloyd Street bridge for homeless people to sleep.

Figueroa knew he had to go check it out. Turning onto the bridge over Highway 41 at N. 47th Street, he called out, "Hey buddy. What's going on?"

"Keep driving," the man hollered back. He was now on the outside of the fence standing on a six-inch ledge overlooking the highway. Figueroa could hear the roar of traffic as it zoomed past below them. At four in the afternoon, it was almost rush hour.

Figueroa knew driving away was not an option. He pulled his motorcycle over and called 911 to report him as a suspicious person.

With the dispatcher still on the line, he approached the man and asked again, "What's going on? What are you doing?"

He noticed the man, who wore a nice leather jacket and appeared to be in his late thirties, was shuffling toward the middle of the overpass.

"Keep going. You're going to cause a scene."

"What's your name? Why are you here today?" Figueroa asked, removing his jacket to reveal his police uniform underneath.

"Go home to your wife and kids."

The conversation went on for about two minutes until the man finally relented.

"I'm trying to get to the middle. I'm going to end my life."

Figueroa's suspicions were confirmed, but he remained calm.

"I've got a potential suicidal subject," he told dispatch. "He's trying to jump off the bridge. Block off 41 in case something happens."

He put the phone on speaker and set it down on the ground preparing to talk the man down.

"Look, it's just you and me talking right now," Figueroa said. "I know there's a lot of struggles out there."

"I control my life. You don't. Just let me get to the middle. I'm going to jump," he repeated, continuing to move toward the center of the overpass.

Figueroa was not about to let him commit suicide right in front of him. He reached through the fence and grabbed onto the six-foot-tall, one-hundred-eighty-pound man's right side jacket pocket and declared, "I'm not letting go."

"I'll give you my wallet if you let go of my jacket," the man pleaded with him.

"Buddy, calm down. Relax. Take a few deep breaths. We can talk about this."

Figueroa had dealt with mentally unstable people before but never anyone suicidal. He relied on his instincts and his basic training in crisis intervention to try to talk to him until help arrived. He knew to communicate with him on a name-to-name basis and to ask him about his problems without getting too personal.

Figueroa could hear the clock ticking in his head while he waited the five or so minutes for police to arrive. It felt like forever.

In addition to clinging onto the struggling man and attempting to talk to him, a million thoughts ran through his head, like what if the man starts fighting him. So far he had not been argumentative or combative, but he wondered how long that would last.

Finally Figueroa heard the wailing of sirens on the way. He was so relieved he felt like he could cry. Still, he knew it was not over. He had to keep hanging onto the man until the firefighters got on scene in case he jumped the thirty or so feet to his death.

Officer Hector Claudio arrived first, followed by Sergeant Michael Pelnar a couple of minutes later. The two, whom Figueroa knew from when he worked at District 3, climbed over the eight to ten foot chain link fence and stood on the ledge to the left of the man.

Claudio also grabbed onto his jacket, but the man leaned back and let go of the fence. Claudio knew they needed to better secure the man so he jumped up on the fence and in an impressive acrobatic feat climbed around to the man's right side to make room for Pelnar on the left.

Now with Claudio and Pelnar on each side of the man and Figueroa across from them on the other side of the fence, the three continued to grasp onto him until the firefighters arrived. Meanwhile, below them, Milwaukee County Sheriff's deputies blocked off freeway entrances and off-ramps.

"I'm going to jump when I get to the middle," the man said again. "Just leave."

He intermittently would let go of the fence and lean back, but the officers and Figueroa tried to maintain his focus by talking to him and asking what was bothering him. All they got out of him was his name; he wouldn't specifically talk about his problems.

The ordeal at last came to an end when the Milwaukee firefighters arrived. They parked their truck on Highway 41, extended a twelve-foot ladder up to the man, and pulled him down when he refused to come down willingly.

As they lowered him to safety, the man's aunt who lived four blocks away drove by and recognized her nephew. She told Figueroa and the others that he had been depressed and family members were out looking for him.

The man was transported to Milwaukee County Mental Health Complex, where he cited car and money problems as the reasons why he tried to commit suicide.

It wasn't until the forty-minute incident was over and his adrenaline went down did Figueroa feel the pain in his fingers from clinging onto the man for that long. He didn't have much time to dwell on that though, as the aunt, other family members, and even neighbors began hugging and thanking him for being in the right place at the right time.

"If I had stayed ten minutes late at work that day or left three minutes early, I never would have seen him jumping off the bridge," the Milwaukee native later said.

His actions on November 1, 2012, also did not go unnoticed by city officials and peers. The following day Mayor Tom Barrett called him on his cell phone, and later Milwaukee County Sheriff David A. Clarke, Jr. thanked him, as did the members of the Milwaukee Common Council.

He was awarded a Lifesaving Merit Award from the Milwaukee Police Department and an award from 8th District Alderman Bob Donovan on behalf of the city of Milwaukee and the city of Milwaukee Common Council known as the Golden Glove Award.

"I didn't do it because I work for the police department. I did it because I saw someone in trouble," said Figueroa, who became a Milwaukee officer in 2013. "I'm glad I saved his life. I hope he gets the help he really needs. I didn't know the guy, and I still haven't met him. I'm just glad I was there to help him."

Milwaukee Police Aide Program

Police aides at the Milwaukee Police Department are uniformed civilian employees who serve in an apprentice-style program designed to prepare them for a career as a police officer.

They help officers with arrest processing and booking, perform administrative and clerical duties, and assist citizens on the phone and in person, in addition to other tasks. They are not allowed, however, to conduct any law enforcement duties on their own. It is a forty-hour a week job, with a salary between $22,862 and $31,587.

Some of the requirements to become a police aide include passing a written test, a physical ability test, an oral interview, a writing sample exercise, and a background investigation. They also have to be at least seventeen years of age and no older than nineteen at the time of appointment.

People cannot become police aides if they have been convicted of a felony or a misdemeanor crime of domestic violence, dishonorably discharged from any branch of the United States Military Service, or failed a Milwaukee Police Department background investigation within the last two years of applying.

Police aides may be hired as police officers once they turn twenty-one and if they receive a favorable recommendation from the chief, serve in the program between two and four years, and earn twenty-four college credits among other requirements.

—Information from the Milwaukee Police Department website.

17

Saved by an Eighth of an Inch

The phone ringing at four a.m. jolted Milwaukee Detective Ted Engelbart awake.

A man reported a bomb dragging from his car at 60th Street and Keefe Avenue on the city's northwest side. Headquarters ordered Engelbart, a member of the ten-person bomb squad, to go investigate.

"Honey, I gotta go. They have a suspicious device," Engelbart told his now awake and concerned wife.

"Be careful, honey. I love you," she said. Although she had grown accustomed to her husband responding to dangerous situations over the years— sometimes even learning about them in the newspaper the next day—she still naturally feared whenever he had to examine a potential bomb.

"I love you, too. Don't worry."

After a hug and kiss goodbye, Engelbart drove the ten-minute ride to the scene, his heart racing. The whole time he kept thinking, *Please don't go off. Please don't go off.* If anything, he wanted the bomb to go off before he got there.

Once on scene he found the car containing the suspected device isolated in the middle of the intersection of the residential street. No one could be near the vehicle in case it was indeed a bomb and it exploded.

Officers had blocked off the surrounding hundred yards, evacuated the residents of four nearby houses, and stood at corners stopping the little traffic passing by that early in the morning. Other officers waited one-hundred-and-fifty feet away from the car behind barricades, as did an ambulance on standby.

"The guy said he saw something there," an officer said to Engelbart, pointing under the car.

Engelbart approached the car alone with bated breath. He kneeled down, and quickly peered underneath. Wrapped to the exhaust pipe were six sticks of dynamite, a blasting cap, a nine-volt battery, and a spring-type clothespin switch. A four-by-four-inch piece of wood tied to a brick kept the clothespin to-gether. When the driver took off, the piece of wood, called a shim, was meant to eject from the clothespin, triggering the explosion.

Engelbart knew this was no longer a suspected explosive device. This was a legitimate bomb.

He hustled over to Detective Terry Datka, his partner who had just ar-rived with the bomb truck, and said, "It looks like dynamite."

Datka took a turn by himself to check out the device, came back, and said, "Yep, you're right."

Ordinarily, x-rays are taken of explosive devices to identify their compo-nents, but in this case it was clear to Engelbart and Datka how this particu-lar bomb was constructed. The detectives—who completed many advanced courses including a month-long training in Huntsville, Alabama, at the Red-stone Arsenal, one of the U.S. Army's training centers—could tell the bomb was not a timing device nor did it possess a secondary switch.

"How are we going to deactivate it?" Datka asked. As members of the bomb squad, he and Engelbart were level headed and pragmatic. They knew they needed to carefully construct their plans or else they could blow their fingers off like a fellow squad member once did—or even die.

"How about one of us grabs the clothespin so it can't close, and the other one take off the blasting cap?" Engelbart suggested. Without the cap—a cy-lindrical six-inch-long object sprouting with wires—dynamite cannot explode.

"I'll grab the clothespin," Datka offered.

"Okay, I'll grab the cap."

Usually, only one bomb squad member neutralizes an explosive device in order to prevent more fatalities in the event it does go off. In this case, how-ever, two were needed so one could use both hands to hold apart the two ends of the clothespin switch while the other removed the blasting cap.

Engelbart and Datka returned to the car and lay underneath it.

It was just his partner, himself, and his thoughts.

This could be it. This could be my last breath, Engelbart thought. He said a little prayer, *Please God help me and be with me.*

If the two ends of the spring-activated clothespin switch made contact, the bomb would explode. One little bump, and they would be dead. This is the part when trusting one's partner comes in.

Moving slowly, Datka reached for the clothespin switch and, trying his hardest to keep his hands steady, clasped onto each end.

"I got it," he said excitedly.

"You got it good?" Engelbart asked cautiously.

"I got it good."

Engelbart exhaled. The bomb didn't go off, and he knew it no longer would now. They were in the clear.

Engelbart removed the cap and unhooked the battery. In five minutes, it was over. They deactivated the bomb, and no one was hurt. He and Datka laughed in relief.

What kept the bomb from going off in this incident, they discovered, was an eighth of an inch. If the clothespin had come together by just that much more it would have exploded.

The only reason it didn't was because the man, frustrated by an argument with his girlfriend, accelerated abruptly as he drove away. The shim did eject from the clothespin as intended, but the clothespin skewed when the car fishtailed leaving it open by that eighth of an inch.

"Make a big donation to your church," Engelbart told the visibly shaken man.

A week later police arrested the ex-boyfriend of the man's girlfriend and charged him with attempted murder. The girlfriend had nothing to do with the plot.

In his twenty years on the bomb squad, Engelbart, now retired after a thirty-year career, responded to over a thousand calls of suspected bombs planted by everyone from organized crime and extreme right wingers to rival gangs and robbers. About a hundred of the bombs turned out to be legitimate, but this particular incident that took place in the late nineties is memorable to him because it was such a fluke.

"You wonder if it wasn't for the grace of God," Engelbart said. "That guy should've been killed. A thousand times in that same scenario it would've blown up."

———•———

Explosives Incidents in the U.S.

The statistics below include bombings, attempted bombings, incendiary bombings, and stolen explosives as reported to the U.S. Bomb Data Center.

Year	No. of Explosive Incidents	No. of Injuries	No. of Fatalities
2012 (Jan. 1–Oct. 31)	4,033	37	1
2011	5,219	36	5
2010	4,897	99	22
2009	3,886	57	4
2008	4,198	97	15
2007	3,143	60	15
2006	3,797	135	14
2005	4,031	148	19
2004	3,919	263	36

—Information from the Bureau of Alcohol, Tobacco, Firearms and Explosives.

———•———

18

The Right Place
at the Right Time

Wausau Daily Herald

Wausau cop in national spotlight

A Wausau Police officer has been nominated for an America's Most Wanted All-Star award for twice saving the lives of young children while on duty.

On Jan. 20, Thomas Peterson revived a 2-year-old girl who had no pulse and was not breathing after she was found facedown in a bathtub. Peterson picked up the child and struck her on the back. The toddler spit out some water and began to cry as ambulance crews arrived at the home.

In October 2008, Peterson performed the Heimlich maneuver on a 7-month-old child who was choking on an unknown object and was not breathing.

Peterson is one of 48 police officers, firefighters and paramedics currently nominated for the award. Each week, the public votes for finalists to be considered for the award winner, which will be selected at a later date.

To see Peterson's nomination and to vote, visit AMW's Web site at www.amw.com/allstar/2010.

Rothschild police officer Trevor Ostrowski was nominated for the award in 2008 for his actions June 17, 2007, after Errol Demmerly allegedly shot at the officer during a traffic stop.

The seven-month-old baby boy stared at Wausau Officer Thomas Peterson with wide, frightened eyes. Foam bubbled from his mouth, and he couldn't breathe.

Peterson, an eleven-year veteran of the department, grabbed the choking child out of his hysterical father's arms, laid him facedown on his left forearm, and delivered back blows with the heel of his right hand until the infant spit an unidentified small object out of his mouth.

A little over a year later, in January 2010, Peterson found himself in a similar situation.

A call came in on the city's northeast side early one afternoon about a two-and-a-half-year-old girl found facedown in a bathtub.

Peterson, who happened to be about two blocks away, rushed to the scene and ran into the unlocked house where he found the screaming mother on the phone with dispatch. She had left the bathroom for a few minutes during which time her daughter went underwater.

Peterson looked down to see the child laying on her stomach on the living room floor naked and soaking wet, her long, dripping hair shielding her face. The bathtub in the nearby bathroom brimmed with water.

"Help my baby! Help my baby!" the woman pleaded.

Without uttering a word, the officer lifted the toddler's limp blue body off the floor and, like the choking infant, laid her on his forearm facedown and gave strong back blows. Suddenly she began spitting out water, coughing and crying much to Peterson's relief. Up until then he wasn't sure if the child would make it or not.

The paramedics arrived moments after he revived the baby and transported her to the hospital. "You know you saved that little girl's life," a doctor told Peterson.

She was ultimately flown to the Ministry Saint Joseph's Children's Hospital in Marshfield where she made a full recovery.

In recognition of the incidents, Peterson received a Lifesaving Award from the American Red Cross, the Medical Director's Award from Ministry Saint Clare's Hospital, and two Lifesaving Awards from the Wausau Police Department. He was also nominated by a citizen in 2010 as an America's Most Wanted All-Star, a contest from the *America's Most Wanted* TV show that asks people to vote for their favorite first responder hero.

"A lot of things came together," Peterson said, of how it felt to save those children's lives. "Just being in the right place at the right time and having the training to know how to handle the situation. I'm fortunate to work for a police department that puts a lot of emphasis on training officers."

Coincidentally, those weren't the only times Peterson saved someone's life. Years earlier in 1987 when he worked as a correctional officer at the Marathon County Sheriff's Department, he performed the Heimlich maneuver on a dispatcher who was choking on a cookie. He subsequently received the Honorable Mention Award from the sheriff's department.

"Yeah it's a little unusual I'd say," Peterson said, about saving not one or two but three lives. "Like with that little girl a lot of things had to line up that day because the nearest person could've been across town and could've been too late. I didn't realize the scope of it until the doctor said 'you saved that little girl's life.'"

———◆———

Children and Drowning

Children ages one to four have the highest drowning rates, according to the Centers for Disease Control and Prevention. In fact, drowning is responsible for more deaths among children in that age group than any other cause except congenital anomalies (birth defects).

In 2009, more than 30 percent of children one to four years of age who died from an unintentional injury died from drowning. Among those one to fourteen years of age, fatal drowning remains the second-leading cause of unintentional injury-related death behind motor vehicle crashes.

Below are safety tips from the United States Consumer Product Safety Commission:

♦ Never leave a baby alone in a bathtub for even a second, and always keep the baby in arm's reach.
♦ A baby bath seat is not a substitute for supervision. Babies have slipped or climbed out of bath seats and drowned.
♦ Never use a baby bath seat in a non-skid, slip-resistant bathtub because the suction cups will not adhere to the bathtub surface or can detach unexpectedly.
♦ Never leave a bucket containing even a small amount of liquid unattended. When finished using a bucket, always empty it immediately.
♦ Learn CPR. It can be a lifesaver when seconds count.

———◆———

CALLS INVOLVING CHILDREN

"*The one call every police officer does not want to go to.*"

—Brown County Lieutenant Dan Sandberg

19

Set Free

Cage/Kids scarred by abuse, therapist testifies

From page 1

for abusing their only daughter.

As the case, which drew national attention, was slated to go to trial, both parents pleaded guilty to four felony charges. In a plea agreement, District Attorney Kenneth Kratz dropped six additional felony charges against each of them.

The other charges, alleging three of their four children were hit with sticks and a metal drain pipe, is being read into the record.

Three police officers sobbed and several spectators wiped away tears as they watched a 40-minute videotape in which the girl and three of her four brothers told of being beaten with sticks, belts and a drain pipe. The children said they were sometimes forced to stand for hours holding boards over their heads.

Their unemotional testimony was taped and played at their parents' sentencing so they would not have to face their mother and father in court.

Both parents "should be punished," their 10-year-old son said, adding that what his mother and father did was "bad."

Speaking in a monotone voice, the little girl said she spent weekends and the hours when she returned home from school locked in the tiny cage, hugging a stuffed animal. Looking directly into the camera, she said she didn't know why she was locked up.

A cage barely large enough to hold a small dog or puppy was displayed on a table Thursday along with 4-inch-thick sticks and a drain pipe used to beat four of the couple's five children. They were seized from the family's home in Brillion after the parents were arrested Nov. 17.

A son, now 12, said on videotape that his parents shopped

ASSOCIATED PRESS

Michael and Angeline Rogers are being sentenced for child abuse after pleading guilty to locking their 7-year-old daughter in this 20-by-24-inch dog cage in the basement of their home nearly every day.

for the cage specifically to contain his sister. He said the cage, which measures 20 by 24 inches, was too small to hold any of the family dogs.

The couple's five children, ages 11, 9, 7, 6 and 18 months at the time, were placed in other homes.

Michael Rogers, dressed in a gray suit, sat slumped in his chair, showing no emotion as the videotape played. Angeline Rogers appeared to bite her fist as she watched her children describe a home life that had gone terribly haywire.

Derozier said Angeline Rogers was like a Venus flytrap who showed "certain nurturing" characteristics, "but she could close in on prey if it suited her."

Meanwhile, Michael Rogers was her opposite. Weak-willed, he did what his wife told him to do, the psychologist said.

Mark Rohrer, an attorney for Michael Rogers, said that in the years leading up to the parents' arrest, three psychologists determined that the girl suffered from "defiant oppositional disorder." Symptoms include

throwing temper tantrums, being angry and resentful and exhibiting spiteful behavior. He said the girl sometimes smeared the house with feces and once dumped the contents of the family's refrigerator into the garbage.

The little girl's tragic predicament came to light when her then-11-year-old brother trudged through 30-degree weather without shoes or a coat to the Brillion police station to

alert authorities about the pligh of his sister.

Though the boy has been hail ed as a hero and his sister's sav ior, he now suffers from "surv vor's guilt," Derozier said. H feels that he contributed to hi sister's problem because h didn't alert authorities sooner.

All of the other children, wit the exception of a boy who wa 18 months old when the Roger were arrested, are deepl scarred by their parents' bizarr treatment of them.

The second oldest son, nov 10, "vacillates between thinkin his parents are jerks and that hi parents are wonderful," Dero zier said. An 8-year-old so thinks the family would hav been better off "if this siste just wasn't around," he said.

The children have thrive since being placed in fost homes, he said. The girl ha grown several inches and ha started to regain self-esteem.

"From January to Augus she's been able to receive lov which means she has begun t trust."

Derozier added that it coul take the girl 20 years to recupe ate from bouts of anxiety an depression she is likely to suffe

The eleven-year-old boy wore no jacket or shoes on that below-freezing November evening in 1997.

Just after dark he walked into the Brillion Police Department and told the school resource officer and Sergeant Daniel Alloy that his mother kicked him and his two younger brothers out of the house and into the cold garage as punishment for eating Halloween candy without permission.

Yet, that was not the most alarming thing about the story.

The boy went on to tell the police that his parents kept his six-year-old sister in a dog kennel in the basement.

Alloy desperately wanted to go check on her, but he had to fight the urge. He needed to wait until he had enough specific information from the boy that the girl's life was in danger to authorize him to enter the house without a warrant.

Once Alloy had enough details, he rushed to the house where he found the two parents in the driveway heading out to look for the oldest son. The two other boys were since allowed back into the house.

"He's fine. He's at the police department talking to another officer," Alloy said of their son. "That's why I'm here. He said a young girl is being kept in a dog cage in the basement. Are you aware of that?"

"I don't think so, but you can go check," the mother answered. She and her husband looked surprised to see Alloy, but he got the sense that they knew they were caught and were now trying to minimize the situation by cooperating.

"Oh, I'm going to go look," Alloy firmly said. He didn't need their permission; he had the community caretaker doctrine on his side.

The parents warned Alloy that the children probably wouldn't open the locked door, but the two young boys who answered threw open the door in excitement when they saw him, as if rejoicing that help had finally arrived.

"Where's your sister?" he asked them.

"In the basement." He fully expected that to be the answer, but his body still tensed up at the anticipation of what he was about to find.

Unable to find the light switch in the old home, Alloy pulled out his flashlight to guide him down the creaky steps. The basement was cold. Not as chilly as outside, but almost. He could tell it was unheated. He stepped over a heap of dirty clothes at the bottom of the steps and continued fumbling around looking for a light. Shining the flashlight around he saw nothing in the unfinished basement except for the pile of laundry and a washer and dryer.

At last he found a light hanging from the ceiling and yanked on the string, brightening the basement. He still didn't see the girl, but he did spot a door to what looked like a food storage area. He pulled open the knob-less door and was assaulted by a wretched smell. The flashlight's illumination revealed human excrement covering the concrete floor and an open-wire mesh kennel.

"Cabbet? Are you there?" Alloy called out into the silence to the child.

He paused waiting for an answer that didn't come. The odor was so foul he almost couldn't breathe.

He decided to pick up the twenty-by-twenty-four-inch kennel, thinking it would be fairly light if empty. Instead it was heavy. Too heavy.

He peered into the kennel and glimpsed a little girl peek out from a dirty blanket inside the kennel.

Brillion Sergeant Daniel Alloy rescued the little girl once known as Cabbet Rogers from a twenty-by-twenty-four-inch kennel (photo provided by Daniel Alloy).

She was underfed and unkempt, but she was not scared. At just six years of age, Alloy could tell she was strong.

Immediately unlocking the kennel, he scooped her out and carried her up the stairs to the bright, warm house to safety.

Alloy was in shock and angry. In his twenty years in law enforcement, he could not believe someone would keep a child in a cage. He never would have thought something as horrific as this would happen in a small midwestern town and that he'd be in the middle of it. *Things like this are supposed to take place in big cities thousands of miles away,* he thought.

At that moment, Alloy did not trust himself to treat the parents in a fair manner, so he instructed the school resource officer who arrived moments after he did to deal with the parents. They were immediately taken into custody and placed into separate squad cars to prevent them from collaborating on a story. The children were given medical examinations, and the child abuse investigation began.

This wasn't, however, the first time the Brillion police had heard of abuse transpiring at the home. Shortly after the family moved to Brillion a month earlier, the police began receiving complaints about the children's living conditions.

The Calumet County Department of Human Services investigated, but found no signs of abuse. In a frustrating twist of irony, the department's letter stating that they found no substantiated abuse arrived at the police department on the very day Alloy rescued the little girl.

Once the police investigated, they discovered all the ongoing physical and mental abuse the five children suffered. Besides Cabbet, who was almost seven, the family consisted of the eleven- and nine-year-old boys, a six-year-old boy, and an eighteen-month-old boy.

The parents, Angeline and Michael Rogers, allegedly kept the food on top of the cupboards out of the children's reach and beat them. After Alloy rescued the girl, the children walked him around the house showing him all the objects—sticks, belts, a rain gutter—used to hit them. They never displayed any sadness while doing so; instead they were talkative, informative, and excited to finally tell someone.

When Alloy met Cabbet as a child, he found her to be smart, polite, and outgoing (photo provided by Daniel Alloy).

The parents also beat Cabbet, Alloy said, but she was the only child they caged. They forced her to live in her makeshift prison for four years, only letting her out to go to school. As soon as she returned, right back in she went until the next morning. She was not allowed to play with other kids, and they did not clean her or see to her personal needs other than occasionally hosing her off while belittling her and calling her names.

She came to school filthy as did the other children, but every time the school would report it and child protection got involved, the family would move to another community to avoid investigation. Alloy said the family moved as many as three or four times to various locales in Wisconsin before coming to Brillion, a city of three thousand near Appleton.

Angeline told police that she kept her daughter in the cage as punishment because she was mischievous, extremely hard to handle, and insubordinate.

Alloy knew that was just a lie though. He found Cabbet to be smart, polite, and outgoing—nothing like her mother had described.

According to the psychologists that interviewed Angeline, the mother imprisoned Cabbet because she perceived her young daughter as a threat. Though Michael complied, Alloy said Angeline was the instigator and ordered her husband and sons to lock Cabbet up.

Alloy believes she would not have survived another winter in the basement cage; she would have died or run away.

Learning about the abuse Cabbet and her brothers had suffered made Alloy, a father to a twelve- and fourteen-year-old at the time, appreciate his family even more. He would never allow for his kids' needs to go unmet—if anything he would be the one to go without—and he wanted to make sure Cabbet and her brothers were taken care of as well.

He and the other Brillion police officers became close to the children. Shortly after the incident, they threw a Christmas party for them complete with a Santa Claus and an abundance of presents donated from people around the United States.

Alloy will never forget seeing Cabbet sitting on the floor playing with a Barbie doll.

"Do you like the dolls?" he asked, taking a seat next to her.

"Oh I love the dolls," she told him.

"Do you have any dolls at home?"

"No I don't have any toys. This is my first Barbie doll."

Not only did she not own any toys, she did not even have a bed. Her only personal possession was that dirty blanket in the cage. It infuriated Alloy that the human services workers never even bothered to ask, "Where's Cabbet's bed?"

Shortly after the Christmas party, the unexpected happened.

The Calumet County Department of Human Services prohibited contact between the officers and the kids, telling them that they didn't want the children to be influenced.

Alloy was heartbroken. He felt as if his own child had been kidnapped.

"They pulled the kids away from us, and we always needed that contact for our healing," he said. "I was never able to put closure to that case."

To make the situation worse, the judge sentenced Angeline and Michael Rogers to one year in jail after they gave up their parental rights and reached plea deals. (Angeline ultimately was sent to prison, however, for escaping after police had arrested her for attempting to get into Mexico. She was paroled in 2006, according to the *Milwaukee Journal Sentinel*.)

"It was like getting kicked in the stomach after months and months of putting this case together and going to court and having to testify and relive the whole thing," Alloy said.

Alloy asked the human services department several times about the children after the parents were sentenced, but the only answer he ever received was that they were fine. All he knew was that the children were separated and sent to multiple foster families until each one was eventually adopted.

Alloy thought about them often over the years, wondering how they were doing and if they needed anything. Finally he resigned himself to the fact that he'd never see the kids again or find out what happened to them.

———

Then one day thirteen years later, Alloy received a call from a *Milwaukee Journal Sentinel* reporter who wrote an update article on the then twenty-year-old Cabbet who—not wanting to be known as the girl in the dog cage—renamed herself Chelsea. The reporter said that Chelsea wanted to get in touch with him, and asked if she could pass on his contact information to her.

Overjoyed, he answered, "Absolutely."

Alloy and Chelsea met in a reunion that he described as a release of emotions. After nearly a decade-and-a-half, he was finally able to get closure. What's more is that he found her to be the same smart, polite, outgoing person that she had been when he met her as an abused six year old.

"She is absolutely beautiful," he said. "Her personality is just what you would always hope one of your children would be like."

Since they reconnected in 2010, Alloy and Chelsea frequently see and talk to each other. His wife babysits her son every Tuesday while she's in class, they go out to dinner, and they spend the holidays together. Her little boy even calls Alloy and his wife Grandpa and Grandma.

"She's our daughter," he said. "Maybe not in court documents but in our minds. They're not going to go without anything. If they need something, they have it."

Alloy, who retired as the Brillion chief in 2013 and is now a park ranger for the Wisconsin Department of Natural Resources, believes Chelsea easily could have become a substance abuser or a nasty person. "No one would've held it against her because of what happened to her, but she never reacted that way. From the day I brought her upstairs and set her on the kitchen table to look at her, she said 'I'm okay' and she has been ever since."

Chelsea—whose goal was once to become a social worker because she wanted to do a better job than the ones did for her—still has some horrible memories of her imprisonment in that dark, cold basement. She and her mother have never tried to contact each other, and she reconnected only briefly with her father (who ultimately divorced Angeline), but didn't ask him why he and her mother abused her.

"I've never really cared for a response. I don't know if what they say is true or sincere," Chelsea said as a guest on *The Oprah Winfrey Show.* "They [her parents] had ten years of probation after their one year in jail, and I think they should have spent those ten years suffering as I spent my seven years suffering."

Now she is focused on giving her son the childhood she never had and living the life she always wanted.

"She said she always dreamed of being part of my family, and I was able to make that come true," Alloy said. "It took a while. But she has what she always wanted, and I have what I always wanted. Things are good now."

For his role in the rescue, Alloy received the Mike McKinnon Humanitarian Service Award in 1998 from the Appleton and Grand Chute Police Chaplains and the Meritorious Service Medal from the Brillion Police Department.

"My biggest award is the love I receive from the little girl that I pulled out of that cage all those years ago and is now a part of my family," he said.

The Community Caretaker Doctrine

Although the Fourth Amendment protects citizens from unreasonable searches and seizures, the community caretaker doctrine is one of three court-defined reasons that allow law enforcement officers to conduct a search or seizure without a warrant.

(The other two are probable cause sufficient for issuance of an arrest or search warrant or "exigent circumstances" and reasonable suspicion of criminal activity.)

The U.S. Supreme Court originally set forth the community caretaking doctrine for searches in the 1973 case of *Cady v. Dombrowski* in the context of a vehicle search.

A Wisconsin officer searched the vehicle of a Chicago officer visiting the state who had been in a car accident. He appeared intoxicated, and the Wisconsin officer searched for a possible weapon in his car to "protect the public from the possibility that a revolver would fall into untrained or perhaps malicious hands."

The U.S. Supreme Court ruled the search legal, as it was the result of the officer's community caretaking function.

Since vehicles and traffic are heavily regulated and there is a high potential for contact between officers and vehicles, the court views the searches of vehicles differently than that of homes, given the sanctity of the home.

The federal appeals court, for instance, rejected the officers' argument that their warrantless entry was justified by their community caretaking function in *Ray v. Township of Warren*. In that case, officers entered a house without a warrant to check on a young girl whose mother received no response when attempting to pick her up from a court-ordered visitation with her estranged husband.

The federal appeals court stated that there could be exceptions in other situations, which would include exigent circumstances, such as the hot pursuit of a suspected felon, the possibility that evidence may be removed or destroyed, or the protection of a child's welfare if the officer reasonably believes that "someone is in imminent danger."

The majority of federal circuits limit community caretaking to vehicle searches, but a minority of circuits upholds warrantless entries into houses due to the community caretaking exception created in *Cady v. Dombrowski*.

These include the Eighth Circuit in *United States v. Quezada* involving a deputy who found an open apartment door and a pair of legs on the floor next to a shotgun, and the Sixth Circuit in *United States v. Rohrig,* when two officers entered a home to abate a significant noise nuisance.

—Information compiled from "The Community Caretaker Doctrine: Yet Another Fourth Amendment Exception" by Mary Elisabeth Naumann, and "Home Searches and the Community Caretaking Doctrine," published in the *AELE Monthly Law Journal.*

20

"If I Die Young"

BRIAN D. BRIDGEFORD / NEWS REPUBLIC

Patrol Officer Michael Pichler describes finding the bodies of 5-week-old Baraboo twins Savannah and Tyler Yates in April 2008 during the first day of the murder trial of their father, Baraboo resident David R. Yates. Monday's testimony kicked off what is expected to be as much as four weeks of witness statements.

Murder trial starts

Witnesses offer emotional testimony

By Brian D. Bridgeford
News Republic

Voices quavered and tears flowed in Sauk County Circuit Court on Monday as witnesses described finding the bodies of infant murder victims Tyler and Savannah Yates.

The twins' father, David R. Yates, faces life in prison if a jury finds he battered his children to death in April 2008, as county authorities charge.

Assistant District Attorney Kevin Calkins made an opening statement, giving the jury an overview of the prosecution's case. A jury was brought from Portage County to hear the case.

He described how the children's mother, Susan Winbun of Baraboo, came by Yates' Lake Street condominium to pick them up after they had been with him for the weekend. After the failure of repeated attempts to get him to answer the door, she asked Baraboo police to check on the children's welfare.

Calkins said a pathologist who

- **OVERVIEW:** David R. Yates, 48, is being tried for first-degree intentional homicide in the deaths of his 5-month-old twin infants.
- **TODAY'S DEVELOPMENTS:** Assistant D.A. Kevin Calkins made his opening argument, outlining the prosecution's case. Witnesses testified about finding the bodies.

examined their bodies estimated the children had been killed between the evening of Saturday, April 12 and that Sunday morning.

Patrol Officer Mike Pichler testified he came to Yates' home after a dispatcher notified him of Winbun's call for assistance. After his own repeated attempts to get someone to answer the door failed, he entered the home through an open patio door.

Pichler said he found Yates laying in the master bedroom and, with some difficulty, roused him. Yates appeared to be lethargic, confused and unsteady on his feet.

When asked where the children were, Yates said they were at a friend's house. When Pichler asked how that could be – given that the children's car seats were still in the condo – Yates said the friend brought his own car seats.

Pichler said he handcuffed Yates and locked him in a squad car after Yates picked up a pair of scissors in a way the officer found threatening.

It was on a second search through the darkened bedroom that Pichler saw a child's foot sticking out from beneath the bed Yates had been laying on. He lifted the dust ruffle to see the twins laying against one another.

Pichler's voice quavered as he said one of the children had a dark, red substance around the eyes, nose and mouth. He touched one child's foot with the back of his hand, and it was cool.

"The children had an ashy, like plastic, skin tone to them," he said. "I specifically looked for whether there was breathing in either child, there was none."

Several times during testimony, prosecutors projected evidence photos on a wall showing the children laying in the bedroom. At those moments Yates turned his face away from

SEE **TRIAL**, PAGE 14

Baraboo News Republic

B *aby killer.*

A woman at the bar hurled that insult at the father of her grandchild, accusing him of allowing his child to roll over on the couch and suffocate.

Baraboo Officer Michael Pichler attempted to handle that harassment complaint downtown on April 13, 2008, when dispatch sent him to a check welfare call at a condominium on the city's southeast side.

He instructed the father and grandmother to leave each other alone and headed off to the check welfare call. *Here we go again*, he thought. He and other officers go on many check welfare calls every week, but at least he figured it'd be quick and easy.

Little did he know how chillingly similar it would be to the call he was just leaving.

The five-year veteran arrived on scene a little after eight in the evening, where he met with a woman named Susan Winbun. Pichler knew her because he had previously arrested her on-again, off-again boyfriend, David R. Yates, on disorderly conduct charges.

Winbun told him she came to Yates' condo earlier that day to pick up their five-and-a-half-week-old twins, whom she had left with Yates for the weekend. He didn't come to the door so she left for a couple of hours before returning later that evening. He still didn't answer the door, but she knew he had to be home because she could see through the front door that the natural gas fireplace and TV were both still on. She grew worried that Yates, an alcoholic, was passed out and not caring for the children, which is when she called the police.

Now that Pichler was on scene he, too, rang the doorbell and knocked on the door to no avail. Puzzled why Yates wasn't coming to the door, Pichler moved around to the back of the condos and peered through a large window, where he glimpsed a man's leg on a bed. He knocked on the window but it wasn't until Winbun rang the doorbell again did Pichler see the leg move a little.

Pichler waited a minute or so for the man he assumed to be Yates to get up before finally deciding he either needed to break a window or climb the deck in order to check on the welfare of the infants and Yates. If he could get up onto the deck, the base of which was at eye-level, he could then enter the house through an open patio door. To do that, however, he needed the authorization of his supervisor.

After the supervisor gave him permission to enter the house without a warrant, the five-foot-six Pichler chose to climb the deck. He jumped three feet over a retaining wall, grabbed onto the spindles of the deck, and pulled himself up over the railing and onto the deck.

"Baraboo Police Department. Anyone there?" he hollered into the house. No response.

He slid the patio door open a little more and repeated, "Baraboo Police. Anyone there?"

Again, no response.

Pichler stepped into the dining room and looked around for the babies, seeing two car seats near the front door. Before he continued his search, he crossed through the kitchen and living room to go unlock the front door. Not only does he hate the sense of being locked in anywhere, he wanted another way of exiting besides jumping off the deck. Climbing it was risky enough.

Once he unlocked the door he headed for the bedroom, passing along the way two more car seats near the threshold of the room. He recognized Yates as the man sleeping in the bed.

"Baraboo Police Department. Wake up," he shouted, shining his flashlight into his eyes. Yates awoke a few moments later groggy and incoherent. He seemed drunk, which Pichler knew would be a probation violation stemming from his fifth offense of operating a motor vehicle with a prohibited blood alcohol concentration.

Pichler instructed him to get dressed and began inquiring about the twins. He asked their birth dates, and Yates gave substantially different dates.

This is making no sense, Pichler thought to himself.

"Where are your kids?" he asked him.

"At my friend Dan's house."

"Why do you have two sets of car seats here then?"

"Dan had car seats."

"Your friend had two car seats to take your infants?"

"Yes."

Before, Yates had said that he had dropped them off; now he changed the story to say that his friend picked them up using his own car seats. All Pichler knew was that nothing Yates said made sense.

When Pichler asked if he was on probation and if he had been drinking, Yates went into the kitchen, grabbed a pack of gum, and pulled a pair of shears from a utensil bucket.

"Put that down!" Pichler ordered. He assumed Yates intended to chew the gum in a misguided attempt to throw the breathalyzer test off. He probably grabbed the scissors to open up the pack, but it nonetheless alarmed him.

Yates set them down, but the whole situation thus far felt wrong. He could feel it in his gut.

Due to the size difference between himself and the six-foot-five Yates, Pichler placed him into handcuffs to lead him outside to his squad car. He again complied, but as they walked past the front door, Yates tried to flip the lock on the door and pull it shut as if to prevent Pichler from getting back inside.

Pichler, wondering why he would do that, quickly stuck his foot in the door to keep it from closing. He didn't want to have to climb over that deck again to get into the house.

Once outside, Pichler tried to administer the PBT (preliminary breathalyzer test), but Yates refused. Pichler, suspecting that he had been drinking, decided to take him to jail where he would attempt the PBT again. The probation violation was the least of his worries right now, but at least it was something to hold him on while he figured out what happened to the babies.

"Where are the kids?" Winbun asked, after Yates was placed in the back of his squad car.

"I don't know yet," Pichler said. During the ten to fifteen minutes that he had been inside the condo, he neither saw nor heard any sign of the babies. Unless they were sleeping, he, himself a father of a two-year-old son, knew they would have been making some kind of noise.

Together they went inside to scour the house for the babies. While Winbun checked the basement, Pichler walked past several rooms into Yates' bedroom. He didn't know why he chose that room first; he just felt the urge. He scanned the room and spotted a red substance on a foam triangular-shaped wedge in the crib. Continuing to survey the room, he noticed a two to three foot gap between the wall and bed. He walked over there, looked down, and saw a foot sticking out from under the dust ruffle.

A baby foot.

Oh shit. He knew what he was about to find, but he had to force himself to look.

He kneeled down on the floor and when he lifted the dust ruffle he found the two babies. Wearing only diapers, they were shoved under the bed, almost stacked on top of each other. One's toes faced Pichler, and the other lay alongside of its sibling in the formation of a sideways L. Neither was breathing, crying, or moving. Their skin was so white they looked like plastic. They were cold to the touch. In their noses and around their mouths was blood. No bruises were visible, but he could tell they had been beaten.

Pichler went into autopilot as thoughts raced through his mind. Yates, the suspect, was outside—out of his sight. The condo was now a crime scene. He had to get Winbun out of the house and break the news to her that her babies were dead.

He asked her to come upstairs and as they exited the condo he called for an ambulance, coroner, and additional units.

"Are my babies dead?"

She already knew by the look on his face, but he still had to tell her that her babies were gone.

She unleashed a bloodcurdling scream that Pichler would hear for years. It was so loud anyone two to three blocks away could have heard it.

Besides handling her, he needed to watch the house and he needed to check on Yates. He knew that Yates would know what he had just discovered. He had to make sure Yates was still alive in his squad or hadn't kicked out the car windows trying to escape.

"You have to try to regain some control of yourself," Pichler told Winbun. "I can't have you like this. I have to watch him, the house, and you. I can't have you going hysterical. You can be upset, but you can't go crazy. I can't do what I need to get done if you're going crazy."

Just like that she went from hysterically screaming to sobbing.

A county officer who is a friend of Pichler's arrived on scene first. Though Pichler hadn't requested backup in emergency mode, his buddy knew something was wrong from the tone of his voice and rushed to the scene with his lights and sirens activated.

Once the rest of the units and the coroner arrived they went inside to move the bed over and to confirm that the babies were dead. Pichler felt sick and briefly stepped outside to collect himself.

Then for the next seven hours he stood at the front entryway until the early morning hours writing his report while Home & Garden television played on in the background.

———

Yates was charged with two counts of first-degree intentional homicide for killing twins Tyler and Savannah. Both babies had suffered blunt force brain injuries, hemorrhages, abrasions, and skull fractures. Tyler also sustained a broken foot and rib fractures. According to Pichler, the coroner equated the babies' injuries to what they would have suffered in a multi-rollover highway vehicle crash.

Pichler thinks that Yates, a first-time father in his forties, didn't know how to deal with them and ended up beating them in frustration at their crying. The coroner estimated that they had been dead twelve to eighteen hours before Pichler discovered them under the bed. *Shoved under the bed like a dirty pair of socks*, he thought.

For the next two-and-a-half years, until the case at last went to trial, Pichler struggled to move on from the incident because he had to keep reliving it in countless motion and preliminary hearings. He almost broke down during one of the "horrible and brutal" testimonies until the judge stopped him. He tried not to cry in court because he didn't want Yates to see how much he had affected him.

"No one tells you at school how to deal with this stuff," Pichler said. "You can take your [uniform] shirt off and your [gun] belt off, but you can't take your eyes and heart out. No one explains to you that you can't undo what you see."

The self-described macho officer, who recalls only crying when his dog and his grandpa died, tried tenaciously to push the memories back. He didn't want to think about it; he didn't want to deal with it. He thought it'd go away, but it didn't.

At least once a day for the next eight-plus months Pichler was haunted by the memory of the babies under the bed. Usually the image would flash in his mind when he'd close his eyes to rinse shampoo out of his hair in the shower. For a year, he intentionally drove around the quiet six-block street to avoid passing Yates' condo.

What's more is that the incident ruined the first year of his daughter's life for him. He had only learned that his wife was pregnant with their second child a few weeks before the call, and once she was born, Pichler was constantly reminded of the twins.

The sight of the triangular-shaped wedge in his baby's crib made him sick. He'd stash it in the changing table first thing in the morning before he'd even pick her up. He'd panic and wake her up immediately whenever she'd fall asleep in her swing and get the same light-colored tone to her skin as the twins had. He always dressed her in a Onesie because it bothered him to see her roll around in just a diaper.

Pichler often got into arguments with his wife, who wanted him to talk to a therapist. As a fellow Baraboo police officer, she had helped him over the years through other harrowing incidents, like the time he was shot at and the Halloween night he witnessed a fatal car accident. The double homicide of the twins, however, was something she couldn't.

"This was too big," he said.

His wife eventually talked to the chief about how upset Pichler was by the incident, and he came to their house one day carrying a bag of donuts. He told him that he had made an appointment for him to speak to a therapist. Pichler went to one session and that was it.

"I wasn't going to sit there and have some guy in his office tell me everything is okay. It's not okay. I can't erase what I saw," Pichler said. "He can tell me he understands, but he doesn't know what it's like to deal with it. I wasn't going to let someone give me out-of-the-book answers."

The Band Perry's "If I Die Young" and tears were what finally comforted him. The country song came on the radio one day a couple of months before the trial, inexplicably causing him to cry.

"For whatever reason, it helped," said Pichler, who went on to listen to the song for what he estimated to be five hundred times.

Right before the trial Pichler also finally received the reaffirmation he desperately sought for the last two-and-a-half years, when the district attorney and assistant district attorney assured him that he did everything 100 percent right.

He had continually chewed himself up trying to figure out what he could have done wrong that would get the case thrown out. The defense attorneys, for one, relentlessly fought to prove his entry into the condo was illegal. If it had been, the entire case would be tossed out because everything he found once inside would be inadmissible.

"I had fifteen minutes to make the decision I did, and five attorneys got two-and-a-half years to find something I messed up on," Pichler said. "I didn't want to be the one who messed it up to let this guy off."

The case went to trial in October of 2010, when Pichler testified for the last time. He drove to the cemetery once he was done, kneeled next to Tyler and Savannah's gravestones, and listened to "If I Die Young" on his iPod. He sat there and cried and said he did everything he could and it was now not up to him anymore. Then he got in his car and went home.

The verdict came in two weeks after the start of the trial: Yates was found guilty of two counts of first-degree intentional homicide and sentenced to two consecutive life terms without the possibility of parole. Yates—who would never look at the photographs of the dead babies during the trial, much to Pichler's immense irritation—pleaded not guilty and maintained Winbun killed the children and drugged him to set him up.

"It was a relief it was over, but I knew it would never be over," Pichler said. "He [Yates] is filing for appeals, and he's very intelligent. The case won't end until he [Yates] dies, but like I said, my country song and tears made things a lot better."

Shortly after the trial, the Sauk County Law Enforcement Officers Association named Pichler the 2010 Officer of the Year for his efforts in the investigation. Pichler—who never grew out of his boyhood dream to become a police officer—would have rather won the award for something else such as saving a family, but he nevertheless treasures the award and feels it helped justify his career to his mother, who did not want him to become a police officer.

"I'm proud of what I did. I feel I should be. I did a good job that night," he said. "I didn't mess that case up. I'm good at my job, but no one ever trains you to go into a house and expect that."

Pichler is still bothered by the incident to this day. He's angry about the time he lost with his newborn daughter. He wishes he could hear Yates admit that he killed his twins. He gets the "goonies" driving by Yates' condo, he becomes misty-eyed whenever he hears "If I Die Young," and he teeters on the verge of crying when he discusses the case in great detail.

"I don't know if it's something you ever totally get over," he said. "I don't know how. It's just one of those things that will be with me forever."

Of all the dangerous, traumatic incidents in which he's been involved, this is the one call Pichler wishes hadn't happened to him.

In a way he's glad it did though, because he wonders if the incident would have broken another officer.

"I've had other people say, 'I couldn't have dealt with it. I would have quit,'" Pichler said. "But I'll be damned to let this guy and what he did not let me do what I want to do. I don't know what else I'd do if I didn't have this job."

When Fathers Kill

Terms
Filicide: refers to the murder of a child up to the age of eighteen that is committed by the natural parent.
Infanticide: refers to the murder of a child under the age of one year by the parent.
Neonaticide: refers to the murder of a newborn within the first twenty-four hours of life by the parent.

History
In ancient times, fathers practiced filicide regularly and without repercussions. Aristotle and Plato both believed that this was done to preserve the integrity and size of the population. In 374 A.D., Constantine, the first Christian emperor, decreed that the murder of a child was equivalent to all other homicides.

Reasons why a father kills a child
- Altruistic filicide: the parent kills the child because it is perceived to be in the child's best interest.
- Acutely psychotic filicide: the parent, responding to psychosis, kills the child with no rational motive.
- Unwanted child filicide: the parent kills the child, who is regarded as a hindrance.
- "Accidental" filicide/fatal maltreatment: the parent unintentionally kills the child as a result of abuse or neglect.
- Spouse revenge filicide: the parent kills the child as a means of exacting revenge upon the spouse/other parent.

How often filicide and infanticide occurs
Roughly half of all filicidal acts are committed by fathers; infants represented about one-fifth of the child homicides committed by fathers.

Who are the perpetrators and victims of filicide
On average, the fathers are in their mid-thirties, the mean age of their victim is five, and they sometimes killed more than one child. Sons and daughters were killed in equal numbers.

Possible reasons for paternal filicide
- (Mis)perception of the child's behavior
- Domestic disputes

♦   Rage
♦   Physical abuse
♦   Neglect
♦   Mental illness (psychosis, depression)
♦   Revenge

Common methods of paternal filicide
♦   Wounding violence (battery, shooting, stabbing)
♦   Head injuries
♦   Strangulation, suffocation, or asphyxiation
♦   Drowning

Fathers who committed filicide were more likely than mothers to:
♦   Inflict wounding violence on victims
♦   Commit suicide
♦   Kill their spouses or commit familicide (the killing of a whole family)
♦   Be more harshly sentenced

—Information compiled from "Fathers Who Kill Their Children: An Analysis of the Literature" by Sara G. West, M.D.; Susan Hatters Friedman, M.D.; and Phillip J. Resnick, M.D., published in the *Journal of Forensic Sciences*, March 2009, Vol. 54, No. 2.

21

The Worst Kind of Call

Toddler killed in driveway accident

By Andy Nelesen
Press-Gazette

GLENMORE — A 19-month-old girl was killed Tuesday when she was run over by her father's pickup truck.

"It's very tragic," said Brown County sheriff's Lt. Scott Semb. "These are the worst. It is very sad."

Michael Van Deurzen, 29, was leaving his farm's driveway at 2810 Pine Grove Road at about noon when he struck his daughter, Laura.

"The dad thought she went inside," Semb said. "He went in the barn and when he came out he didn't see her. He got

"This was absolutely an accident. We investigate every fatal, but there doesn't seem to be anything here other than an accident."

— Scott Semb, Brown County Sheriff's Lt.

in his truck and pulled forward."

Semb said the little girl had stepped either in front of or under the truck, out of view of the driver's seat.

Deputy Dan Sandberg, who was at the scene Tuesday to investigate, said the vehicle was parked next to the barn before the tragedy.

Van Deurzen had gone inside the barn and put some feed into his truck.

"We're not exactly sure where (Laura) was," Sandberg said. "When (Michael Van Deurzen) went in the barn, he saw her in the back yard next to the house."

Van Deurzen, a volunteer firefighter, called 911 and started cardiopulmonary resuscitation immediately. Rescuers arrived at the town of Glenmore home and rushed the toddler to St. Vincent Hospital where she was

Green Bay Press-Gazette

T he day started out badly for Brown County Deputy Sheriff Dan Sandberg. He had plans with his six-year-old and three-year-old children, but he got forced in early to work at eleven a.m. instead of three p.m.

Then it got worse.

His first call on that late summer day in 2000 was for a nineteen-month-old child hit by a car in a driveway.

He and another deputy rushed out to the Glenmore farm four miles outside of Green Bay. Sandberg always drives faster any time a call involves a child, hoping those extra seconds will make a difference.

Although he doesn't have a good memory, what he found once on scene would be burned into his brain for the rest of his life. In the backyard, a young father covered in blood was kneeling on the ground over his motionless daughter furiously performing CPR.

The mother stood at the back door, blocking her three other little kids from seeing what was happening to their sister. A look of relief washed over her face when she saw Sandberg, as if thinking, *Good. The police are here. She'll be okay.*

The little girl had been outside playing, and the father didn't see her when he got into his pickup truck to leave. He pulled forward, knocking her down with the front bumper. Then the back tire ran over her head as he turned the wheel.

Sandberg ran to the toddler and checked for a pulse that wasn't there. Not wanting to waste any time, he didn't even bother to put on gloves.

As the other deputy gave updates over the radio, the father, who happened to be a volunteer firefighter, gave her breaths while Sandberg did chest compressions.

When Sandberg learned how to perform CPR years ago, he hoped that he'd never have to do it on a child. Seeing the lifeless little girl in front of him was the worst day of his law enforcement career.

Sandberg and the father fervently continued doing CPR until the county rescue workers arrived. Sandberg stepped back and watched as they loaded the toddler into the ambulance. He was pretty sure she was dead.

After the family left for the hospital, Sandberg looked down at his bloody hands. He rinsed them off with a nearby garden hose and then noticed the girl's little white tennis shoe laying on the ground. It was covered in blood.

That's not right. That can't stay there.

He didn't want the parents to come home and have to relive the tragedy.

Sandberg washed the blood off her shoe, set it on the steps, and cleaned the area as much as he could without damaging the scene for the crash reconstruction specialists who were on the way.

———

The little girl, named Laura, was pronounced dead in the emergency room. Head injuries were the cause of death, according to the medical examiner.

Sandberg was in a haze the rest of the day. He can't remember anything else that happened other than going to his parent's house after the call. His mom gave him a big hug, and he "let loose there a little bit." Since becoming an adult, the former military man can count on one hand the number of times he's cried, and this was one of them.

When he was done with the call, he had to put in another eight hours as he had a twelve-hour shift that day. Looking back, he said that he probably should have gone home that day as he was too distraught to be of much use.

He was so shaken up over the situation that he made twelve or so mistakes on his report—more than he's ever made in his fourteen years on patrol.

Due to the trauma of the incident, Sandberg and his partner were required to talk to a counselor afterward. When the partner was asked what he remembered most about the incident, he said that each time Sandberg did a compression he heard a gurgling, sucking sound.

Up until then, that memory was something Sandberg had blocked out. Now, it's something he can't forget.

He later wrote in his journal where he documents his daily calls, "Sometimes this job really sucks."

———

Throughout his nearly nineteen-year career, Sandberg—who has worked countless Green Bay Packer games and is now a lieutenant at the Brown County Sheriff's Office—has seen everything: gunshot victims, car crashes, and suicides. Yet, nothing tears him up like a child does.

"Some people don't realize that first responders get impacted by these incidents, too," Sandberg said thirteen years later. "Those are the types of incidents that no law enforcement officer ever forgets. They remember exactly who was there and what happened."

As a child, Sandberg remembers his mother, who worked as a nurse in the maternity ward, crying at the table at night over the babies she saw die.

"I always wondered why she was so upset. She was just doing her job and had no connection, but it's horrible—just terrible."

As the years went on he always wondered what had happened to the family and if they were doing okay. Eleven years later he told the story to a group of people at a bonfire, one of whom turned out to be the brother of the father. He told him the parents went on to have another child, and they were doing as well as could be expected.

Despite the closure that update gave him, Sandberg still remembers the call like it happened yesterday. He could sketch out the house, the locations of everyone, and where the girl's little shoe laid.

"When it deals with a child, that is the one call every police officer does not want to go to," Sandberg said. "We despise those calls more than any others. We hate seeing children like that, but it happens so infrequently that hopefully not too many have to deal with it.

"I love this job. It's the greatest job in the world. I would never want to do anything else, but there have been a handful of times that you wish you weren't seeing what you see out there."

The Dangers of Children and Cars

At least fifty children in the United States are hit by vehicles backing up every week, with at least two of those fatally injured, according to KidsAndCars. org, a public safety awareness website. The predominate age of the victim is one years old, and over 60 percent of backing up incidents involve a large vehicle such as a truck, van, or SUV. A parent or close relative is behind the wheel in over 70 percent of the incidents.

Here in Wisconsin, this safety issue made news when State Senator Dave Hansen, D-Green Bay, accidentally drove over and killed his two-year-old granddaughter in 2007.

According to preliminary figures provided by the Wisconsin Department of Transportation, a total of 110 pedestrians aged one to nine were injured and one pedestrian aged one to nine was killed after getting struck by a vehicle in 2013.

Below are safety tips from KidsAndCars.org:

- Walk around and behind a vehicle prior to moving it.
- Know where your kids are.
- Teach children that "parked" vehicles might move.
- Install cross-view mirrors, audible collision detectors, rearview video cameras, and/or some type of backup detection device.
- Measure the size of your blind zone area behind the vehicle you drive.
- Be aware that steep inclines and large SUVs, vans, and trucks add to the difficulty of seeing behind a vehicle.
- Teach children to never play in, around, or behind a vehicle and always set the emergency brake.

22

Living in the Dark

It was three a.m., the time town of Beloit Sergeant Pat Stergos' shift was supposed to end, but he had to stay late because he received a call of a woman in labor. Knowing he wouldn't be going home anytime soon, he prepared to snap on the rubber gloves and go help deliver a baby.

When he arrived at the single-story house, he found a woman standing at the front door wearing a baggy winter coat with a purse slung over her shoulder. She looked like she was waiting for someone to pick her up.

"Did someone just call about a woman in labor?" he asked her. She appeared to be in her mid-twenties, perhaps only a few years younger than himself.

"Yeah, I just gave birth," she replied calmly. For a woman who had just delivered a baby, Stergos didn't think she appeared to be in a lot of pain.

As he stood in the entryway talking to her, he looked around the house scattered with beer bottles and drug paraphernalia. It was quiet. Too quiet.

"Where's the baby?" Stergos asked.

"In the toilet," she nonchalantly answered.

"Why? Why is the baby in the toilet?" he asked, his voice edged with anger and concern.

"I think it was born dead," she said, as if the baby was a piece of trash.

"That's not a good enough answer," said Stergos, fighting the urge to slam her into handcuffs. "Why is the baby still in the toilet?"

After instructing her to sit down, Stergos and a paramedic rushed to the bathroom and discovered a full-term baby lying in the fetal position in the toilet.

It was a little boy.

He was submerged in the water, his umbilical cord still attached to the placenta. The evidence of cleanup—the bloody towels and rags in the bathroom—bothered him almost as much as seeing the dead baby. The mother had taken the time and effort to wipe up the blood, yet hadn't bothered to remove her child from the toilet.

Stergos couldn't help but think of his six-month-old daughter when he saw this defenseless baby.

The paramedic lifted the infant from the toilet, checked for vitals, and determined he was dead. Raging with anger, Stergos stomped back out to the entryway where he found the woman now surrounded by paramedics and two rookie officers.

"Based on what I just saw and what you told me, you are under arrest," he declared.

"For what?" she scoffed.

"Looks to me like murder."

———

During the investigation, Stergos learned that the woman was prostituting herself for dope when she accidentally got pregnant by her john.

Friends said that she was angry throughout the pregnancy, but unable to get an abortion. She was too far along by the time she discovered she was pregnant. So while other expectant moms began taking prenatal vitamins and eating healthier, this mom-to-be continued snorting cocaine and smoking marijuana because, as Stergos believed, she wanted her baby dead.

He believed the infant was born alive, but was proven wrong when he attended the autopsy. The doctor removed the baby's lungs and placed them in a water-filled glass. If the lungs floated, that meant the baby took a breath, the doctor explained. If the lungs sank, no breath was ever drawn.

The lungs sank.

Even if the baby had lived, the doctor told Stergos that because he was full of cocaine, he would have suffered severe brain damage and would have become a drug addict just like his mother.

Although the district attorney's office ruled it was not a homicide because the baby never drew a breath, Stergos viewed the death as a slow murder.

"If there is a God, He can judge her when it comes her time," Stergos said. "Most cops are pro-death penalty and don't see why someone should be allowed to take another breath and walk amongst us after doing something like that."

It's not uncommon, he says, for many police officers to lose trust in people—even people as seemingly innocent as scoutmasters—due to the amount of cruelty and tragedy they see on the job.

Stergos read about the scoutmaster theory in a book called *Emotional Survival for Law Enforcement: A Guide for Officers and Their Families*, written by Dr. Kevin M. Gilmartin, a behavioral scientist specializing in law enforcement-related issues. In it, Gilmartin asserts that when many officers hear the word "scoutmaster," they automatically associate it with "pedophile," "child molester," or "sex offender." Civilians, on the other hand, perceive the term positively, thinking of an adult interested in helping youth primarily through outdoor activities.

"Cops' thinking is almost in the negative all the time," Stergos said. "They're always thinking, 'What's the worst that could happen?'"

It took about two or three years for Stergos, who became a cop at the age of twenty-four, to start thinking that way.

"In the first year, you're so gullible as a cop thinking that you can go out and change the world and crush crime," he said. "Then you realize as you get into it, it's just the job and crime will always be there."

Life will also always be there, and Stergos said that he learned from Gilmartin's book to continue living life by staying involved in hobbies. This helps him stay balanced because most cops are continually riding what Gilmartin calls the Hypervigilance Biological Rollercoaster.

It's perfectly reasonable and expected for a cop to go above what he likens to a baseline while he or she is at work, as their sense of alertness should be heightened. It's impossible for their heart rates not to skyrocket when responding to a report of shots fired, for instance. The problem, however, is that when cops return home from work they crash and dip below the baseline.

They become tired, detached, isolated, and apathetic, according to Gilmartin. They often come home and turn on the TV, incessantly flipping through the channels and zoning out. It generally takes eighteen to twenty-four hours for the officer to return to what he describes as the normal phase of social interaction, emotion, and perception. Yet the cycle inevitably resumes when the officer goes back to work and back to a state of hypervigilance.

To combat the Hypervigilance Biological Rollercoaster, Stergos has followed Gilmartin's advice to stay active. He lifts weights, fishes in the summer, and rides his ATV.

When cops get caught up in the rollercoaster and don't remain active, Gilmartin and Stergos assert that it can lead to marital problems, alcohol abuse, and the tendency to only socialize with others cops, thereby closing out everyone else.

Still, Stergos maintains that cops don't need to be "Officer Friendly" to the general public. He learned that when a suspect grabbed his own flashlight from him and struck him in the head with it three times, splitting his head open. Stergos vowed then and there that he would do everything he can to prevent injuries to himself and other officers.

"It's not gray to me. It's 'Is there a problem or not a problem?'" he said. "I'm not going to kiss the public's ass just because I'm a cop. We're there to protect the public, but I'm not into hugging babies."

Out of all the incidents he has dealt with throughout his eighteen-year law enforcement career, Stergos—who went on to work in patrol and drug investigations at the neighboring Beloit Police Department—remembers that call where he found the dead baby as the most horrendous.

"I was so pissed at her [the mother]," Stergos recalled a decade later. "I don't think I've ever been so mad at somebody." While the baby embodied pure innocence, to him the drug addict mother represented pure evil.

When he finally closed the case on that call twenty hours later, Stergos returned home and gave his baby daughter an extra hug and kiss.

"When you're a parent, you give children the most protection, and then here's this baby disposed of in a toilet."

* The officer interviewed for this story requested a pseudonym due to the sensitive nature of his story.

———◆———

What Police Officers Need to Do
to Become Emotional Survivors

From cynicism to apathy, a law enforcement career can have negative effects on the lives of officers. *Emotional Survival for Law Enforcement: A Guide for Officers and Their Families* by Dr. Kevin Gilmartin offers expertise on how officers can become "emotional survivors." Here's some tips:

Maintain control of their personal lives
Many police officers find it difficult to be in charge of their personal time because of changing work shifts, training schedules, forced overtime, and court subpoenas, but Gilmartin says they need to recognize that their individual roles as officers should not be 24/7. To maintain control of their personal lives, they should be proactive in making decisions, opposed to acting reactive as they are on the job, schedule plans in advance, and make time for themselves and their loved ones.

Practice physical fitness
While officers are alive, alert, energetic, involved, and humorous on duty, they become tired, detached, isolated, and apathetic off duty, according to Gilmartin. He asserts that these two opposite worlds result in what he named the Hypervigilance Biological Rollercoaster. For officers to move up from the bottom of the rollercoaster back within the normal range necessitates a physical intervention, which he says can be accomplished by moderate aerobic exercise. Physical exercise not only raises the behavioral activity level of the officer, but it can also prove beneficial in stress and anger reduction.

Balance the multiple roles in their lives
According to Gilmartin, one of the most difficult aspects of being a law enforcement officer is balancing one's professional role with the role of friend, spouse, or parent. Being the best law enforcement officer one can be is important but so is being the best mother, father, husband, wife, community member, etc.

———◆———

10-50 Fatal Accident

"... that just showed the love between the father and the daughter that the last thing they did was reach out to each other and make that connection."

—Retired Wisconsin State
Patrol Trooper Casey Perry

23

An Untold Story

Judge gives Powell 25 years in prison

By DAN KITKOWSKI
EagleHerald regional editor
dkitkowski@eagleherald.com

MARINETTE — In what a judge hopes will be a stern message about drinking and driving, a Marinette man convicted of killing seven people, including two unborn children, was sentenced to 25 years in prison Tuesday in Marinette County Circuit Court.

Richard A. Powell, 40, 700 Main St., was sentenced to five years each in connection with a crash that killed Joel Rivas, 44, Wrightstown, Wis., and four of his children on the evening of Jan. 18, 2009, near the Taco Bell/Shell Station at U.S. 41 and Country Meadows Road.

"A substantial sentence is necessary to put us all on notice that if you drink and drive recklessly, there are severe consequences," Circuit Judge Tim Duket said.

The four children killed were Nancy Rivas, 19; Elina Rivas, 16; Karen Rivas, 15; and Nicandra Rivas, 12.

Powell had pleaded no contest to causing seven deaths — the five previously mentioned victims and two unborn children. Two of Rivas' daughters — Elina and Karen — were pregnant.

For each death, Powell was charged with homicide by intoxicated use of a vehicle, homicide by negligent operation of a vehicle, and homicide by use of a vehicle with a prohibited alcohol count above 0.10 percent.

All but five of the 21 felony counts were dropped in a plea deal, but two of those — homicide by use of a vehicle killing an unborn child — were read in at sentencing.

Following the prison sentence (which could be reduced to less than 19 years through a Risk Reduction program), Powell will be under extended supervision for another 15 years. He also must adhere to 500 hours of community service per year

EagleHerald/Rick Gebhard
Richard Powell faces a lengthy prison term for his role in the deadliest drunken driving accident in Wisconsin history.

while under extended supervision.

Family and friends of the victims called for the maximum combined sentence of 75 years in prison, followed by 50 years extended supervision. Powell's supporters, including his attorney Kevin Musolf of Appleton, Wis., asked for much less — jail time with work release, followed by extended supervision and community service.

Duket said it was one of the most difficult cases he's had to wrestle with in his 20 years on the bench.

"I cringed when this case was assigned to me," he admitted. "Nobody did anything intentionally to anyone. It was recklessness."

The judge said it was much easier to sentence Scott Johnson (the Niagara bridge shooter who killed three people) and Joseph Evans (a Marinette man convicted of killing his wife) to life in prison in the last year because the defendants clearly had intent.

According to court records, Powell was driving about 77 to 81 mph in a 45 mph zone of snow-covered U.S. 41. His alcohol level was 0.238 percent — almost three times the legal limit — and he was supposedly adjusting his radio when his pickup crashed into Rivas'

See POWELL, A3

Emotions run high at sentencing

By DAN KITKOWSKI
EagleHerald regional editor
dkitkowski@eagleherald.com

MARINETTE — A gentle giant who wouldn't hurt anyone or a terrible killer responsible for seven lives?

Emotions ran hot Tuesday in Marinette County Circuit Court during the sentencing hearing for Richard A. Powell, who late last year pleaded no contest to five counts of homicide by intoxicated use of a vehicle relating to a January 2009 crash.

Judge Tim Duket's courtroom was overflowing with approximately 35 people in support of Powell and another 25 there for the victims — Joel Rivas and four of his children, including two who were pregnant.

Duket said he received waves of letters (about 70) in support of the defendant, and several unflattering letters. He said the presentence report was a lengthy 23 pages.

Alma Rivas, Joel's sister from California, was the first to speak. She described her brother as a "confidant" and a person to look up to.

"He was my mom's favorite child," she said. "He was always there for her. He'd call her every day even if he lived across the country."

Alma Rivas looked directly at Powell and said this wasn't an accident, but a choice he made on that fateful night.

"This was an avoidable crime," she said. "He deserves a lengthy incarceration."

Christine Schad, a friend of the family, read a statement from Joel's wife, Patri-

See SENTENCE, A3

A drunk driver slammed into a car one winter evening in Marinette County, killing all five family members plus two unborn babies.

The medical examiner believed that the victims died on impact, but Wisconsin State Patrol Trooper Casey Perry is convinced otherwise.

Upon surveying the wreckage, he found the father's hand touching his daughter's. He believes they were alive for just a few moments after the crash, during which time the father reached for her hand in the back seat.

"To me that just showed the love between the father and the daughter that the last thing they did was reach out to each other and make that connection," Perry recalled four years later.

The January 18, 2009, accident remains the deadliest drunk driving accident in Wisconsin history to date, due to the number of deaths in one family.

Joel Rivas, forty-four, of Wrightstown, was killed along with his children, Nancy Rivas, nineteen, of Green Bay; Elina Rivas, sixteen, of Kaukauna; Karen Rivas, fifteen, of Kaukauna; and Nicandro Rivas, twelve, of Wrightstown. The mother, whom was divorced from Joel, and two other children were not in the car.

The Rivas family was killed after an intoxicated Richard Powell slammed his GMC Sierra pickup truck into their Kia Sephia on January 18, 2009 (photo provided by Casey Perry).

The first-time drunk driver, Richard Powell of Marinette, was sentenced in 2010 to twenty-five years in prison. Powell, whose blood alcohol content was almost three times the legal limit, pleaded no contest to five counts of homicide by intoxicated use of a vehicle. The other initial sixteen felony charges were dismissed as part of a plea deal. The two counts of homicide by intoxicated use of a vehicle killing an unborn child were dismissed but read in, meaning that the court could consider the charges when determining the sentence for Powell's other crimes.

Perry, who lived in Green Bay but was assigned to the Wausau post, was one of three members of the reconstruction team to investigate the accident, which occurred at the intersection of U.S. Highway 41 and Country Meadows Road in the town of Peshtigo.

Of all the crashes that he's investigated in his thirty-one years with the state patrol, this is the one that had the most impact on him.

Not only was this the longest he'd ever spent investigating an accident—nearly four months opposed to the normal couple of weeks—but it was also the one with the most inconsistent, unreliable, supposedly "eyewitness" accounts that made up or concealed facts.

It began with the misreported first 911 call.

A man initially told the dispatcher that he was driving behind the car that got hit, a pickup truck ran over the car, and the car did not stop at the stop sign.

Subsequent interviews with the man, as well as a surveillance video from a nearby Shell gas station, proved that none of those things were true.

Furthermore, the man also gave a wrong street name and a wrong landmark on the 911 call. He said he was near a K-Mart even though that store is located in Menominee, Mich. Those mistakes resulted in ribbing from his friends who heard the 911 call played on the radio and TV.

"The media right off the very start of the case went for open records and obtained the 911 tapes to get the story," Perry said. "They pretty much ran with the dispatcher asking [the man] what happened and poisoned the listeners and viewers into thinking that the family ran a stop sign in front of this driver that happened to be drunk."

According to Perry, the media never corrected the information or followed up.

Complicating the matter, the man told a woman who rushed to the scene after the crash that the car did not stop. This woman had been at the gas station with her two sons when the accident occurred.

She then repeated that to someone else on the scene, telling him that she and her sons witnessed the crash and that she had said to her kids, "Oh my god what is that car doing? They are not stopping for the stop sign." She also went on to talk to the media and the insurance company about what she saw, when in actuality Perry discovered that she and her sons only *heard* the accident. They then looked up to see the vehicles in their final resting spots.

Joel Rivas; his four children Nancy, Elina, Karen, and Nicandro; and two unborn babies were killed in the car accident. Powell, whose blood alcohol content was almost three times the legal limit, was sentenced to twenty-five years in prison (photo provided by Casey Perry).

When witnesses try to piece together what happened with each other in the moments after an accident they contaminate each other, Perry said. Each person may have shared or listened to the opinion of others, and then they pass on the wrong information to countless other people.

Witnesses also tend to give inaccurate statements because of their brains working to fill in the gaps by plugging in something they may have seen on TV, for example, or because of their poor emotional states, according to Perry. The latter was said to be the reason for the erroneous initial statement from an employee at a nearby fast food restaurant.

He initially told police he was "... looking at the intersection when the crash happened." He recalled the car traveling eastbound (opposed to westbound), that it was struck on the passenger side (opposed to the driver side) and that truck was "... going too fast for road conditions."

When later interviewed, however, he admitted that his supervisor had told him what to put in the statement. It was eventually determined that neither he nor his supervisor saw the collision.

The employee ultimately attributed the discrepancies in his statements to his poor emotional state, telling Perry, "My mental condition was bad. I was crying and shaking a little."

"Initial statements are taken when they [witnesses] are still in shock. If you interview them again you'll get a different story, which we did," Perry said. "It's not unusual for witnesses not to recall facts correctly when in stressful situations."

Thus, what's frustrating to Perry is when the media does not give witnesses space after an accident such as this.

"The news media was trying to get the scoop and the 911 call, and they didn't give the witnesses any time for their stress levels to go down," he said.

Besides the media leading the public to believe Joel Rivas ran a stop sign, the public sentiment was that the Rivas family members were illegal when, in fact, none were.

Joel, a franchise owner of a janitorial service who also owned and operated several rental properties, was born in Mexico but obtained permanent resident status in the United States in 1989. Karen and Elina, also born in Mexico, became citizens in 1998, and Nancy and Nicandro were born in the United States. When the accident occurred, the family was on their way home from cleaning a health clinic with which Joel had a cleaning contract.

Besides assuming that they were illegal, the community also judged them harshly because the sixteen-year-old and fifteen-year-old daughters were unmarried and pregnant. Perry thought that was unfair because both the girls were close to their next birthdays and becoming mothers at young ages is accepted in their culture.

"Anytime the news media would do a story on the next part of the case it would generate another new blogging experience for people still saying he [Powell] didn't do anything wrong and if the [Rivas] family was not in this country this wouldn't have happened," Perry said. Without an actual witness it is not known whether or not Rivas stopped at the stop sign; however, the car's speed range of ten to sixteen miles per hour at the time of impact, as well as the timeframe established by the surveillance footage from the gas station, indicates that he had.

The real reason for the crash was determined to be Powell's high rate of speed—seventy-seven to eighty-one miles-per-hour in a forty-five mile-per-hour zone. He also had an alcohol level of 0.238 percent.

During his investigation that included twenty-five-plus interviews, Perry discovered that Powell, then thirty-nine, had been at a local tavern where his estranged wife worked since just before noon that day. He interviewed the wife as well as the other bartenders to find out how much alcohol he had consumed to support the blood alcohol level, and while doing so he uncovered more about Powell's life.

For instance, he learned that Powell was abusive and suicidal and that his wife was going to leave him the next day.

"We'll never know, but personally I believe that he left the tavern parking lot with the intention of getting involved in an accident. I don't know if he wanted to kill himself or just get injured so that she'd stay with him," Perry said. "When you look at it all, it sure seems to add up that way."

Take the event data recorder, a piece of equipment more commonly known as the black box, in his pickup truck, for example, or the position of the truck's tow hooks. According to Perry, the black box did not record Powell braking and the tow hooks struck the Rivas car at a dead center. "Even people who are intoxicated will steer or brake at some point unless they're passed out, but he never braked, steered, or did anything to prevent it. He drove right into them," he said.

When asked if justice was served in Powell's twenty-five-year prison sentence, Perry said yes.

"Looking at his age, he will be in for a long enough period of time that hopefully there will be no more additional problems," he said. "But it also sends a message to the rest of us out here in the world that if you're driving drunk there are consequences. And if you injure someone, it goes up a level; if there's a death, it goes up another level; and if there's multiple deaths, there are greater levels."

———

Perry, who received a certificate of commendation from the Marinette County District Attorney for his investigation of the accident, retired from the Wisconsin State Patrol in 2010. He now works as an investigator for the law firm of Habush, Habush & Rottier in Green Bay.

In addition to his job as a state trooper, he also served as the executive director of the Wisconsin Troopers Association, the chairman of the National Troopers Coalition, and the president of the state patrol union.

Through his various positions, he testified before members of Congress and lobbied bills concerning law enforcement officers and public safety, drafted concepts of bills for members of Wisconsin's Legislature, and lobbied on many other bills. Consequently, he has met many governors, as well as Presidents George H.W. Bush, Bill Clinton, and George W. Bush.

———

Though Perry never felt as though the Rivas family's story was told, he was at last asked to present the story behind their deaths at a juvenile death review panel three-and-a-half years after the accident.

"It gave us some closure because we were able to tell our story," Perry said of himself and the other troopers who investigated the crash.

This case not only had an effect on the community but all of northeast Wisconsin, according to Perry, as this was a time period in the United States when a record number of illegal immigrants were deported. "Therefore, many people still believe they were illegals and ran a stop sign causing the fatal crash."

The incident remains Perry's most memorable call, and the photograph of Joel's hand touching his daughter's is one he'll never forget.

"That picture will always have a lasting impression."

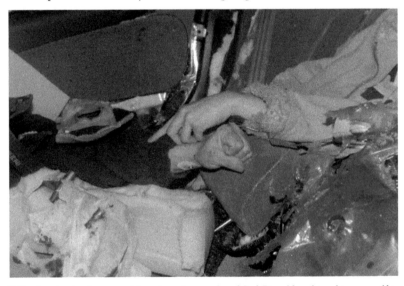

Following the deadly car accident, investigators found Joel Rivas' hand touching one of his daughter's. "... that just showed the love between the father and the daughter that the last thing they did was reach out to each other and make that connection," said retired Wisconsin State Patrol Trooper Casey Perry (photo provided by Casey Perry).

Drunken Driving in Wisconsin

Wisconsin has the highest rate of drunken driving in the nation, according to the Wisconsin Department of Transportation. The latest figures show that 223 people were killed and 2,907 were injured in alcohol-related crashes in 2012.

Counties with the highest number of fatalities resulting from drunken driving accidents

1. Milwaukee: 27
2. Dane: 16
3. Rock: 10
4. Waukesha: 10
5. Fond du Lac: 7
6. Ozaukee: 7
7. Pierce: 7
8. Portage: 7
9. Vernon: 7
10. Washington: 7
11. Brown: 6
12. Manitowoc: 6
13. Marinette: 6

The counties with no fatalities resulting from drunken driving accidents are Ashland, Barron, Clark, Crawford, Door, Dunn, Grant, Green Lake, Iowa, Iron, Kewaunee, Lafayette, Menominee, Pepin, Price, Rusk, Trempealeau, and Wood.

Counties with the highest number of injuries resulting from drunken driving accidents

1. Milwaukee: 350
2. Dane: 184
3. Kenosha: 148
4. Brown: 139
5. Waukesha: 124
6. Rock: 112
7. Winnebago: 95
8. Racine: 91
9. Washington: 79
10. Outagamie: 77

Menominee was the only county with zero injuries resulting from drunken driving accidents.

24

Two Minutes Later

"Look at that jerk driving a motorcycle in this weather," said Milwaukee Officer Tom Schmidt. Glancing up from his papers, his partner peered at the helmeted driver zooming down Bluemound Road, a well-lit thoroughfare near downtown Milwaukee. "Sucks to be him."

It was shortly after eleven p.m., and the two had just started their shift. After picking up their free coffee from the George Webb restaurant, the two parked in the lot of a closed Enco gas station and, with the assistance of an overhead light, began reviewing paperwork detailing the day's earlier calls.

It had been a warm, sunny April afternoon, but late that night the weather suddenly and unexpectedly worsened. The temperatures dropped and it began snowing and sleeting in what turned out to be the prelude to a blizzard that shut the city of Milwaukee down for three days.

Schmidt watched the motorcyclist pause at a flashing stoplight and then continue down Bluemound. Looking away, the twenty-five-year-old officer continued sipping coffee and reading until dispatch jolted him two minutes later.

"Motorcycle accident 10-17. Hawley and the freeway."

"Holy shit!" Schmidt exclaimed.

They instantly knew who it was.

Cussing, the two sped off to the accident scene at the intersection of Bluemound and Hawley Roads, three blocks south of the gas station.

Any available officer is required to respond to 10-17 calls, and Schmidt and his partner were the first on scene, arriving within seconds in a squad/ambulance combination vehicle. Similar in appearance to a Chevy Suburban, the vehicle was set up with oxygen and a gurney in the back. It was 1974, and at the time Milwaukee didn't use the fire department for ambulatory services, but instead depended on officers—who were given basic first-aid training—to tend to patients and rush them to the hospital in a process the cops referred to as "snatch and run."

Although Schmidt didn't always work the squad/ambulance, the seven-year veteran was accustomed to responding to accidents. This one, however, was unlike the others. This one he would remember his whole life.

The motorcyclist had lost control taking the curve onto Hawley Road and flew off, slamming into the grille of a chocolate brown 1972 Pontiac Grand Prix. After the impact, the motorcycle slid about two hundred feet before coming to a stop. Other than a few scrapes, it was undamaged. The same could not be said for the Pontiac, whose whole middle front was pushed inward. That sight was nothing compared to the motorcyclist though. Clad in a letter jacket with a white shirt and tie underneath, he lay motionless on his back with his face down on the cold, icy street. His head was still attached, but it had rotated 180 degrees. Flakes from the steady snowfall glistened on his lifeless body.

When Schmidt and his partner turned him over, they heard the sickening sound of his bones crunching. They lifted him onto the gurney with his open-faced helmet still on and laid him on his back before rotating his head as much as they could. His head was smashed, and his open eyes stared blankly at Schmidt. Surprisingly, there was very little blood.

The officers didn't attempt to give him CPR because the Red Cross didn't recommend it at the time, but Schmidt nevertheless began applying oxygen—even though he knew without a doubt that he was dead. At least he didn't suffer, Schmidt thought. He knew his death must have been instantaneous.

As the frantic sound of police cars grew closer and closer, his partner said, "That oxygen really isn't going to help much." Schmidt looked up to see a smirk on his face. Although it might seem insensitive, it is crucial for cops to use black humor in situations like this in order to keep their sanity.

"I'm just doing it for show," Schmidt replied, glancing toward the panicked onlookers. Although late at night, a moderate amount of vehicles slogged past on the slushy street. Occupants from at least a dozen cars on both sides of the road had stopped to help. The scene was so horrific that two or three people immediately fainted upon stepping out of their cars, requiring more squad/ambulances to respond.

Ignoring the bystanders, the officers rushed the motorcyclist to the county general hospital in Wauwatosa where he was pronounced dead, brought down to the morgue, and given his last rights—all while still wearing his helmet.

Schmidt guessed he was in his early twenties and, based on his clothes, was perhaps a manager at a fast-food restaurant on his way home from work that night.

While Schmidt and his partner were at the hospital, other officers arrived on scene to handle the investigation part of the accident, which Schmidt didn't envy. Called "thirteen pointers" because there are thirteen steps to them, fatality accident investigations can take at least a day or two to complete. It's an arduous process where officers must find out such information as whether the victim had been drinking and who was the last person to talk to him or her.

The officers also interviewed the driver of the Pontiac. Schmidt had been so busy tending to the motorcyclist that he hadn't even noticed whether the driver was a man or a woman or how he or she reacted to the accident. Whoever it was, Schmidt felt sorry for the driver because the situation was out of his or her control. It was like a deer coming out of nowhere and hitting your windshield.

———

Thirty-seven years later, Schmidt, who no longer works at the Milwaukee Police Department, said he never felt like he could've prevented the accident. "He had a right to drive," he said.

Schmidt never knew his name, but he would always remember his face—even nearly four decades later.

"I saw the guy in my dreams for years," he said. "Not nightmares where I'd wake up screaming, but it bothered me. Even now I can imagine what he looked like, and it was forty years ago."

Someone once asked him how he coped with that trauma, and he simply said, "Life just goes on. There's nothing you can really do."

One way of dealing with the pressures of the job, however, was to drink.

"Drinking was completely different back then," he said, referring to the late sixties and early seventies. "Everyone drank like ten times what they do now."

When Schmidt was hired in 1967, the police world was very different than it is now. For instance, officers could only be men (the first female officer, Ada Wright, was not hired until 1975), and they had to be at least five-foot, eight-inches, weight-proportionate, and have 20/20 vision. Out of seventy-two people who applied when he did, Schmidt said he was only one of four hired. Soon after, however, he said the police department lowered the standards because not enough cops were eligible to be hired.

In the late sixties, not many people wanted to be cops either, he added.

"No one wanted to be a cop back then," Schmidt said. "They were hated and called pigs because of the race situation." At the time, Milwaukee was one of the most segregated cities in the nation.

Schmidt, however, was inspired to become a police officer by the cops who used to come in for their free food at the McDonald's where he worked as a teenager. He planned to attend McDonald's Hamburger University in a Chicago suburb to become a manager of his own franchise, but changed his mind.

"The cops said, 'Why don't you become a cop?' and told me about the police aid program."

Schmidt became a police aide right out of high school at the age of seventeen. Less than a month later, the Milwaukee Riots broke out on July 30, 1967, and Schmidt was responsible for loading ammunition and going downtown with the prisoners.

Brought on by racial tensions, the riots resulted in widespread looting, fires, and sniping. Mayor Henry Maier declared a state of emergency and called in the National Guard. Eight days later, more than fifteen-hundred people were arrested and four people were killed, including Patrolman Bryan Moschea, according to the Milwaukee's Finest website. The riots also left Patrolman John Carter blinded and seven other officers wounded.

Schmidt found himself involved in yet another historical event a year later when the Vietnam War draft began. He drew number seventy-six and would have been sent to war, but he was exempted because of occupational deferment, meaning he didn't have to serve in the military because he was already in an occupation vital to American safety.

"God was looking out for me," Schmidt said.

The big man upstairs was also watching out for him when he himself was involved in a motorcycle accident on his way to work one day in the late 1960s. A woman blew a stop sign and plowed right into him. Schmidt, who wasn't wearing a helmet, flew into the windshield of the car. He sustained bruises, and a hospital worker had to cut his class ring off his swollen finger. That was the last time he rode a motorcycle.

Motorcycles were known around the police department as "death machines," according to Schmidt. The motorcycle cops—who received an extra thirty dollars a month to ride them—joked that their mothers dropped them on their heads as babies. All the other officers thought they were nuts for riding them because motorcycle cops often got hit and one cop even lost a leg.

Schmidt is certain that the motorcyclist in the fatal accident that spring night in 1974 didn't even know what happened. To Schmidt, the weather—something as simple as that—is what killed him.

"Life can be over with really quick," he said, adding that he'll take that accident to the grave with him. "You can say goodbye to somebody, and that might be it. Freak things happen just like that."

"I don't know if we [cops] appreciate life any more [than civilians], but you know that life can end real quick," he continued. "You have to enjoy what you got because you just don't know when it's going to be done."

Motorcycle Crashes in Wisconsin

♦ In 2012, 112 motorcyclists, including passengers, were killed in traffic crashes. That is up 40 percent from 80 fatalities in 2011 and 44 percent higher than the 78 in 2002.

♦ In 2012, 2,398 motorcyclists were injured in Wisconsin, up 14.2 percent from the 2,100 injured in 2011 and 17 percent more from 2002. An additional 136 non-motorcyclists were injured in crashes involving motorcycles in 2012.

♦ Alcohol and/or speed were the primary contributing factors in 56 percent of fatal single unit motorcycle crashes in 2012 and in 31 percent of all single unit crashes.

♦ Motorcycle helmets were known to have been worn by 25 (22 percent) of the 112 motorcyclists killed in traffic crashes in 2012.

♦ Nine out of ten motorcycle crashes occurred on dry pavement in 2012.

♦ Saturday and Sunday are the two most common days for alcohol-related and non-alcohol-related motorcycle crashes. More than half of the alcohol-related crashes occurred on these two days.

♦ More motorcycle crashes occur between 1 p.m. and 7 p.m. than any other six-hour time period.

♦ In general, more fatalities occur in the more densely populated southeast area of the state than in any other region in Wisconsin.

♦ The five most frequent possible contributing circumstances in both fatal and non-fatal motorcycle crashes in 2011 were: Failure to control; inattentive driving; speed too fast for conditions; driver condition; and exceeding speed limit.

—Information compiled from the Wisconsin Department of Transportation's 2012 *Wisconsin Motorcycle Safety Facts* book.

STRANGER THAN FICTION

---

*"I've had a lot of interesting calls and goofy things,
but not a bull and now I can't say that anymore."*

—Denmark Chief Ron Towns

25

The Case of the Purple Bus

Publication:The Oklahoman;Date:Apr 27, 2007;Section:Front page;Page Number:1 A [Continuation]

Questions on mysterious bus raid lead to ...

DEAD END

By Ken Raymond,
Augie Frost and Jay F. Marks
Staff Writers

What happened to 17 or more people seized by federal and Wisconsin authorities Wednesday at a gas station along Interstate 40 in Oklahoma City?

Where is the bus in which they were riding? Why were they stopped? Who are they?

Whoever knows isn't talking.

"It's a big mystery," said Mark Myers, Oklahoma County sheriff's spokesman.

About 1:45 p.m. Wednesday, the bus pulled up to the pumps at a TravelCenters of America truck stop at I-40 and Council Road. In an instant, law officers from a variety of agencies surrounded the vehicle, removing the passengers at gunpoint and binding them

with handcuffs or plastic ties, a witness told KWTV NEWS9.

Two large bags of cash may have been seized, along with the passengers' wallets and cell phones, NEWS9 reported. Drug-sniffing dogs checked out the baggage compartment.

About an hour later, most of the detainees got back on the bus. Their hands were freed.

The bus drove east on I-40 with a caravan of marked and unmarked law enforcement vehicles around it. At least one bus passenger was driven in an unmarked beige van.

The bus was taken to the northeast Oklahoma City headquarters of the Central Oklahoma Metro Interdiction Team, a multi-agency task force, Oklahoma County

See BUS, Page 3A

What happened?

Analysis from former U.S. Attorney Robert McCampbell:

■ "The officers/agents have fairly broad discretion when it comes to stopping a vehicle, detaining a person and securing the people and objects for purposes of officer safety. It is not unusual, for example, that the officers would have guns drawn and would handcuff everyone at the outset."

■ "As for searching the occupants and the bus, the officers may have had a warrant. For example, a magistrate in Wisconsin could have issued an arrest warrant for some of the people on the bus, a search warrant or both. Even without a warrant, it would not be unusual to see a vehicle searched in this circumstance. The key concept is that there is a lower expectation of privacy in a vehicle than in one's home."

■ "Under the Supreme Court case of Terry v. Ohio, an officer can temporarily detain a person if the officer has 'reasonable suspicion' that the person is engaged in a violation. During the period of temporary detention, the officer can conduct a reasonable gathering of facts to determine if there is probable cause to support an arrest or if the person should be released. Thus, some of the people seen in handcuffs may have been only temporarily detained ... and may not be charged."

■ "I see that drug dogs were at the scene. For the drug dog to sniff around the bus is not technically a 'search' and requires no warrant. If the drug dog 'hits,' that is probable cause to believe drugs have been present."

The Oklahoman

H e erased his fingerprints and underwent nine plastic surgeries to alter his appearance.

The Detroit drug lord named Adarus Mazio Black went to these extreme measures to avoid arrest, but even so his attempts were in vain. Agents from half a dozen multi-state agencies busted him for his sophisticated drug smuggling operation using tour buses in an investigation that took them halfway across the country and resulted in the seizure of nearly $4 million.

But it all got started in Milwaukee with an informant's tip to one Wisconsin special agent.

The investigation began on the evening of St. Patrick's Day in 2007, a holiday that fell on a Saturday that year.

Special Agent Tim Gray's cell phone rang. "Hey Tim, I know this guy who has a bunch of money stashed."

The last thing Gray, from the Wisconsin Department of Justice's Division of Criminal Investigation, wanted to think about that night was work. He was at a friend's house drinking beer after participating in a bowling tournament earlier that evening.

"Why don't you get his name and let me know?" Gray said.

He figured it'd take a couple days for his informant to get back to him, but half an hour later he called again.

"His name is Kelvin. He's got a storage place on the south side [of Milwaukee]."

"How do you know this?"

"Because I'm messing around with his girlfriend. She's mad at him because he left for Vegas."

"Why don't you have her take you and show you where this storage facility is?"

"Tim, that's your job."

"Call me back when you have more information."

Gray, now at a bar continuing the festivities, was surprised when the informant called again.

"Do you have a last name?" Gray asked.

"Yeah, it's Jones. Kelvin Jones."

"Ask the girlfriend if she has the name of the storage facility."

"Tim, come on," said the exasperated informant. "Fine, I'll call you in the morning."

The next day at seven-thirty in the morning he woke up a hung-over Gray.

"She's got a rental contract. Here's the number for the storage facility."

"Okay," Gray sighed. He hung up and rolled over, knowing he had to go deal with this.

———

Gray called the property manager of the storage facility that Sunday morning to inquire about Jones and his rental unit.

"You better come with an army," the anti-cop manager told him.

"We'll be seeing you soon," said Gray. A threat like that didn't bother the no-nonsense cop, ironically an army veteran himself.

With the details on Jones and the large sum of money, Gray had all he needed to obtain a subpoena from the Milwaukee District Attorney. Then he, along with a K-9 handler from the Milwaukee Police Department, headed out to the storage facility to serve it.

They obtained documents providing information on one Kelvin Jones and a surveillance video showing that Jones and his girlfriend—the one who provided the information to Gray's informant—had visited the storage facility the previous day. Gray noticed that Jones made the woman wait in the car for him so she wouldn't see the location of his unit.

The handler ran his K-9 past the storage units, and it hit on Jones' unit, giving Gray enough probable cause for a search warrant. He went back to the D.A. and returned with the search warrant for Jones' storage unit.

Packed into a blue plastic bin he discovered $1.1 million.

$1.1 million neatly arranged into bundles and labeled with the initials of people who paid the money.

Gray had one good informant.

———

Late that night Gray and other DCI agents executed a search warrant on Jones' suburban Milwaukee house, resulting in the seizure of a motorcycle and a couple of expensive cars, records and documents of a lavish lifestyle, and lastly one mysterious photo of a purple bus.

They lured Jones to his house and arrested him at three in the morning on charges of money laundering. He ended up partially cooperating, telling Gray about a man with the last name of Washington who owned a bus company in Chicago. He said Washington (whose full name is James Washington Jr.) gave him the money to hold onto for him.

"Why did he give it to you?" Gray asked. He knew Jones was lying.

"I don't know. He just wanted me to hold onto it."

"How much is there?"

"I don't know."

"Yeah you do. We watched the video," Gray said, referring to the storage facility's surveillance video that showed him taking money from the plastic bin. In addition to Gray's informant information and the expensive merchandise they found in Jones' house, the bin containing the money was the only thing in the storage unit. He had to have known how much money was in there.

Jones went on to explain that Washington's bus company had two buses— a purple one and a red one—used for smuggling drugs. He hired people to ride on them as covers in exchange for giving them a thousand dollars per trip and a free night in an Arizona hotel. The passengers are given instructions that if the bus is pulled over by the police they should say they are on their way to Las Vegas.

Investigators, including Wisconsin Department of Justice Special Agent Tim Gray, trailed this purple bus from Chicago to Detroit to Tucson, Arizona, where they uncovered $1.4 million (photo provided by Tim Gray).

In actuality, the bus first travels to Detroit to retrieve the cash that will be used to buy the drugs and then back to Chicago to pick up the passengers before driving to Arizona. Once in the Grand Canyon state, the passengers spend the night in a hotel and then get back on the bus the next day. About ten minutes before the bus gets to a location near Tucson the passengers are instructed to lie down on their seats while the bus backs up and the drugs get loaded onto the bus.

Ten minutes later they're told to sit up again, and the bus cruises back to Detroit where they repeat the process. The passengers are told to lie down in their seats for about ten minutes while the drugs get offloaded from the bottom of the bus. Then the bus departs back to Chicago.

Jones knows this routine because he had ridden before as a passenger.

"Okay, let's go to Chicago, and you can point this place out," Gray said.

———

On the way to Chicago, Gray learned that there was more to the story.

"Hey, Tim. There's something I didn't tell you," said Jones, in a move to lessen his money laundering charges.

"Yeah what's that?"

"It's about my dad."

"What about your dad?"

"He's a bus driver."

Jones figured out the Detroit-Arizona routine after riding as a passenger on the bus his father drove. With the help of his dad, Jones carried out a robbery he had planned with his friends on one of the trips.

The bus drove to Detroit, picked up a passenger who threw on a few duffel bags full of money with the zippers glued shut, and headed back to Chicago to pick up the cover-up passengers. In Chicago, Jones and his friends jumped onto the bus, robbed it at gunpoint, and hit Jone's father over the head with a pistol just to make it look good.

Jones and his friends split with the money—the $1.1 million Gray found in the storage unit.

————

DCI agents set up a 24/7 surveillance on the bus barn with the help of a friend from the Illinois State Police who works with the Narcotics and Currency Interdiction Team (NARCINT). Within thirty minutes, one of the buses rolled out of the barn. They followed it to Detroit.

Yes, it's our lucky day.

The bus driver met with someone at a hotel, turned around, and came right back to the Chicago bus barn.

False alarm.

Even though it was a bust, it confirmed to Gray the importance of his agency maintaining control of the investigation because he'd be willing to bet that had there been multiple bosses involved, someone would have wanted to pull the bus over, thereby ruining the investigation.

Agents continued conducting 24/7 surveillance for the next two or three weeks until the director of his agency limited the surveillance to two shifts due to astronomical overtime costs.

Then one day when the daytime shift arrived, one of the buses was gone. The agency administrator was ticked, ordering the 24/7 surveillance to resume.

They planned to install a camera across the street from the bus barn and place tracking devices on the buses, but when Gray was on his way to the Chicago district attorney's office to swear on the affidavits for the equipment, the action started—one of the buses had just pulled out.

"Follow it," Gray told the surveillance agents.

The agents followed the bus to Detroit to the very same place Gray had previously trailed it. The bus picked up a passenger, but now instead of going back to Chicago it headed toward Indianapolis. They knew it was on its way to the West Coast.

Gray happened to be working with Milwaukee Police Officer Dean New-port at the time on an unrelated wiretap case and told him, "We gotta go."

They drove to southern Illinois as fast as they could, where they met up with an Illinois state trooper. They were parked for no more than five minutes when they spotted the purple bus rumbling down the highway.

While the trooper pulled the bus over to write a warning ticket for speeding, Gray and Newport slid under the bus and set up tracking devices.

———

Gray requested assistance from the Arizona Department of Public Safety, and the next day he, his boss, the director of his agency, another agent from his office, and Newport flew to Arizona. Just as they landed in Arizona, Gray got a call from the surveillance agents in Chicago informing him that the second bus, the red one, had left the barn and was headed for Detroit.

Gray instructed them to follow it and then called the agents in southern Illinois who had been planning to go home and redirected them toward Indianapolis.

Meanwhile, out in Arizona, Gray and the others followed the purple bus using the tracking devices they had installed. They lost it for a while due to no cell coverage and had to compute a time-distance analysis to determine when the bus would arrive in Tucson. Serendipitously, an off-duty local cop who lived next to the interstate happened to hear the unfolding incident on the radio and saw a purple bus go by as he sat on his porch drinking coffee.

He called in to report the bus sighting, and Gray and the others soon tracked it to a restaurant in Tucson. As soon as the passengers unloaded and went into the restaurant, a Toyota Avalon pulled up to the bus and the bus driver pulled up the panels.

Oh yeah, there's the money transfer.

Once the driver of the Avalon left, an Arizona Department of Public Safety agent followed the car to an apartment where he watched a man unload four black duffel bags. The agent followed the car when it left again, pulled it over, and obtained probable cause for a search warrant. After they had the search warrant, they found no evidence or money at the apartment until an officer happened to spot the duffel bags lying outside next to the garbage can. It looked like someone tossed them out of a window and missed aiming for the trash.

Stashed inside the bags was $1.4 million.

———

Within half an hour of conducting the search at the apartment, Gray ordered the agents trailing the red bus that left Chicago bound for Arizona to pull it over. They had been surveying the bus for eighteen hours, with different agents switching on and off following it as to go unnoticed.

With Gray's go-ahead, agents at last swarmed the bus when it pulled into an Oklahoma City truck stop.

"You go first," a Hispanic agent told another agent. "They're going to think I'm trying to rob them."

The agents swarmed the bus and discovered $1.1 million on board.

Images of the agents, clad in their Wisconsin police jackets, played all over the news, as local citizens and media remained flabbergasted at what happened and why.

"What happened to seventeen or more people seized by federal and Wisconsin authorities Wednesday at a gas station along Interstate 40 in Oklahoma City?" asked staff writers in an article from the *Oklahoman* dated April 27, 2007. "Where is the bus in which they were riding? Why were they stopped? Who are they? Whoever knows isn't talking."

———

Out in Arizona, Gray and the other agents interviewed the bus passengers and the two men who took turns driving. The drivers quasi-cooperated and ex-

Gray followed up on a tip that led to the seizure of $1.4 million in Arizona and $1.1 million in Oklahoma (photo provided by Tim Gray).

plained how they drove to Detroit, picked up one person with bags, and then drove to Arizona, where they offloaded bags into a waiting car. They talked about how much they were paid and said that Washington would give them money to cover the passenger expenses and hotel stay.

They discussed the most recent trip, as well as previous trips, but they didn't admit to specifically transporting the drugs. One said that he didn't know what kind of drug was involved, and the other said he suspected drugs but didn't ask because he needed the money. (The bus drivers were each reportedly paid $2,000.)

They released the drivers, the passengers, and Washington after he provided some decent information. They did not hear from him until a month later when Gray learned from an informant that someone put a hit out on Washington.

Washington's attorney insisted to Gray that the attorney had not heard from nor knew the whereabouts of Washington, which Gray knew was a lie.

"I don't believe you. This is the real deal. There's a hit out on his life. Even though you haven't heard from him, make sure he knows that," Gray told him.

Thirty minutes later the attorney called Gray back.

"Okay, he wants to know what's going on."

———

Around the time that Gray learned about the hit on Washington, the two drivers of the buses that got busted in Tucson and Oklahoma City got summoned to Detroit under what Gray believes was the pretense of discussing another smuggling run. They were instructed to pull off the road at a specific location in Detroit and to raise the hood of the car as a signal.

At that point a hit man named Vincent Smothers arrived and shot them to death.

Smothers' life of crime has been well chronicled in publications, including the *New Yorker* and the *Huffington Post*, which detail the series of murders to which he ultimately pleaded guilty. One of the murders was of a woman that her police officer husband had hired him to kill for $50. Smothers was sentenced in 2010 to fifty to a hundred years in prison for eight murders.

Gray believed that the same criminal organization was behind the hits on the bus drivers and the attempted hit on Washington, but he didn't learn the identity of the ringleader until he received a call from a federal drug agent from Michigan.

"Is this your case?" he asked Gray.

He told Gray that the Drug Enforcement Administration officials were angry that he [Gray] had not involved their agency in his investigation, but the Michigan agent laughed and said, "I would've done the same thing."

The federal drug agents in Michigan had already been investigating Adarus Mazio Black for the deaths of two rival drug dealers in Detroit before Gray began his investigation.

The DEA ultimately tracked Black to California where U.S. Marshals arrested him. The criminal who had nine plastic surgeries and erased his fingerprints didn't go willingly. En route to a court appearance he kicked out the window of the transport vehicle and dived out onto the Interstate.

———

Black received a life sentence in 2009 for drug trafficking and escaping custody. Washington, who turned himself in to police after Black put the hit on him, was sentenced to seventy months in prison for money laundering. Finally, Jones was sentenced to twelve months and one day in prison. Jones' father was not charged and neither were any of the passengers.

———

Of all the investigations Gray has conducted throughout his eighteen years at the Wisconsin Department of Justice, the case of the purple bus is his most memorable, as it was the largest amount of money that has ever been seized in Wisconsin on a drug case.

"It was a once-in-a-lifetime case," said Gray, who won the Narcotics Officer of the Year Award from the Wisconsin Narcotic's Officer Association. "It was a fun investigation, and a lot of things came together well."

Division of Criminal Investigation

The Division of Criminal Investigation is an agency belonging to the Wisconsin Department of Justice overseen by Attorney General J.B. Van Hollen.

Charged with a purely criminal investigative mission and function, the DCI employs special agents in its headquarters of Madison as well as Milwaukee, Appleton, Wausau, and Eau Claire. The special agents are sworn law enforcement officers possessing statewide jurisdiction and tasked with the responsibility of investigating crimes that are statewide in nature or importance.

They work closely with local, county, state, and federal officials to investigate and prosecute the following crimes:

♦ Homicide
♦ Arson
♦ Financial crimes
♦ Illegal gaming
♦ Multi-jurisdictional crimes
♦ Drug trafficking
♦ Computer crimes
♦ Homeland security
♦ Public integrity
♦ Government corruption
♦ Crimes against children
♦ Special investigations requested by the governor or legislature

DCI also provides extensive training to local, state, and federal officers on current issues in law enforcement.

—Information from the Wisconsin Department of Justice website.

26

Saint Michael Pray for Us

B eloit Officer Tom Halvorsen knew the man was going to be dead. He was ill and elderly. No one had seen or talked to him in over a week. The mail was piling up. The answering machine was full.

On this hot, late summer afternoon in 2004, Halvorsen headed over to the city's west side for a seemingly predictable check welfare call that turned out to be anything but.

As Halvorsen drove to the call, he traveled through Beloit's small downtown and turned north, driving parallel along the Rock River before heading west into a residential part of town. The house Halvorsen rolled up to was a fairly well-maintained, average-looking two-story house with a three-season porch and detached garage.

He started out by knocking on the front door, the urgency increasing in each knock.

No answer.

Still no answer.

At his feet lay about four days of mail and newspapers.

I hate dead guy calls, the four-year veteran said to himself, thinking about how much more he'd rather be out arresting people than writing the dreaded death investigation report.

Most death scenes that he's been called to are natural deaths, which means there's actually no investigating. Instead, he just ends up baby-sitting the body until the coroner arrives.

This body in particular was going to reek, too.

Dead bodies have an unpleasant odor as it is, but this sweltering day was only going to make it worse. Plus, he knows from experience that there's a certain stink you can't get off your clothes.

Knowing the man must be dead inside the house, Halvorsen began searching for an entry point into the house by checking for any unlocked doors or windows. He also looked for any kicked-in doors or windows signifying forced entry, which could mean that foul play was involved.

Meanwhile, his sergeant and another officer arrived on scene, which the latter learned from neighbors that the man had a son who lived with him occasionally.

The three of them continued walking around the house searching for an entry point when suddenly a light "tap, tap, tap" came from a first-floor window.

The elderly man whom everyone suspected was dead was lying in a bed next to the window and had just pulled the curtain back.

"Oh my God, he's actually alive," Halvorsen said, completely surprised. He found himself feeling giddy. Instead of having to generate a case number and write a time-consuming report, now all he had to do was add some minimal notes to the laptop in his squad and be on his way. The paramedics would take it from there.

While he knew that it was the jerk inside himself that was excited about having less work to do, the kindhearted part of him acknowledged, *Sweet, he's alive. We can let the family know he's okay.*

Okay was a bit of an overstatement though.

Standing outside looking through the window at the man, Halvorsen thought he looked like a concentration camp survivor. The man, who appeared to be in his seventies, could not speak and was frail and pasty with sunken eyes and cheeks and greasy, thinning gray hair. Halvorsen assumed it had most likely been several days since the man ate, drank, or used the bathroom. Despite his poor physical shape, the man animatedly motioned for them to come inside.

Halvorsen knew that the man needed to be seen by the paramedics right away, but there still wasn't a way to get into the house because the man was unable to stand up, let alone walk to the door and open it.

Dubbed the "burglar" by his coworkers because of his knack for finding a way into secure houses, Halvorsen at last managed to get the door of the three-season porch open.

After that, he was able to pry open a window into the house, at which time he was abruptly struck in the face by a dead person odor. It was like getting smacked with a board.

It's impossible to fully describe the smell of a dead person because words alone cannot do it justice. It simply takes your breath away.

Halvorsen expected the house to be absolutely disgusting because the man had probably been defecating and urinating on himself, but why the dead person odor when the man turned out to be alive?

He moved aside the curtains and began to climb through the window, keeping his head up to watch for any threats. Then all of a sudden he glanced down and saw a dead man lying flat on his back with his legs spread apart on the couch directly below the window. He was naked except for one brown boat shoe.

Just like that Halvorsen went from *Yay the guy's alive, no report,* to *Oh crap.*

He instantly knew the man was 10-42, cop code for dead, because rigor mortis and lividity had already set in. The latter was evident by the purplish color of the skin where it had made contact with the couch.

It appeared that the man, who looked to be in his late thirties, had been dead for several days. He was even sticking to the cushions of the couch.

Halvorsen had seen plenty of dead people before, but the sight and smell of this one sent him coughing and cringing.

"You've got to be shitting me," Halvorsen said.

"What?" asked his sergeant.

"There's a naked, dead guy right here."

"Are you serious? Are you sure?"

"Sure looks like it."

"It must be his son," the other officer said, remembering that the neighbors had told her a son was known to live with him.

Considering it was his call and he was the most agile of the three—at five-foot-ten and a hundred-forty pounds, he's always the one at the police department getting jammed into little crawlspaces—Halvorsen knew what he had to do.

He had to climb over the dead, naked guy to get inside the house to attend to the elderly man whom he was there to check on in the first place.

This figures, he thought to himself, marveling at the irony of going on a check welfare call only to find a *different* dead man. *This could only happen to me.* After all, Halvorsen is known around the police department as a "cluster magnet," to the point where he can turn a barking dog into an armed standoff.

It reminded him of what happened on the first Christmas Eve he worked when he got sent to what he still calls the "Oompa-Loompa" incident, referring to the round, short-statured workers in Willy Wonka's chocolate factory.

Like the other call, this one also started off as a welfare check. The tenants in a downstairs apartment unit noticed strange liquids seeping through the ceiling. They went upstairs to ask their neighbor what was going on, but he didn't come to the door. At that point, they realized they hadn't seen him in a while so they called the police.

After officers arrived and gained entry into the apartment, they found the man dead. It turned out the strange liquids seeping into the ceiling were actually his bodily fluids. As if that wasn't gross enough, then Halvorsen and the other officers couldn't get the man into a body bag because he weighed over four hundred pounds. They ended up wrapping two car tarps around him and securing them with rope, but the rope broke as they were pulling him through the doorway and he slid down the stairs.

The runaway corpse wasn't the end of the story though.

The gurney collapsed and broke under the man's weight.

Halvorsen shuddered at the memory as he prepared to climb over the dead, naked man on the couch.

It wasn't so much climbing to him, though, as it was giving the man a lap dance. It could also be viewed as the worst reverse limbo contest ever, he thought. Halvorsen turned out to be a good limbo player, however, since he managed not to touch the body.

Despite the stench, he didn't bother holding his breath as he entered the house. He knew he'd have to contend with it anyway because he had three other rooms to go through to get to whom he referred to as the "alive guy."

He unlocked the door for the other two, and together—guns out—they began clearing the house. Even though it didn't appear that foul play was involved in this case, police treat all death investigations as homicides until they can be proven otherwise.

As they walked through the disheveled, dirty house, Halvorsen sweated from the intense humidity caused by running water. A leak from the bathroom had flooded the kitchen and dining room, leading to a foot of standing water in the basement. The dining room floor subsequently buckled, raising the floor by about eight inches. Halvorsen felt like he was walking across a wooden bubble. The moist floor throughout the house was full of animal feces, which he thought, coupled with the smell of the dead man, made for quite the nauseating fragrance.

In the kitchen sat partially ripped-open bags of dog food and grocery bags still full of food, as well as about twenty empty bottles of vodka strewn all over. Since the elderly man was immobile, Halvorsen surmised that it was the dead man who had gone grocery shopping and then drank himself to death.

Upon entering the elderly man's bedroom, Halvorsen discovered the animals. A small dog stood on the bed next to the man shaking and barking, as a cat darted across the room and under the bed. Both animals were thin and dirty with gross, matted hair. They looked traumatized. Even worse was the dead dog Halvorsen spotted curled up in a small pet bed on the floor next to the man's bed. He could tell it was a small, long-haired dog, but it had been somewhat cannibalized.

As a dog-lover, Halvorsen felt sorry for the animals, but he also found himself really grossed out by that partially eaten dog. He wondered if there were any more animals in the house, but he didn't go out of his way to check because the house was so disgusting. Even the thought of kneeling down to look under the bed was revolting to him.

Halvorsen walked across the room to the bed and told the elderly man, "It's okay. We're going to get you help. The paramedics are on their way."

The man just groaned.

The paramedics arrived and took the man out of the house through the back to keep him from seeing his dead son on the couch.

Halvorsen believes the elderly man probably ended up in a group home or a nursing home, but he never found out what was wrong with him or what happened to him. He knew he was taken to the hospital, but aside from that he didn't care to find out. Although fully aware that might sound calloused and cold to civilians, he later said that cops can't allow themselves to become emotionally involved in cases. They need to have some semblance of separation. If they didn't, they probably wouldn't be doing the job very long.

Next, employees from the humane society arrived to retrieve the animals, and after that there was one more thing to do before Halvorsen could leave and that was the thing he had dreaded from the moment he rolled up to that fairly well-maintained, average-looking house: baby-sit the smelly, dead body until the coroner arrived.

Halvorsen finally returned to the police department around midnight, about eight hours after the call began, to write the equally dreaded report. Before he sat down to do so, though, he immediately stripped and changed as much clothing as he could and shoved it all in a bag. At about three a.m., four hours after his shift was supposed to end, Halvorsen at last went home, carrying with him that bag of stench-ridden clothes.

———

Seven years later that call remains memorable to Halvorsen because he believes it is one that could only happen to him: the "cluster magnet." Throughout his career, chaos and trouble have followed him like an obstinate shadow.

To deal with his bad luck, Halvorsen wears a gold chain adorned with a pendant of Saint Michael, the patron saint of law enforcement, tucked under his shirt every day. Smaller than a dime, the circular-shaped, golden pendant depicts a winged warrior wielding a sword. Around the pendant is inscribed, "Saint Michael Pray for Us."

Halvorsen also has a Saint Michael figurine displayed above his kitchen cupboards, along with half a dozen other police figurines, including a uniformed officer, a SWAT member, and a motorcycle cop. In the corner sit two large figurines of German shepherds, which are a common police dog breed and also the kind of dog Halvorsen owns. His beloved thirteen-year-old German shepherd, Aron, is named after a police dog from Nashville who sacrificed his life to save his handler. Aron's heroic story is recounted in a poem, of which Halvorsen owns a copy.

Despite Saint Michael's inclusion among his prized police memorabilia, Halvorsen doesn't know or seem to care about the saint's religious back story. Appearing a number of times in scripture as an archangel of protection, Saint Michael is once referred to as "the great prince, the protector of your people." In the Bible's Book of Revelation, Saint Michael provides protection for the Kingdom of God and defeats Satan in a war in heaven.

To Halvorsen, though, all that matters is that he's the patron saint of law enforcement.

Saint Michael has played an integral role in Halvorsen's life, as he has worn the necklace every day since a former girlfriend gave it to him as a gift in the late '90s, when he became a correctional officer.

"If it broke or fell off or got lost, I would probably have to call in sick and not go in to work," he once said.

Halvorsen knows of other officers who possess good luck charms, such as one cop who dons a Saint Michael patch and a Superman "S" on his bulletproof vest.

"I'm sure everybody probably has something they won't leave the house without. But we're just not going to go out to the bar and say, 'Thank God I had my pendant.'"

Like many civilians, officers also harbor apprehensions regarding Friday the thirteenth and full moons. Yet, he said these superstitions are magnified for the police because of the nature of the job. For instance, they could hurt themselves just by responding to a call or end up taking someone's life in a deadly force incident.

The only times Halvorsen takes off his Saint Michael necklace is when he tans or gets X-rays for all the injuries he's sustained on the job. Over the years, he has suffered a concussion, back and knee injuries, broken fingers, a dislocated shoulder, and a broken nose.

"You name it," he said, of all the injuries he's had. "I've been to the hospital quite a bit." All these injuries were the result of physical altercations and from the time a suspect intentionally struck him with a car.

Although the validity of his good luck charm could certainly be questioned due to all the injuries he's sustained while wearing it, Halvorsen doesn't see it that way.

"I'm still alive, aren't I?" he countered. "I haven't shot anyone, and I'm still employed. Things might snowball, but you get through it. Everything's survivable. If I didn't have this good luck charm, imagine the type of luck I could have. Something worse probably would've happened if I wasn't wearing it. The necklace is a peace of mind that every night I'll go home."

Superstitions in Law Enforcement

Like Beloit Officer Tom Halvorsen, many law enforcement officers have their own superstitions, rituals, or lucky items they carry with them.

"I have a cop buddy who committed suicide. I have his picture inside my vest, and a picture of him in my squad by the visor so he is riding with me every shift."   **—Sergeant Craig Freitag, Randolph Police Department**

"You never want to say 'quiet' because then things go bad."
—Officer Thomas Peterson, Wausau Police Department

"I'm a true believer in the moon. If there's a full moon there's going to be some action."
—Lieutenant Rodney Stearns, Eau Claire County Sheriff's Office

"A really good friend of mine gave me a silver dollar. I've carried it in my uniform pocket every second of every shift every day. It's as much a part of my uniform as my pistol. If it gets me through my career and I don't die, I'm going to drill a hole through it and make a necklace out of it."
—Chief Ron Towns, Denmark Police Department

"I always felt naked and unprotected if I was not wearing a cross of some sort. Additionally, often times I would ask the 'big guy' to help put words of wisdom in my mouth and/or help me get through a sticky situation."
—Retired Detective Kim Pierce, Milwaukee Police Department

"I superstitiously set up the cargo pants of my uniform the same way every day. My squad key, search gloves, latex gloves, cheat sheet of city ordinances, Chapstick, handkerchief, backup key. Everything's the same."
—Officer Nate Becker, Madison Police Department

"The one thing I tell guys whenever I sign off with an email or on the phone is to stay safe, especially when I know they're going to work. Be safe and get home."   **—Lieutenant Dan Sandberg, Brown County Sheriff's Office**

27

Raging Bull

Shootin' the bull

By Matt Kapinos
The Denmark News

A thirteen hundred pound bull escaped from its pen Thursday morning, crashing through a gate, leaving one man with minor injuries.

The pen is operated by American Foods Group, and this bull was of particular concern because of its aggressive nature. Workers notified authorities immediately, and the Brown County Sherrif's Office, Denmark Police Department, and Eagle III helicopter were dispatched to the scene. The helicopter was called so the animal could be tracked from above if it decided to bolt.

The animal was spotted a few hundred yards off of County Highway R.

Denmark Police Chief Ron Towns was quoted by WTAQ radio saying, "It was extremely dangerous and very aggressive. If the bull came into contact with some poor soul on foot, that per-

son would probably be seriously injured or killed."

As with the term 'raging bull', these animals are notoriously difficult to bring down. Towns retrieved his own .300 Winchester magnum, which he said he hadn't fired in ten years. "I figured it would be able to do what we needed it to," said Towns.

Eyewitnesses say Towns took the shot from over 300 yards, and hit and dropped the animal. The animal got up once more, staggering, when Towns took a second shot, felling the animal again. Authorities then finished putting the animal down near County Highway P.

Towns says he joked with authorities about the legend being born, "20 years from now the people in Denmark will talk about the chief that shot a bull at a thousand yards at a dead run while standing on his head backwards looking through a mirror with a six gun."

The Denmark News

Police are occasionally called upon to shoot dangerous or injured animals like deer, dogs, or raccoons, but one sunny summer day in 2012, Denmark Chief Ron Towns found himself aiming at an unexpected creature: a bull.

The fourteen-hundred-pound animal escaped from a barn operated by American Foods Group, located approximately two miles east of Denmark. This rural village of about twenty-two hundred is surrounded by farmland in the southeast corner of Brown County. Dispatch initially sent county officers to the call, but since Towns was closer, the sheriff's office asked him to respond as well. All Towns knew was that the call involved a problem with an extremely dangerous animal near County Highway P.

"Ron, we've got a real problem here," a panicked man at the barn told him when he arrived. A bull was roaming at large somewhere in the nearby high cornfields or woods. It was ten-thirty in the morning, but they wanted to make sure they found it before dark.

"Do you have a rifle?" the man asked.

"No. I have my sidearm and shotgun," Towns replied.

"You can't go out on foot with a shotgun."

"I have no intention of doing that."

They both knew his 12-gauge shotgun didn't have enough firepower to fend off a bull in close quarters, especially an aggressive one such as this. Before disappearing, it ran over an employee, fortunately leaving him only with bumps and bruises. That's not always the case though. A local farmer known to be excellent at handling his livestock was found stomped to death by one of his bulls a couple of years earlier. And even though this particular bull on the loose was not as large as others—bulls can weigh up to a ton—it's the smaller ones who tend to be more aggressive and quick.

Some employees driving around in a Gator utility vehicle looking for the bull had a .30-06 rifle and a Brown County sergeant had a .223 rifle and a pistol, but none of those weapons were capable of bringing down the animal either.

The officers set up a perimeter around a square mile section to keep the bull contained and called in an Eagle III helicopter to track the animal from the air. Then Towns drove to his house a couple of miles away to retrieve his personal .300 Winchester Magnum and some ammunition.

He hadn't used it in about twenty years, and recently lent it to a friend for hunting so he didn't even know if the scope was sighted properly and where it would shoot.

Back at the scene, Towns quickly loaded three rounds into the rifle and then spotted the bull in the treeline approximately five hundred yards out.

"I got a vision on him and a clear shot," Towns said over the radio. "I'm going to take it." He figured he would see dirt fly or some other indication of where the weapon shot, and he would go from there.

As he got ready to fire, the bull glanced up at the helicopter overhead. Then it looked at Towns and moved toward him from a thirty-degree angle.

Knowing the bull wasn't coming over to socialize, he knew he'd better start shooting. He put the scope out in front of the animal and thought he'd let it trot into it. When the timing was right—*BANG!*—he shot once.

Much to Towns' surprise, the animal went down. The bullet hit it with one ton of force, knocking it off its feet.

"Chief, that was a jaw-dropping shot," said the sergeant.

Towns didn't want to tell him it was probably sheer luck, but before he could rejoice any further, the bull tried to get up.

He hit him once; he'd now try again. This time he positioned the crosshair at the base of the animal's neck thinking that if he struck either high enough in the neck or low enough in the body cavity, he'd have a vital shot. *BANG!* He struck it again.

One of the men got off the Gator and approached the bull thinking it was dead, but when he was about twenty to thirty yards away, it started to get up again.

Oh crap. Towns shot one more time before the man on the Gator fired the final shot.

The group of eight to ten people standing around applauded in excitement, and one of the sergeants commented on how everyone would remember that day, joking that, "Twenty years from now the people in Denmark will talk about the chief that shot a bull at a thousand yards at a dead run while standing on his head backwards looking through a mirror with a six-shooter."

Towns garnered a lot of attention for his marksmanship, with even a TV crew from Channel 2 arriving on scene to cover the incident. The reporter asked to see the shell casings, and Towns offered one for her to keep. "She was so excited you'd think that I gave her a diamond ring," he later said.

Afterward, Towns was curious to know the distance of the bull when he shot. Using the laser in his squad car, he determined the bull was three-hundred-and-thirty yards out, or about three football fields.

Still assuming that he just made a lucky shot, he took his Winchester to a local gun shop to see where the scope was sighted. The owner checked it and said, "Chief, it was dead on." The scope was sighted for three hundred yards.

For the next six weeks, the bull incident continued to be the topic of conversation in Denmark. A semi-hauler driver from Dubuque, Iowa, passing through town asked if "this is the place where the guy shot that bull," and a local engineer who used to be a sniper in Iraq shook Towns' hand and told him he made a hell of a shot.

"Of all the people who could've complimented me, a professional sniper counts for a little bit," said Towns, adding that he grew up in the Upper Peninsula of Michigan "where mothers have their children shooting guns by the time they're a couple days old."

In all seriousness, Towns said the loose bull was a serious situation, and it was fortunate no one was seriously injured or killed, which could have been the case had the bull come across a child playing in the woods or if it was struck by a vehicle. Hitting a fourteen-hundred-pound bull would be like slamming into a brick wall.

In Towns' nineteen years of experience in law enforcement, he had never shot a bull or any kind of domesticated animal, nor had he ever used his personal weapon on duty.

Shooting a bull, however, is indicative of what it's like to be a cop in a small town.

"It's almost an art form," Towns said. "I always tell my young officers that we're not as much police officers as peace officers. We're a little bit police officer, guidance counselor, priest, dad—a lot of things."

Towns, now in his mid-sixties, only became a police officer at the age of forty-five. Prior to that he worked as a truck driver, electrician, construction worker, and owner of a rig company. It wasn't until he moved to Green Bay to work for a paper company that he met some police officers who encouraged him to become a cop.

Towns worked as an officer at the two-person Denmark Police Department for six years until he became the chief in 2000, which is when he discovered the notoriety that comes with serving as the chief of a small town.

His wife soon discovered that people she hadn't even met knew the names of their children and dog, and Towns realized they couldn't go anywhere—whether it was Green Bay, Appleton, or even as far as Minocqua two-hundred miles away—without being recognized.

"It reminds me of a sheriff in a little town," Town said. "I'm never offended by someone referring to me as Andy from Mayberry. A lot of people would take offense to that, but I know how hard it is to keep order in a small society. It's difficult to walk that fine line of enforcing the laws in a small community without getting everyone pissed off at you. Andy Taylor did a hell of a job in Mayberry. He was a little bit philosopher, marriage counselor, a little of this and that. If you can do all those things a little bit, then maybe you'll be successful in a small community."

Towns himself has done everything from performing CPR to responding to a call for a loose llama and from helping a frantic mother with a choking child to dealing with a drunk dressed as a cowboy at a tractor pull.

"I've had a lot of interesting calls and goofy things, but not a bull, and now I can't say that anymore," he said.

Wisconsin Law Enforcement Agencies A-Z

With a police chief, one full-time and one part-time officers, and two crossing guards overseeing around 2,000 residents, the Denmark Police Department is one of the smallest law enforcement agencies in Wisconsin.

The Milwaukee Police Department, conversely, is the state's largest police department. According to its website, the agency is comprised of over 2,000 sworn officers and 700 civilians, serving a city of nearly 600,000 residents.

The Madison Police Department, protecting the state capital's roughly 240,000 residents, consists of 449 commissioned personnel, approximately 109 civilian personnel, and approximately 19 crossing guards, according to its most recent annual report.

There are in total approximately 954 law enforcement agencies in the state, according to the 2014 Wisconsin Law Enforcement Directory maintained by the Wisconsin Department of Justice's Training & Standards Bureau.

The directory includes a wide variety of law enforcement agencies, including police departments, sheriff's offices, district attorney offices, victim assistance programs, and state departments such as the Department of Natural Resources, Department of Corrections, and Department of Transportation.

28

State Trooper Movie Star?

"Hey, you're in a movie."
From troopers all over the state to his family back home in Australia, about a hundred people called Wisconsin State Patrol Sergeant Nate Clarke to tell him, "Hey, that's you. Have you seen that movie?"

The film in question was the 2011 comedy *Bridesmaids*, featuring a charismatic cop character named Nathan Rhodes who serves as Kristen Wiig's love interest. Played by Chris O'Dowd, the cop is a Wisconsin state trooper with an Irish accent who works in the area between Milwaukee and Chicago.

Clarke, who came to the United States from Australia when he was sixteen, was skeptical at first. *There is no way that there's a character in a movie that resembles me*, he recalled thinking.

Then he watched the movie and found himself struck by the similarities between himself and Rhodes. Even his wife suspiciously turned toward him on the couch like, "Want to tell me about this one?"

Beyond the many obvious likenesses, most people didn't know there were even more.

Around thirteen years previously, Clarke had met a woman when he was working as a trooper in Racine, located between Milwaukee and Chicago. He pulled her car out of a ditch during a snowstorm and afterward found himself in some of the same predicaments as Rhodes did.

For example, Wiig's character Annie doggedly tries to get the attention of an upset Rhodes by committing wild antics. One of them, driving past the officer ducked down in the driver's seat to give the appearance of no one behind the wheel, was something this woman did to Clarke.

In fact, she purposely got herself pulled over three times by Clarke, trying to talk to him.

Clarke can't verify if the woman was indeed Wiig (a co-writer of *Bridesmaids*), who perhaps went on to base the character Rhodes on Clarke because his agency didn't retain the reports from that many years ago, but he nevertheless finds it peculiar.

"I can tell you I've never been in a bar drinking with my uniform on," Clarke said, of some of the more embellished, not-so-realistic parts of the movie, "but it appears to be too coincidental given the accent, the location, [the first name], and the agency."

Classic Cop Characters in Cinema

Officer Nathan Rhodes as played by Chris O'Dowd in the 2011 film *Bridesmaids* is just one of the many law enforcement officers to grace the silver screen. Here's a list of some of the most popular ones from the last twenty-five years.

1. Sheriff Ed Tom Bell (Tommy Lee Jones) from *No Country for Old Men* (2007)
2. Commissioner Jim Gordon (Gary Oldman) from the *Batman* series (2005 on)
3. Inspector Frederick Abberline (Johnny Depp) from *From Hell* (2001)
4. Officer Bud White (Russell Crowe) from *L.A. Confidential* (1997)
5. Chief Marge Gunderson (Frances McDormand) from *Fargo* (1996)
6. Detective David Mills (Brad Pitt) and Detective Lieutenant William Somerset (Morgan Freeman) from *Se7en* (1995)
7. Detective Mike Lowrey (Will Smith) and Detective Marcus Burnett (Martin Lawrence) from *Bad Boys* (1995) and *Bad Boys II* (2003)
8. Deputy Marshal Samuel Gerard (Tommy Lee Jones) from *The Fugitive* (1993)
9. Lieutenant Raymond Tango (Sylvester Stallone) and Lieutenant Gabriel Cash (Kurt Russell) from *Tango & Cash* (1989)
10. Officer John McClane (Bruce Willis) from the *Die Hard* series (1988 on)

COMIC COP STORIES

"Thank goodness I didn't run away.
I never would have lived it down."

—Retired Wisconsin State Patrol
Trooper James H. Smith

29

Not a Zombie

One spring morning at about three a.m., Officer James H. Smith spotted a pair of headlights in the cemetery while out on patrol.

Figuring some mischievous kids were tipping headstones, the Wausau suburban police officer pulled into the cemetery to investigate.

With his window rolled down, he navigated along the twisted roads listening for any suspicious activity. Coupled with the misty rain and the thick fog rolling in off the Wisconsin River next to the cemetery, he could only see about seventy feet ahead of him, and he wound up facing the pickup truck instead of approaching it from behind as he had intended.

Smith peered over the headlights into the truck, but didn't see anyone. Still seated in his squad, he looked to his left, and at the limit of his visibility glimpsed a man's head on the ground in front of a headstone.

Smith shook his head, thinking he must be seeing things. He looked again only to find the head staring right back at him. "I wondered when you would get here," it said.

Up out of the ground emerged a dirt-covered hand and arm; then came the other blackened hand and arm. The man pulled himself out of the ground and began walking toward Smith's squad car.

Holy cow! Smith thought. He looked like a zombie crawling out of the earth in a horror movie.

"Now it seemed to me that if a man comes out of the grave to get you, bullets weren't going to do much good," Smith later said, recounting the incident.

While the officer scrambled to think of the best course of action, the man calmly said, "I thought someone would call about me being out here."

He went on to explain that he was the gravedigger—not a grave robber, as he assumed had been reported to the police. He had a grave half dug and had the hole covered with a sheet of rusted metal, which blended into the muddy ground. He had been burning tires to thaw the ground so he could finish digging the hole in the morning, but the rain had extinguished the fire. He slid the metal back just far enough to crawl under it and was trying to restart the fire when Smith drove into the cemetery.

Not wanting the gravedigger to know that he had thought he was a zombie, the officer attempted to carry on the conversation with him normally.

"He was totally unaware of the image he projected crawling out of the ground like that," said Smith, who retired as a state trooper in 2007 and now works as a police communications operator for the Wisconsin State Patrol. "Thank goodness I didn't run away. I never would have lived it down."

Wisconsin State Patrol

♦ The Wisconsin State Patrol enforces traffic and criminal laws; helps motorists in need; inspects trucks, school buses, and ambulances; and helps local law enforcement agencies with natural disasters or civil disturbances.

♦ Services provided by the Wisconsin State Patrol include: size/weight inspection, motor carrier safety assistance, ambulance inspection, school bus inspection, crash reconstruction, and mobile data communication.

♦ The state patrol is comprised of the Public Security and Communications Bureau, the Field Operations Bureau, the Transportation Safety Bureau, and the State Patrol Academy Office.

♦ The state patrol originated from the Motor Vehicle Department, which was created by a statute passed by the Wisconsin legislature in 1939.

♦ The training academy in Fort McCoy was established in 1955, which presently educates state patrol officers as well as county and municipal law enforcement officers.

♦ In addition to the training academy, the state patrol operates sixteen safety and weight enforcement facilities.

♦ Headquartered in Madison, the state patrol has posts in the southwest region of DeForest and Tomah, the southeast region of Waukesha, the northeast region of Fond du Lac, the north central region of Wausau, and the northwest region of Eau Claire and Spooner.

♦ As of December 2011, the state patrol employed 345 troopers and 99 inspectors.

♦ In 2011, troopers issued 135,291 citations, made 218,704 motor vehicle stops, investigated 5,804 traffic crashes, and completed 4,015 safety inspections.

—Information compiled from the Wisconsin Department of Transportation website.

30

Blue and Brown

All new police sergeants are notorious for their arrogance, according to Russ Steeber.

"You get promoted and try to prove yourself to your peers, so you can get a little headstrong," he said. "I'm the first one to admit that sometimes I could get pretty stubborn."

That trait was on full display one fateful day in the late 1980s when this new sergeant at the Rock County Sheriff's Office responded to a double fatality accident between a semi-truck and a car on Interstate 90 near a town north of Janesville called Newville. Road construction had shut down the two northbound lanes, and the semi-truck driver reportedly crossed over one of the southbound lanes and crashed head-on into the car.

The Rock County Sheriff's Office arrived on scene first, and Steeber got to work right away calling in the coroner and the wreckers and instructing his deputies to take photographs and interview witnesses.

"Then the state patrol shows up and ruins everything," Steeber recounted nearly twenty-five years later, a lilt in his voice.

"I've got everything under control," he told the lead trooper, only to discover that he was as obstinate as himself.

Steeber was already annoyed, but he exploded when the trooper instructed dispatch to cancel the wreckers.

"You want this mess, it's all yours," Steeber barked. He ordered his deputies to leave the scene and stomped back to his squad car.

He waited a few moments while a female trooper struggled to yank an orange and white construction barrel off the road so he could pull back into traffic, but he quickly wore out of patience. He rode over the barrel in a huff, narrowly missing her.

———

A few years later Steeber attended an instructor development class at the Wisconsin State Patrol Academy in Fort McCoy. Every day he sat next to a female trooper whom he later exaggeratingly described as "ice cold" and a "real bitch."

He finally asked her after two or three days, "Did I do something wrong?"

"You're one of those Rock County guys," she coolly replied. "I can't stand the deputies from Rock County."

The trooper went on to talk about this jerk of a sergeant she had encountered a couple of years earlier who almost ran her over. Steeber realized, with a lump in his throat, that he was that stubborn Rock County guy.

Instead of her hating him even more, it turned out that his admission resolved the tension and the two realized how much they had in common. Russ and Lauri got married a year later.

"Somehow he managed to get me to change my perspective about those Rock County guys," Lauri said.

———

After a thirty-three-year career, Russ—who retired in 2011 from the sheriff's office at the rank of captain—called that call his most memorable.

"It had the most profound and long-lasting impact on me," he said. "It's interesting how fate plays out. We grew up twenty-five miles apart (she in Green Bay, he in Manitowoc County), we ended up down here by happenstance, and the rest is history."

Over two decades later, the Steebers say that their marriage comprised of two law enforcement officers has proven to have its benefits, complications, and even friendly competitions.

"You have no authority, but I do," Lauri would say to Russ when they crossed the county line.

"Okay, now I have rank," Russ would retort upon returning to Rock County.

Other times, Lauri enjoyed using her more vibrant uniform color to her advantage.

"What color do you like better, blue or brown?" she once asked her son's fourth grade class, referring to her blue trooper uniform and Russ' brown sheriff's uniform.

"What fourth grader is going to say they like brown better?" Russ interjected in the present.

Besides stirring up competition, their uniforms also caused some inquisitiveness.

"Who wears the pants in your family?" asked their dry cleaner one day.

"People are curious about that when you're both in law enforcement," said Lauri, who retired as a lieutenant after twenty-three years with the state patrol working in Sauk, Dane, and Walworth Counties as well as the state headquarters.

Their careers also led to some leeriness among people, in particular their son's baseball coach, who called one day asking to speak to one of them only to hear that they couldn't come to the phone because they were in the garage cleaning their guns.

He didn't know, however, what they did for a living.

"He thought we were some sort of terrorists," an amused Russ recalled.

Two parents in law enforcement certainly gave their three daughters and son a different childhood than most.

Sometimes it proved to be detrimental, such as the time a girlfriend of a boy Lauri had arrested broke the nose of one of their daughters.

Other times it made it difficult to get away with things.

One night shortly after midnight, their son returned home and woke up Russ and Lauri to tell them a cop stood outside waiting to talk to them. The officer had busted their son for driving sixty-five miles per hour in a thirty mile-per-hour zone.

"It's embarrassing, especially if it's someone you know who stops your kid or if you hear their name being called over the radio," Lauri said. "It's just a matter of time before we'd find out."

Like the time Russ and Lauri returned home after a weekend getaway and discovered her squad car dented across the passenger side.

"I go in the house and ask, 'Okay guys, what happened?'" said Lauri, laughing about it now.

Two parents in law enforcement also made for unusual routines for the family.

Russ and Lauri's "evening," for instance, was actually in the morning when they worked third shift. They would arrive home around seven in the morning and open a bottle of wine as their high school-aged kids got ready for school. Then they'd go to bed around eight or nine in the morning.

Due to Russ' and Lauri's schedules, their family also sometimes had to open Christmas presents or eat Thanksgiving dinner on another day.

Still, Lauri said the holiday isn't about the day.

"It's about when you make it as a family," she said.

It wasn't until one of their daughters testified at a senate hearing about the importance of a state law enforcement memorial that Lauri realized the concerns their children had for them.

"I didn't realize how much the children worried about us when we went to work and how much it bothered them," she said. "They really worried about us coming home."

Although Russ and Lauri didn't worry about each other on the job, they found their marriage to a fellow law enforcement officer helpful to each other in dealing with the pressures.

"I think only another cop can understand the stress of the job," Lauri said.

The general public, for instance, might not be able to empathize with her about a horrific car crash to which she responded, but to Russ it would make sense.

"You felt like you were talking to someone you could vent to and be personal and intimate with about your feelings, but you knew they wouldn't chastise you for how you felt and you knew it wouldn't get back to the person like if you went out with a coworker," Russ added.

A marriage between law enforcement officers from different agencies, however, could lead to some conflict, according to the Steebers, because each agency has different ways of handling issues.

Nevertheless, Lauri emphasizes the importance of talking about non-work related issues and pursuing other interests, especially as a family, in order to maintain a healthy relationship.

For example, the Steebers and their children were actively involved in Special Olympics Wisconsin, a statewide organization providing people with intellectual disabilities with year-round sports training and competition.

While many police officers are also involved in the organization, Russ said it's a positive activity in the law enforcement world that gives them a respite from work.

One element of the job that they're okay with bringing home with them? The 10-code.

"The kids don't understand it," Lauri said. "So once they knew how to spell, we moved to the 10-code."

———

Lauri, of course, is not still mad at Russ for almost running her over the day they met all those years ago; but, she did feel the need to prove a point by bringing home an orange and white construction barrel one day about four years after they got married.

"I pulled it off the concrete just to prove I could do it, damn it. I never told him where I got it."

The 10-Code

Originating in the early 1920s when public safety radio was in its infancy, the purpose of the 10-code is for officers to communicate concisely and quickly in order to reduce radio traffic, according to the National Institute of Justice. The use of 10-codes is also beneficial because it helps to prevent suspects who are within earshot from understanding what officers and dispatchers are saying.

Though they vary across jurisdictions, below is a widely accepted list of 10-codes.

- 10-0 Caution
- 10-1 Unable to copy—change location
- 10-2 Signal good
- 10-3 Stop transmitting
- 10-4 Acknowledgement (OK)
- 10-5 Relay
- 10-6 Busy—stand by unless urgent
- 10-7 Out of service
- 10-8 In service
- 10-9 Repeat
- 10-10 Fight in progress
- 10-11 Dog case
- 10-12 Stand by (stop)
- 10-13 Weather—road report
- 10-14 Prowler report
- 10-15 Civil disturbance
- 10-16 Domestic disturbance
- 10-17 Meet complainant
- 10-18 Quickly
- 10-19 Return to ...
- 10-20 Location
- 10-21 Call ... by telephone
- 10-22 Disregard
- 10-23 Arrived at scene
- 10-24 Assignment completed
- 10-25 Report in person (meet) ...
- 10-26 Detaining subject, expedite
- 10-27 Drivers license information
- 10-28 Vehicle registration information
- 10-29 Check for wanted
- 10-30 Unnecessary use of radio
- 10-31 Crime in progress
- 10-32 Man with gun
- 10-33 Emergency
- 10-34 Riot
- 10-35 Major crime alert
- 10-36 Correct time
- 10-37 (Investigate) suspicious vehicle
- 10-38 Stopping suspicious vehicle
- 10-39 Urgent—use light, siren
- 10-40 Silent run—no light, siren
- 10-41 Beginning tour of duty
- 10-42 Ending tour of duty
- 10-43 Information
- 10-44 Permission to leave ... for ...
- 10-45 Animal carcass at ...
- 10-46 Assist motorist
- 10-47 Emergency road repairs at ...

- 10-48 Traffic standard repair at ...
- 10-49 Traffic light out at ...
- 10-50 Accident (fatal, personal injury, property damage)
- 10-51 Wrecker needed
- 10-52 Ambulance needed
- 10-53 Road blocked at ...
- 10-54 Livestock on highway
- 10-55 Suspected DUI
- 10-56 Intoxicated pedestrian
- 10-57 Hit and run (fatal, personal injury, property damage)
- 10-58 Direct traffic
- 10-59 Convoy or escort
- 10-60 Squad in vicinity
- 10-61 Isolate self for message
- 10-62 Reply to message
- 10-63 Prepare to make written copy
- 10-64 Message for local delivery
- 10-65 Net message assignment
- 10-66 Message cancellation
- 10-67 Clear for net message
- 10-68 Dispatch information
- 10-69 Message received
- 10-70 Fire
- 10-71 Advise nature of fire
- 10-72 Report progress on fire
- 10-73 Smoke report
- 10-74 Negative
- 10-75 In contact with ...
- 10-76 En route ...
- 10-77 ETA (estimated time of arrival)
- 10-78 Need assistance
- 10-79 Notify coroner
- 10-80 Chase in progress
- 10-81 Breathalyzer
- 10-82 Reserve lodging
- 10-83 Work school xing at ...
- 10-84 If meeting ... advise ETA
- 10-85 Delayed due to ...
- 10-86 Officer/operator on duty
- 10-87 Pick up/distribute checks
- 10-88 Present telephone number of ...
- 10-89 Bomb threat
- 10-90 Bank alarm at ...
- 10-91 Pick up prisoner/subject
- 10-92 Improperly parked vehicle
- 10-93 Blockade
- 10-94 Drag racing
- 10-95 Prisoner/subject in custody
- 10-96 Mental subject
- 10-97 Check (test) signal
- 10-98 Prison/jail break
- 10-99 Wanted/stolen indicated

31

The Naked Detective

At 4:03 a.m., Beloit Detective Doug Anderson woke up to his dog barking softly.

"Shut up, Talbot," he said sternly.

He rolled over and closed his eyes, trying to fall back asleep.

The bullmastiff, named after Anderson's wife's favorite clothing store, continued to bark.

"Talbot. Shut up!"

As he rolled over once again, he suddenly heard the noise himself. He immediately sat up in bed and told Talbot to once again shut up—this time so he could better listen to the noise.

As one of two detectives assigned to the drug and gang unit where he would often execute search warrants, Anderson grew accustomed to receiving empty threats from criminals.

"We know where you live Anderson. Next time we'll come pay you a visit," they would taunt him.

He first reached for his gun, then exchanged it for a flashlight thinking maybe the noise just came from a cat.

As Anderson crept down the stairs listening to the noise, the hair on his arms stood up.

Once downstairs, he saw the door leading to an enclosed porch rattling and the doorknob twisting and turning. Behind the glass stood a silhouette.

The only thing keeping the intruder out of his house was a slide latch.

Anderson felt a twinge of fear, but that quickly turned into a bolt of adrenaline.

Let's play, he thought, going into what he described as "full-on ninja mode."

With the flashlight in hand, Anderson swung the door open, reached up and grabbed a handful of the intruder's hair, and slid the perpetrator across the floor.

He placed the person in a perfect three-point control system, with the wrist compressed, the elbow pinned in the small of the back, and his shin across the shoulder blades.

"Buddy, you picked the wrong place to break into," Anderson snarled.

Coming from underneath him, he heard a muffled, high-pitched voice proclaim, "I'm a girl."

"Well, you still picked the wrong place to break into."

As he continued to detain the intruder, Anderson yelled up to his wife who was still in the bedroom.

"I called 911," she hollered.

"Good, but Kate ..."

"And I called Dan," she said, referring to their neighbor, who happened to be a sergeant at the same police department as Anderson.

"But Kate ..."

"What?"

"Bring me my robe."

Anderson had a habit of sleeping in the buff and had just enough time to slip on his robe before Dan bounded in wearing rectangular, green glasses and a T-shirt cut off at mid-thigh, holding a gun in one hand and a flashlight in the other.

Once the patrol officers arrived on scene, they burst out laughing and asked, "What idiot would break into your house?"

It turned out that the "intruder" was an intoxicated college girl coming home from a party who mistook his house for hers. He only lived about two blocks from the college.

To relieve Anderson of the embarrassment sure to come in the local newspaper, a sergeant said he'd hang onto the police reports.

That all sounded good to Anderson, until he realized the mistake his wife made.

When she called 911 that night, the dispatcher insisted that she stay on the line until she finally blurted out that she had to go because her husband was naked and needed his robe.

Subsequently, the dispatcher wrote in the call notes—which can be viewed by any other officer in the county—"Naked detective needs help with female."

A short game of telephone ensued with an officer passing on that information to a newspaper reporter, who then called up Anderson saying, "I can't find the report on what happened at your house last night. You tell me what happened or I'll print what was told to me."

He conceded, and the next day the story ended up in the city newspaper and the following day in an adjacent city's newspaper before finally the Associated Press picked up the story a week later.

Eventually, Anderson's mid-sized midwestern police department fielded calls from media outlets from as far away as Miami, all wanting interviews with "the naked detective."

About nineteen years later, Anderson—who retired from the department in 2005 after twenty-three years—is still baffled at the sureality of that night.

"It was so crazy," he said. "No one could make that up."

To him, it exemplifies just how absurd the life of a cop can be.

As an instructor at Blackhawk Technical College's police academy since his retirement, Anderson always tells his new crop of students about "the naked detective" on their first days.

"The intimidation factor isn't there anymore for the academy students," he joked.

The other thing to take away from the story?

"Don't visit me at 4:03 a.m. unless you want an image you don't want to see."

———•———

Burglaries in Wisconsin

Although Retired Beloit Detective Doug Anderson didn't actually come across a burglar at his house that early morning, there are thousands of burglaries reported in Wisconsin each year.

Green Bay, population 106,080
January–June 2013: 235
January–June 2012: 355

Madison, population 237,508
January–June 2013: 534
January–June 2012: 640

Milwaukee, population 599,395
January–June 2013: 2,819
January–June 2012: 2,976

—Information compiled from the FBI's Preliminary Semiannual Uniform Crime Report, January–June 2013.

———•———

Award Index

Hilary Dickinson is a writer originally from Waukesha, Wisconsin, who formerly covered the police beat for the *Beloit Daily News* in Beloit, Wisconsin. Through that role, she became interested in police work and was inspired to write this book. A magna cum laude graduate in journalism from the University of Minnesota, she has written for publications including the *Minneapolis Star Tribune, Milwaukee Magazine,* and *Rockford Woman* magazine. She is the author and photographer of the *Dogs of Door County* published in 2013.